President Johnson's War on Poverty

David Zarefsky

President Johnson's War on Poverty

Rhetoric and History

The University of Alabama Press

Library of Congress Cataloging in Publication Data

Zarefsky, David.
President Johnson's war on poverty.

Bibliography: p.
Includes index.
1. Economic assistance, Domestic—United States.
2. United States—Politics and government—1963–1969.
I. Title.
HC110.P63Z36   1985   338.973   84–24098
ISBN 0–8173–0266–2

For Nikki and Beth

Contents

Preface

In the early evening of November 23, 1963—his first full day as president—Lyndon Johnson met with Walter Heller, chairman of the Council of Economic Advisers, to discuss the council's research on poverty in the United States. Only four days earlier, President Kennedy had decided to make antipoverty policy a major component of his 1964 legislative program, instructing Heller to develop the outline of a program for review shortly after Thanksgiving. Now instructions were needed from the new president concerning the direction the council's work should take. From his suite in the Executive Office Building, Johnson gazed across to the West Wing of the White House, reflected on the dedication of the White House staff to sustain the motion of government amidst national tragedy, and told Heller to proceed. "That's my kind of program," he is reported to have said. "It will help people."

More than twenty years have passed since President Johnson declared "unconditional war" on poverty and summoned Americans with his vision of a Great Society. In the climate of the 1980s such talk seems a stale throwback to another time, naive at best and suspect at worst.

Currently it is fashionable to stress the limits, not the possibilities, of what government can do. The past two decades have introduced a discontinuity in thought and judgment, so that Johnson's grand vision appears as arrogance approaching hubris. This change begs for explanation, and the key turning points can be found within the dates of the Johnson administration itself.

Although the inception of the program was not without difficulties, in the beginning there was heady optimism. Barely two months passed between the president's call for action and the introduction of the antipoverty bill in Congress. Five months later, the Economic Opportunity Act became law. How such a cause rose so fast is one of the main concerns of this book. But there is another side to the story.

Once antipoverty programs were under way, they were quickly mired in difficulties. They stood accused of not doing enough for the poor and of doing too much. They were criticized both for compromising with local politicians and for antagonizing them. They were charged both with dampening the morale of the poor and with inspiring the poor to riot. They were attacked as inadequately funded and as extravagant. They were tarred with the stigma of public welfare programs. By 1967, only three years after war had been "declared," the future of the antipoverty program was very much in doubt. How could a program which began with such strong support have fallen so far? And was there some *connection* between the quick ascendancy and the rapid demise? Did the methods that contributed to the early success of the War on Poverty actually hasten its decline?

Much has been written about these questions by scholars examining specific programs or decisions as problems in public administration, organizational behavior, or local government. With respect to the War on Poverty as a whole, however, the answers tend toward shibboleth and cliché. Conservatives proclaim that the War on Poverty shows the futility of throwing dollars after problems; liberals decry that not enough was spent.

Perhaps the most common explanation is that the War on Poverty became a casualty of the war in Vietnam. This claim is not without truth, since the increasing urgency of the Southeast Asian conflict reduced the time and energy which the president could devote to the War on Poverty. The controversy surrounding the foreign war also made domestic issues seem less significant or less pressing. But it would be a facile oversimplification to attribute the demise of the Office of Economic Opportunity solely to the demands of the Department of Defense. Many of the difficulties plaguing the antipoverty effort not only were unrelated to the military escalation in Southeast Asia but actually preceded it.

This study suggests a different explanation. It locates the problems of the War on Poverty in its *discourse*. The basic assumption is that language plays a central role in the formulation of social policy by shaping the context with which people think about the social world. In this case, President Johnson's decision to call the effort a *war* had significant symbolic implications. It called for total victory yet instilled confidence that the war was winnable; it influenced the definition of the enemy as an intergenerational cycle of poverty rather than defects in the individual; it led to the choice of community action, manpower programs, and prudent management as weapons and tactics. Each of these implications involved a choice of symbols and language, a decision about how to characterize and discuss the world.

The central thesis of this book is that each of these

rhetorical choices was helpful to the Johnson administration to obtain passage of the Economic Opportunity Act of 1964 but that each also contained the seeds of its own destruction. In some cases, the choice invited redefinition or reinterpretation of a symbol in a way which threatened the program. In other cases the original rhetorical choices depended upon ambiguities which could not be sustained or distinctions which did not hold up. In still other cases, the rhetorical choice involved a way of thinking which easily could fall victim to conflicting habits and styles of thought. For whatever reason, though, the very choices of symbolism and argument which had aided the adoption of the program were instrumental in undermining its implementation and in weakening public support for its basic philosophy.

The plan of the book follows from the foregoing statement of the thesis. The first chapter offers a theoretical framework for viewing definition as a significant symbolic choice linking public policy to rhetoric and for evaluating the progress of symbolic choice through phases of inception, rhetorical crisis, and consummation. These phases form the motif of chapters 2 through 6. The second chapter explicates the significance of the military metaphor and its implications for choices of objectives, enemy, and weapons and tactics—all choices which were beneficial in 1964. The middle chapters trace the unintended effects of each symbolic choice which brought it into contradiction with itself, hampering the program's defenders and hurting its public image. Chapter 6 brings the story through 1967. In that year, supporters of the War on Poverty were able to resist efforts to dismember or dismantle the program. But their victory was ironic, if not Pyrrhic. They were forced to concede virtually every one of their original doctrinal assumptions, with the result that programs were left without a clear sense of mission, without a vision of how their goals might be achieved— and without a workable rhetoric. The war ended in stalemate. The final chapter attempts an overall assessment and uses the War on Poverty to illustrate the impasse of the liberal argument in contemporary American politics.

It is necessary to speak briefly about the term "War on Poverty," since its scope is difficult to identify with precision. Sometimes it was used as a summary term to designate all social welfare programs of the Johnson administration, ranging from increased Social Security benefits to federal aid to education. For the most part, however, it referred to the Economic Opportunity Act of 1964 and its subsequent amendments, and especially to Titles I and II of the act. These titles, pertaining respectively to training programs and to community action programs, were both the most innovative and the most controversial of the administration's antipoverty initiatives.

Since the poverty program had been in the planning stages well before Johnson took office, it is difficult to identify a precise starting date for the War on Poverty. With respect to public discourse, January 8, 1964, is probably the most appropriate date. On that day the new president delivered his first State of the Union address in which he announced a declaration of "unconditional war." This book focuses primarily on the attempts by the executive branch to persuade the Congress to initiate and sustain the program. It is a study of the communication within and between the executive and legislative departments of the federal government and of the messages from government officials to the public. The study is concerned only indirectly with the actual operations of individual antipoverty projects and with the long-term results of the War on Poverty. When these matters are discussed, they are treated as evidence or support which could be drawn upon by the administration or its antagonists in the struggle for adherence from the legislature.

In the short run, the Johnson administration must be judged amazingly successful at its rhetorical task. Over a period of but a few months, strong support was obtained for measures for which there had been no public clamor or demand. Tragically, however, the very rhetorical choices which were so useful in gaining initial support proved to be dysfunctional in the long run. The examination of these two propositions—short-term rhetorical success and long-term rhetorical failure—is the purpose of this book.

I began investigating these questions fifteen years ago in preparation for my doctoral dissertation. My original thinking on the War on Poverty was sharpened by the questions and advice of the members of my dissertation committee, Leland M. Griffin, Robert D. Brooks, and Roy V. Wood. Since that time, colleagues and students too numerous to list have contributed to my sense of the rhetoric of the 1960s. My research was greatly facilitated by the able assistance of the archivists at the Lyndon Baines Johnson Library in Austin, Texas. This manuscript was read in its entirety by Dan Nimmo, E. Culpepper Clark, and my colleague Thomas B. Farrell, who made many excellent suggestions for improving the work. I am particularly indebted to Stephen P. Depoe who provided invaluable assistance with the organizational structure of the final version. Our discussions of the liberal argument in American politics have contributed greatly to my thinking. The final manuscript was ably typed by Janice Greene. My greatest debts, as always, are to my wife and daughter, who encouraged this work and understood its demands on my energy and time.

Evanston, Illinois   D.Z.

Chronology

May 22	Johnson speaks at University of Michigan; sets forth his conception of the "Great Society."
July 2	Civil Rights Act of 1964 signed into law.
July 16	Barry Goldwater nominated for president by the Republican party.
July 23	Senate passes Economic Opportunity Act of 1964.
Aug. 2	Attack on USS *Maddox* by North Vietnamese patrol boats in the Gulf of Tonkin.
Aug. 4	Johnson reports to American people of renewed aggression in the Gulf of Tonkin.
Aug. 7	Congress passes Gulf of Tonkin Resolution with only two dissenting votes.
Aug. 8	House passes Economic Opportunity Act of 1964.
Aug. 20	Economic Opportunity Act signed into law.
Aug. 27	Johnson accepts presidential nomination of Democratic party; selects Hubert Humphrey as running mate.
Oct. 14	Nikita Khrushchev ousted; replaced by Soviet leadership of Brezhnev and Kosygin.
Oct. 21	Johnson campaigns in Akron: "We are not going to send American boys away from home to do what Asian boys ought to be doing for themselves."
Nov. 1	Vietcong attack American base at Bienhoa; Johnson resists pressure for escalation.
Nov. 3	Johnson receives landslide in election against Goldwater.
Dec. 24	Vietcong bomb American officers' billet in Saigon; Johnson again resists pressure for escalation.

1965

Jan. 4	State of the Union message focuses on quality of life.
Jan. 7	Johnson sends special message to Congress on hospital insurance for the aged.
Jan. 12	Johnson sends special message to Congress proposing federal aid to education.
Jan. 20	Johnson delivers inaugural address.
Jan. 27	Defense Secretary Robert McNamara and National Security Adviser McGeorge Bundy recommend escalation in Vietnam.
Feb. 7	Vietcong attack American installation at Pleiku; Johnson approves retaliatory bombing of North Vietnam.

Feb. 24   Sustained bombing of North Vietnam begins.

Mar. 2   Johnson sends special message to Congress on cities; proposes rent supplements and new cabinet department.

Mar. 8   Marines land to defend Danang airfield; first U.S. combat troops in Vietnam.

Mar. 15   Johnson speaks to joint session of Congress to appeal for Voting Rights Act.

Apr. 7   Johnson speaks at Johns Hopkins University; pledges $1 billion in American aid to rebuild North and South Vietnam.

Apr. 11   Johnson signs Elementary and Secondary Education Act.

Apr. 18   Shriver responds to criticism of War on Poverty by Congressman Adam Clayton Powell, who labeled it a "giant fiesta of political patronage."

Apr. 24   Military junta takes control of Dominican Republic.

Apr. 28   Johnson orders U.S. troops to Dominican Republic.

May 23   Article in *New York Herald Tribune* contains first reference to Johnson "credibility gap."

May 26   Shriver addresses National Conference on Social Welfare; criticizes social workers and praises "inspired amateur" in War on Poverty.

June 2   U.S. Conference of Mayors shelves resolution accusing Office of Economic Opportunity of "fostering class struggle"; mayors assured by Vice President Humphrey that they will have greater role in poverty program.

June 4   Johnson delivers commencement address at Howard University; calls for "equality as a fact and a result."

July 28   Johnson approves General Westmoreland's request for forty-four additional combat battalions in Vietnam; first major increase in troop levels.

July 30   Johnson signs Medicare legislation in Independence, Mo.

Aug. 6   Voting Rights Act signed into law.

Aug. 11   Outbreak of riots in Watts area of Los Angeles.

Sept. 18 Memorandum from Budget Director Charles L. Schultze proposes abandoning the goal of organizing the poor politically; Johnson accepts recommendation.

Oct. 9   Johnson signs Economic Opportunity Act amendments,
            including funding for fiscal 1966.
Dec. 2   Shriver addresses American Public Welfare Association;
            defends "criticism, experimentation, and even mis-
            takes" but makes peace with social workers.
Dec. 25   Johnson suspends bombing of North Vietnam.

1966
Jan. 12   State of the Union message; Johnson announces that the
            United States is strong enough to pursue both guns and
            butter.
Jan. 15   People's War Council Against Poverty meets in Syracuse;
            speakers denounce Office of Economic Opportunity.
Jan. 26   Johnson sends special message to Congress proposing
            Demonstration Cities program, later renamed Model
            Cities.
Jan. 31   Resumption of air strikes against North Vietnam.
Feb. 8   Johnson confers in Honolulu with South Vietnamese
            leaders Thieu and Ky.
Feb. 18   Senate Foreign Relations Committee concludes hearings
            on Vietnam.
Apr. 14   Shriver heckled at Citizens' Crusade Against Poverty
            meeting; defends record of OEO.
June 21   Shriver testifies before Senate Labor and Public Welfare
            Committee; says War on Poverty can be won "in about
            ten years."
June 29   Bombing of oil depots near Hanoi and Haiphong.
Aug. 29   Congressman Adam Clayton Powell calls for Shriver's
            resignation.
Oct. 7   Johnson calls for rapprochement with Eastern Europe.
Nov. 8   Economic Opportunity Act amendments signed into law,
            including funding for fiscal 1967.

1967
Jan. 10   State of the Union message proclaims this to be a "time of
            testing."
Jan. 23   Johnson proposes increases in Social Security.
Mar. 14   Johnson submits special message to Congress on rural and
            urban poverty.
May 2   Johnson requests supplemental antipoverty funds, espe-
            cially for summer programs.

June 5   Outbreak of war in Middle East.
June 22   OEO Research Director Robert A. Levine tells Senate Labor and Public Welfare Committee that War on Poverty never can be won as currently fought.
June 23   Johnson holds summit meeting with Kosygin at Glassboro, N.J.
July 12   Outbreak of riots in Newark.
July 18   Senator Winston Prouty of Vermont reads telegram from Newark police director alleging that Newark community action agency employees were ordered to picket or lose their jobs.
July 20   House defeats bill to allocate funds for rat extermination in urban ghettos.
July 23   Outbreak of riots in Detroit.
July 24   Johnson authorizes use of federal troops in Detroit.
July 27   Establishment of Advisory Commission on Civil Disorders, chaired by Illinois governor Otto Kerner.
Sept. 3   National election in South Vietnam; Thieu elected president, Ky elected vice president.
Sept. 29   Johnson, in San Antonio speech, offers to stop bombing of North Vietnam in exchange for "productive discussions."
Oct. 5   Senate passes Economic Opportunity Act amendments of 1967.
Oct. 11   House excludes OEO employees from general pay raise for federal workers.
Oct. 23   House excludes OEO from routine "continuing resolution."
Nov. 15   Reversing earlier trends, House passes Economic Opportunity Act amendments of 1967.
Nov. 30   Senator Eugene McCarthy announces his candidacy for president of the United States in 1968.
Dec. 23   Following conference committee action, Johnson signs Economic Opportunity Act amendments of 1967, including funding for fiscal 1968 and two-year authorization.

1968
Jan. 17   State of the Union message.
Jan. 23   USS *Pueblo* seized by North Korea.

Jan. 31   Tet offensive begins throughout South Vietnam.

Feb. 29   National Advisory Commission on Civil Disorders sub-
          mits report; describes America as moving toward "two
          societies, one black, one white, separate and un-
          equal."

Mar. 1   Clark Clifford sworn in as secretary of defense, succeed-
          ing Robert McNamara; initiates review of Vietnam
          policy.

Mar. 10   *New York Times* publishes report that General West-
          moreland has requested 206,000 additional troops in
          aftermath of Tet offensive.

Mar. 12   Senator McCarthy receives unexpected 42 percent of vote
          in New Hampshire presidential primary.

Mar. 16   Senator Robert F. Kennedy enters presidential race.

Mar. 22   Sargent Shriver nominated to be ambassador to France;
          subsequently, Bertrand Harding named acting director
          of OEO.

Mar. 26   Senior statesmen and diplomats (group identified as the
          "Wise Men") urge Johnson to reassess Vietnam pol-
          icy.

Mar. 31   Johnson announces that he will not be a candidate for
          reelection.

Apr. 3   In response to Johnson's March 31 speech, North Viet-
          namese agree to open talks.

Apr. 4   Martin Luther King, Jr., assassinated in Memphis; subse-
          quent rioting in major cities; U.S. troops sent to Wash-
          ington, Baltimore, and Chicago.

June 5   Robert F. Kennedy assassinated in Los Angeles after
          winning California presidential primary.

June 26   Johnson nominates Abe Fortas to be chief justice.

June 28   Johnson signs bill for 10 percent tax surcharge and $6
          billion cut in domestic spending.

July 1   United States and Soviet Union sign Nonproliferation
          Treaty.

Aug. 8   Richard M. Nixon accepts Republican nomination for
          president.

Aug. 21   Soviet Union invades Czechoslovakia.

Aug. 28   Hubert H. Humphrey nominated for president by Demo-
          cratic National Convention amid chaos in Chicago.

President Johnson's
War on Poverty

1

Rhetoric and Public Policy
The Force of Symbolic Choice

In his now-classic work on the subject, Richard Neustadt wrote that presidential power is "the power to persuade."[1] To that formulation might be added that the power to persuade is, in large measure, the power to define. To exercise this power, the president chooses among available symbols to characterize a situation and influences the choice of symbols by others. This view rests on two premises, which are the foundation of this book: the symbolic interactionist belief that reality is socially constructed, and the emergence in the twentieth century of the "rhetorical presidency."

I

The facts of an episode in political life are not "given" or univocal; they are not present in the external world awaiting discovery by political actors. To be sure, certain conditions exist independently of the will of any public official. One person may be out of work, another may carry a placard condemning nuclear weapons and join others in a march, and a third may be unable to obtain a home mortgage. But the *meaning* of these events depends upon how they are characterized in public discourse. The person out of work may be a "casual job seeker" or a victim of "the worst recession since World War II." The person who marches may be a "nervous Nellie" or may bespeak "the conscience of the nation." The person who cannot get a mortgage may be seeking to live beyond his means or may be a casualty of a national "credit crunch." Each of these alternatives suggests quite different attitudes about the situation and appropriate public policies which might respond to it. And yet no alternative is intrinsically the "right" way to view the situation. Which alternative prevails will depend upon *choices* made by political actors themselves, as they define situations in their own minds and exchange their views with others.

What is true of politics in this respect is true of human behavior generally. While there certainly may exist an objective world independent of the human will, the events of that world are given meaning and significance through the exercise of human choice. Truth may be "given," but reality is socially constructed.[2] People participate actively in shaping and giving meaning to their environment. What any element in that environment "is" will depend on what it "means."

The medium for exchanging individual meanings is the symbol. A symbol, broadly put, is anything which stands for or indicates something else. The "objects" of our world are made meaningful through the symbols which indicate them. As Joel Charon defines the term in his study of symbolic interaction, "A symbol is any object, mode of conduct, or word toward which we act as if it were something else. Whatever the symbol stands for constitutes its meaning."[3] Symbols serve three closely related functions: they define a situation, they shape our response to the situation, and they make possible our interaction and communication with others.

Since the meaning of a situation is not intrinsically given, it must be chosen. By selecting which symbols indicate the situation, people define what it means.[4] They do so first by making indications to themselves, making sense of the world by creating a symbol system which defines and explains it. As J. Robert Cox explains in his study of definition of the situation, "Such *naming* of objects imbues them with meaning, power, and attraction. Through the naming of social objects, then, actors construct the basis for understanding a situation."[5] This understanding will determine the appropriate response to the situation. If the phenomenon of a person lacking work is symbolized as indolence, sloth, or sinfulness, then stern admonition might be called for but public employment programs would seem extremely inappropriate. Conversely, if the same phenomenon is seen as a specific manifestation of a maladjusted economy, then moralizing or temporizing would seem ineffective if not hypocritical; the situation clearly calls for public action.

Interaction with others both influences the individual's choice of symbols and tests and refines that choice. Symbolic choices are not random; they are products of a perspective and world view fashioned through interaction with significant others. When these world views partake of many similar elements, it is possible to speak of the symbol system, or definition of a situation, employed by a society as well as by an individual. The society's symbol system is constantly tested and modified through social interaction. Definitions of a situation which cannot square with experience will be modified or rejected, as happened when President Carter in 1979 was thought to characterize the national mood as "malaise." On the other hand, definitions which are congruent with experience and world view will come to be accepted, incorporated into the world view even as they modify it. For example, President Nixon's early call for "negotiation" rather than "confrontation" with the Soviet Union responded well to the paradox of the time. Americans remained distrustful of their adversary yet sought relief from the tensions of the world. To characterize superpower relations as "negotiation" was to remove the symbols of belligerence and threat associated with "confrontation" yet retain the symbol of "hard bargaining." Gradually, however, the symbol modified our national expectations about the Soviet Union, such that the president could portray détente not as appeasement or surrender but as a major foreign policy triumph.

Increasingly, scholars of politics have recognized the importance of symbolic action. There has been a growing awareness that citizens do not respond passively to stimuli but participate actively in the political world of which they are a part. Studies from this perspective have examined individual actions as well as institutional roles. The choice of "unconditional surrender" as the objective of World War II is an example of the former; Robert E. Denton's study of the symbolic dimension of the presidency illustrates the latter.[6] Perhaps best known is the work of Murray Edelman, who has described American politics generally as symbolic action, focusing on impulses to arousal and quiescence.[7]

What is less generally recognized, however, is the central role of rhetoric in the construction of social reality. In political life, the term "rhetoric" often is taken to mean only the catchy slogan, the vivid phrase which embellishes a public statement. Sometimes the term is used to refer to the public pronouncement which is issued as a "front" to conceal the darker machinations of government. But, as used here, the term's meaning is far broader and more neutral—rhetoric may be taken to be the study of the process of public persuasion. It is the study of how symbols influence people.[8] It encompasses a concern for the terms in which issues are defined, since a definition will highlight some aspects of an issue while diminishing others, and the choice of what is highlighted will make the issue more or less persuasive. Rhetoric involves the selection of symbols which will represent ideas, since those symbols evoke support or opposition by virtue of their association with an audience's prior experience and belief. Rhetoric includes the choices among possible appeals and arguments, since these choices influence whether audiences will be convinced that a proposal is in their interest. And rhetoric includes decisions about how to explain ambiguous situations, so that they may be taken as evidence for one's point of view rather than the opposite.

To view a question of public policy as a problem of rhetoric, then, is to focus on the creation and exchange of symbols through which issues are perceived, defined, addressed, and resolved. In a government based on consent, any policy proposal can be examined from a rhetorical perspective. Ways must be found to persuade relevant audiences to support the proposal. Hence the audiences must be identified, their values and presuppositions examined. This process—which the astute politician often performs instinctively—makes it possible to predict how the audience is likely to characterize a situation and hence how it will act in response to it. Then, strategies must be imagined and symbols generated to associate the policy proposal with the audience's values and predispositions. What is involved here is neither pandering to the audience nor passively laying a proposal before an audience in the confidence that the merits are self-evident but an active process of mutual adjustment. Both the audience and the proposal are somehow changed as a result. A rhetorical perspective on events focuses on what happens to ideas and to people in the course of such transformations.[9]

A rhetorical perspective need not imply that the historical advocates consciously think of what they do as a process of public persuasion. Sometimes they are quite conscious of their audience analysis, but often—like skilled artists in any field—their method and strategy are instinctive. To examine public discourse is to *interpret* events, not necessarily to describe how the actors consciously viewed the events. The working assumption is that motives may be revealed to the sensitive critic through the discourse itself.[10]

In the broadest sense, the approach of a rhetorical study of public policy relies on a problem-solution structure. The first steps are to examine the situation and to determine which elements pose problems in persuasion. Who needs to be convinced of what? What prior beliefs or values make the task difficult or constrain the advocate's choices? Then, the focus shifts to the processes of making and using symbols by which people characterize the "reality" of the situation. What were the advocates' patterns of symbolic choice, their evident strategies? How did they work? What immediate and long-range consequences did they have? And how well did they resolve the problem in persuasion?

II

Any such analysis must begin with the realization that in modern American society the presidency is the primary source of symbols about public issues. The agenda-setting power of the presidency has been noted often, meaning that the president's actions affect what issues people regard as important. The symbol-making activity of the president and his aides also influences how people define those issues and situations and consequently the predispositions with which they respond to them.

Ceaser, Thurow, Tulis, and Bessette traced what they call "the rise of the rhetorical presidency" to Woodrow Wilson's assertion that the president should be the "one national voice" who would arouse public opinion by articulating the public's wishes and feelings, and then would draw on public opinion to pressure Congress to adopt his program.[11] But implicit in Wilson's theory was the belief that the president's rhetorical task was to speak "not the rumors of the street, but a new principle for a new age; . . . so that he can speak what no man else knows, the common meaning of the common voice."[12] In other words, the president's task is to understand the situation and tap the national character in order to give expression to previously latent thoughts that would serve to unify and inspire the people. The job is to find the "deep structure" of symbols which are shared by people who otherwise speak in "the accidental and discordant notes that come from the voice of a mob"[13] and then to associate those symbols with his own policy or program. As Ceaser and his colleagues summarize, "the picture of leadership that emerges under the influence of this doctrine is one that constantly exhorts in the name of a common purpose and a spirit of idealism."[14]

Many twentieth-century presidents—one thinks immediately of Wilson, both Roosevelts, Kennedy, Johnson, and even Reagan—governed according to this formulation of the rhetorical presidency. Their programs required

congressional action in response to situations whose
"meaning" was never self-evident. Their primary weapon
was public opinion mobilized by their own efforts to see a
situation defined in a certain way. Whether it is Kennedy
enlisting support for civil rights by characterizing the
problem as a moral issue or Reagan pleading for his
economic program by defining the American ills as excessive taxation and regulation, the objective is to symbolize a situation so as to attract public and congressional
support.

If anything, the trend toward the rhetorical presidency
has been intensified by the prominence of the electronic
mass media, requiring that the president address diverse
audiences at once; by the weakening of traditional interest groups and political parties, which previously had
provided bases of support; by the elongated presidential
campaign, which draws constant attention to building and
maintenance of political coalitions; and by the increasingly complex nature of political issues, which has been
unmatched by any noticeable public willingness to believe
that problems are complicated and solutions beyond our
grasp. Increasingly, the president functions as the chief
inventor and broker of the symbols of American politics.

III

Definition is the president's greatest asset in filling this
role. Language is not a neutral instrument; to name an
object or idea is to influence attitudes about it. Hence it
can be said that to choose a definition is to plead a cause.
Indeed, the skillful choice of definitions can enable a
rhetor simultaneously to plead more than one cause, as
audiences with different interests and agendas are at-

tracted to different aspects of a definition. Defining terms is an important resource for any advocate who faces conflicting or contradictory demands, as the modern president always does.

Approaches to defining terms are legion, but three theories are particularly important for the analysis here. In their analysis of rhetoric as argumentation, Chaim Perelman and L. Olbrechts-Tyteca describe *dissociation* as a means for redefining terms by breaking links between concepts.[15] A seemingly unitary concept is divided by pairing it with two philosophically opposed terms, one of which is a value generally thought to be preferred over the other. An example of such a "philosophical pair" is theory/practice; after all, of what use is a theory that does not work in practice? The originally unitary idea is then equated with the less preferred member of the philosophical pair, and the speaker's reformulation of the idea, with the more preferred term. The original term, with all its heritage and connotations, thereby takes on a different referential meaning. Lyndon Johnson effectively dissociated the term "poverty" when he argued that poverty was not really just a lack of money but a whole culture and a way of life. He used the philosophical pair appearance/reality to change the referent of "poverty." It *appeared* to be only a matter of money income (which would have required politically unacceptable measures of redistribution), but Johnson argued that it *really* was a lifestyle (which his proposed programs could address without being politically threatening).[16]

Schematically, the process of dissociation can be represented in the following steps: (1) Prior to argument, B is generally regarded as the equivalent of A, so that A is taken to mean B. (2) B is now argued to be only some *aspect* of A, and a relatively undesirable aspect at that—

only the "means" to an end, the "letter" of A, the "appearance" of A, and so on. (3) In contrast, a new term, C, is argued to be the more desirable aspect—the "true end" of A, the "spirit" of A, the "reality" of A. (4) Hence A effectively is redefined as designating C rather than B. Dissociations are employed when the formerly unitary term comes to seem self-contradictory or to lead to unacceptable results but cannot be altogether abandoned.

A second, and closely related, theory of definition is provided by Charles L. Stevenson's discussion of the persuasive definition. Briefly, a persuasive definition is one in which the favorable or adverse connotation of a term remains constant while the specific denotation of the term is changed.[17] In this manner the attitudes surrounding the original term are maintained even though the referent for the term is shifted. The definition is called "persuasive" because it conveys not only meaning but attitude. Johnson employed persuasive definition in labeling the antipoverty effort as war. On the theory that the symbol of war during the early 1960s encompassed such positive attributes as national unity, total mobilization of effort, selfless dedication to a cause, and all-out assault on the foe, Johnson tried to transfer these favorable connotations to his antipoverty program.

The war metaphor also illustrates the third general theory of definition, the distinction drawn by Edward Sapir between *referential* and *condensation* symbols.[18] With referential symbols, it is fairly clear what is indicated by the symbol. Physical objects and social roles are often indicated by referential symbols. In contrast, condensation symbols designate no clear referent but serve to "condense" into one symbol a host of different meanings and connotations which might diverge if more specific referents were attempted. Abstract objects, ideas, or principles are often indicated by condensation symbols. The American flag is for many people a condensation symbol, coalescing such diverse emotions as personal pride, respect for the dead, self-confidence, loyalty to the government, and identification with the heroes of the past. Condensation symbols are particularly useful when applied to ambiguous situations, because they enable an individual to focus on the specific aspects of the situation that are most meaningful. One person might highlight personal pride, another, respect for the dead; but both "read into" the condensation symbol those aspects of its meaning that are most important to them.

The function of presidential definition is primarily to shape the context in which events or proposals are viewed by the public. Context does not absolutely *determine* response, but it contains presumptions. A presumption is a person's predisposition to think or act in a certain way in the absence of compelling reasons to the contrary. The burden of proof is on the advocate who would disrupt or overturn presumption. Consequently, the president's goal is to place ambiguous situations into a context such that the presumed response is congenial to his purpose.

As the rhetorical critic G. Thomas Goodnight has argued, much of American politics can be seen as the tension between liberal and conservative presumptions.[19] The liberal presumption sees change as both inevitable and desirable and assigns to government an active role in its stimulation and direction. Liberals, in this view, will generally favor policies grounded in these judgments. The conservative presumption, in contrast, veers toward stability and is suspicious of an active governmental role. Although one or the other presumption may dominate during a given period of time, the long-term effectiveness of the political system depends upon its ability to encompass both. Claims which veer unabashedly toward either pole, without acknowledging the legitimacy of the alternative presumption, are likely to be dismissed as unreasonable.

In certain periods of United States history, notably the eras of Progressivism, the New Deal, and the Great Society, the liberal presumption has been dominant. It has been reflected in an impatience with social conditions, which are thought to be perfectible, in the assumption that the political system is capable of adjustments which will make it work better, and in the belief that the task of government is to stimulate action directed toward this end. Never, though, has this presumption been given completely free rein. Arguments for the abolition of capitalism, the equalization of wealth, or the abandonment of the work ethic are generally dismissed as unreasonable. Each of the four twentieth-century presidents whom John Morton Blum has described as "progressive"[20] advocated his programs in large part on the grounds that the program *preserved* important values or represented an *alternative* to more drastic action which might be taken otherwise.

In like manner, a political administration which is predominantly conservative must counterbalance appeals to the liberal and the conservative presumptions. Calls for strengthening individual initiative, references to the impossibility of drastically changing society, and admonitions for less government interference in people's lives are seldom absolute. Were conservatives to call for the wholesale dismantling of major governmental efforts—the logical extension of their philosophical system—their arguments would be rejected as unreasonable, as Barry Goldwater discovered in 1964 when he proposed to sell the Tennessee Valley Authority and to make participation in Social Security voluntary.

In short, then, it is the dialectical tension between the liberal and conservative presumptions which sustains political institutions and furnishes the context for argument within them. But the president's definition of a situation can help to make arguments tending toward one or the other presumption seem more reasonable. Perhaps the most effective means for weighting an issue on the side of the liberal presumption is to be able to define a situation as a *crisis*. By their nature, crises cannot be resolved through "business as usual"; it is precisely the failure of normal processes to resolve a problem that transforms an ordinary issue into a crisis. Crises do not admit of time for reflective deliberation; the situation is urgent. A presumption for action is established. Action, to be successful, must reflect centralized control, clear direction, and efficient movement. These considerations all exalt the role of the federal government in planning and implementing change. Even if the change is made to *preserve* values and beliefs, the impetus for change comes from the liberal belief in the perfectibility of man and the benign nature of governmentally sponsored change. The War on Poverty was launched within this framework, drawing heavily on the consensus of modern liberalism, yet eventually exposing its dilemmas and drawbacks.

IV

The president has considerable power to shape public perceptions through his choice of symbols with which to define the situation, but his power is not absolute. The symbol must strike a responsive chord among various publics if it is to stay alive. Otherwise it may go the way of Richard Nixon's vaunted "New American Revolution," Jimmy Carter's "national malaise," or Ronald Reagan's dubbing the MX missile the "peacekeeper"—all instances in which a symbol not only failed to take hold among the American people but exposed its author to public ridicule.

The process by which symbols are picked up and used by wider audiences has been described by Ernest Bormann. Drawing an analogy to the process of group fantasizing, Bormann referred to the fantasies captured in the symbols of public discourse. These dramatizations, he wrote, "are worked into public speeches and into the mass media and, in turn, spread out across larger publics, serve to sustain the members' sense of community, to impel them strongly to action . . . and to provide them with a social reality filled with heroes, villains, emotions, and attitudes."[21] The power of the symbol, then, is not automatic upon its formulation but depends on its "chaining out" as it speaks to the needs of wider audiences.

Within the sphere of political rhetoric, three aspects of this "chaining out" process especially warrant attention. First, key audiences begin to use the term and also to articulate its ancillary symbols and images. The "New Frontier" proclaimed by President Kennedy became a meaningful symbol when it received widespread use and when the related images of discovery, exploration, charting a course, and pursuing the unknown were given expression. This symbolic lexicon provided the means for people to develop and display the implicit dramas to which Bormann referred. After Kennedy's assassination, the symbol of Camelot and its associated images served the same purpose. Likewise, when President Johnson was searching for a phrase to characterize *his* administration, the difference between "Better Deal" and "Great Society" was that the former was ignored whereas the latter encouraged other symbols of idealism and hope and came to stand for major improvements in the quality of American life.[22] In the case of the War on Poverty, the symbol of war became important as it was picked up by influential audiences and as it gave rise to the related symbols of soldiers, ammunition, a battle plan, and an enemy.

Second, political symbols create expectations. The president moves people to action by holding out a vision of what might be. This vision is necessarily based in the future, and there is a gap between what is and what might be; indeed, it is this very gap on which the president relies for forceful persuasion. But to locate the gap is also to create the expectation that it will be closed.[23] Political symbols, in other words, not only define the situation but create standards for public judgment. Here the rhetor in politics confronts a difficult choice. If the vision is not grand enough, it will not impel people to action, especially if sacrifice is required. In part because economic conditions changed, but also because he never managed to portray the conquest of inflation as lofty or noble, President Ford failed to inspire support for his campaign to "Whip Inflation Now." On the other hand, an extravagant vision may be impossible to achieve in practice. Even if people are better off than they were before, they subjectively perceive themselves to be worse off because of the great gap between their actual situation and the promise held out to them. Some have argued that President Johnson courted this fate by calling for such grand objectives as "full educational opportunity," the conquest of disease, and the goal of "total victory" in an "unconditional war" on poverty.

Third, as condensation symbols chain out in the political sphere, their symbolic force dissipates. The reason is that their strategic ambiguity proves difficult to sustain. Ambiguous symbols enhance the adoption of laws; they retard implementation. A condensation symbol is attractive during the process of enactment because people of divergent attitudes may unite by use of a common symbol. But the divergent attitudes do not go away. Decisions must be made about how to administer a law, priorities must be set, and tangible results must become available for inspection. The vision and force which powered the condensation symbol become channeled into administrative routine; Kenneth Burke has referred to the process as "bureaucratization of the imaginative."[24] These results are perceived and judged from different vantage points. People who adhered to a symbol because it suggested one meaning will become disenchanted if it comes to suggest something else. Some may continue to support a program; others may believe it is misdirected; and still others may conclude that it was well-intentioned but that it defaulted or "sold out" on its original promise. A kind of symbolic entropy characterizes the career of many condensation symbols in politics.

Avoiding this entropic transformation requires luck or deliberate intervention, or perhaps both. Though it is highly unlikely, a political program could be fortunate enough to continue to satisfy all the attitudes which its symbols unify, so that its support is not fragmented or weakened. One would be hard put, however, to identify any political program that has been so lucky. In the modern era, perhaps Social Security is the closest approximation. Born in controversy, it quickly acquired a bipartisan consensus of support and for many years was thought to be politically unassailable. Recently, however, even Social Security has come under fire, the result of both demography and inflation.

If not through luck, then, the power of a condensation symbol can perhaps be sustained by active intervention to reassert the vision and to force the evolution of the symbol. Successive redefinitions may be used so that the focus of the symbol gradually shifts while its force remains. The natural dissipation of symbolic force is checked by redefinition, which offers an imperceptibly different vision responsive to changing circumstances. During 1981 and 1982, for example, President Reagan gradually redefined the symbol of the "social safety net" for the "truly needy" to sustain the impression that his policy was both frugal and compassionate at the same time.[25] President Roosevelt in the 1930s modified the meaning of the New Deal to move it leftward while retaining its symbolic power. The prerequisite for any successful intervention is that the symbol must not be an empty slogan, such as candidate John Kennedy's "A Time for Greatness" or candidate Ronald Reagan's "A New Beginning." Interestingly, both slogans were quickly abandoned once the election was won. Rather, the symbol must embody a vision to which audiences respond and yet which has enough fuzziness to permit imperceptible shadings in its referent without loss of its symbolic force.

This discussion of "chaining out" and symbolic transformations suggests that the implications of symbolic choice develop over time. Yet most studies of public discourse are not longitudinal in nature but focus on one or more texts, either as static entities or as one-time responses to an immediate situation. The primary exception is the research literature on the rhetoric of social movements, with its emphasis on their development and decay over time. Although an insurgent social movement and an "establishment" public policy are quite different entities, many of the principles that explain the rhetoric of social movements also explain the discourse produced by "establishment" efforts as well.

In two separate essays, Leland Griffin has described the rhetorical development of movements. Movements may be *pro,* attempting to arouse public opinion to the creation or acceptance of a new idea, or *anti,* aiming for the destruction or rejection of an existing institution. In either case, a study of the movement will identify *aggressor* rhetors, who seek in the former case to establish and in the latter to destroy, and *defendant* rhetors, who seek to resist the impetus of the *pro* movement or to preserve the status quo against the *anti* movement. Chronologically, the movement passes through three rhetorical phases: a period of *inception,* during which the aggressor rhetors reject the existing state of affairs, choose an alternative, and propagate this alternative in search of converts; a period of *rhetorical crisis,* in which it becomes impossible to maintain a mental balance between aggressor and defendant rhetors and hence members of the audience must make choices; and a period of *consummation,* during which a decision is persevered in—either the movement was successful and the aggressor rhetors may abandon their efforts, or the cause was lost and further appeals are useless.[26]

The rhetorical trajectory of a social movement may also be applied to other persuasive ventures. Groups out of power may conceive of themselves as "movements" in order to convey a sense of destiny which sustains the adherence of the faithful. Groups in power may see themselves as "movements" in order that greater significance may be attached to their actions. Advocates may define a given situation as consensus or conflict not because they are the rulers or the oppressed, but because definition serves the strategic purpose of widening or narrowing the scope of conflict.[27] The essence of a democratic polity is that it is open to a multiplicity of speakers and modes of advocacy. As Paul Wilkinson aptly summarizes, "The rhetoric of movement may almost be said to have its own momentum."[28] That being the case, the chronology of symbolic choice and transformation might usefully be explored by tracing public discourse through the periods of inception, rhetorical crisis, and consummation. In what follows, the War on Poverty is examined in such a fashion. It enjoyed a period of inception when President Johnson proclaimed the war and the Congress considered and passed the Economic Opportunity Act. It underwent rhetorical crisis between 1965 and 1967 as all the key symbols—the objective, the enemy, and the weapons and tactics—were transformed. Finally, it experienced consummation in 1967 and 1968 when Congress chose not to emasculate the Office of Economic Opportunity (OEO) yet so compromised the original vision that the Johnson administration ended the war in stalemate.

V

The War on Poverty offers a fitting case study in which to examine the force of symbolic choice, the role of rhetoric in public policy. In some respects it is atypical. Major social policies usually are adopted only after a long and difficult campaign. The path from conception to enactment often takes many years in which a wider public is attracted. But the War on Poverty was initiated within the government by a task force inherited from President

Kennedy. There was no collection of supportive interest groups, and the public was not sanguine about the prospects for success. So the president had to enlist support from across the country. Nor did the cause require many years for its consummation. Barely two months passed between the president's call for action and the introduction of the antipoverty bill in Congress. Five months later, the Economic Opportunity Act became law.

Yet the War on Poverty was in many ways the apex of the liberal reform efforts of the 1960s, clearly embodying the assumptions of the liberal argument: society was benign; "fine tuning" could provide opportunities for those left out, without seriously threatening the interests of the well-to-do; opportunities would translate into results; the values of the middle class were shared by the poor; an expanding economy made it possible to alleviate poverty without redistribution of income or wealth; and the federal government was a fit instrument for carrying out these purposes. All of these assumptions have been challenged if not overtaken by events; few have survived into the 1980s. The War on Poverty offers a case study of what went wrong with the liberal assumptions. And, since it offers a clear case of shaping context through the use of definitions, with symbolic transformations which can be identified and analyzed, it throws into sharp focus the relationship between public discourse and policy.

In the chapters which follow, the Johnson administration's definition of the situation is traced through the periods of inception, rhetorical crisis, and consummation. The military metaphor suggested choices about how to describe the objective, the enemy, and the weapons and tactics. Each of these choices was helpful in obtaining the passage of the Economic Opportunity Act of 1964, but each also contained the seeds of its own destruction. The account in this book should help to explain how.

2

Inception

The War Is Declared

The decision to call the antipoverty effort a war was made at the Johnson ranch during the Christmas holidays of 1963. Although the choice of language might seem casual, Johnson maintained in his memoirs that it was deliberate. He wrote, "The military image carried with it connotations of victories and defeats that could prove misleading. But I wanted to rally the nation, to sound a call to arms which would stir people in the government, in private industry, and on the campuses to lend their talents to a massive effort to eliminate the evil."[1] His intentions were publicly announced in his first State of the Union message, on January 8, 1964. Perhaps the most newsworthy element of the speech was the president's confident assertion that "this administration, here and now, declares unconditional war on poverty."

I

Instinctively, the president sensed the need to inspire and rally the nation and found in the war metaphor the means to that end. Aroused by President Kennedy's untimely death, many Americans longed for redemption through sacrifice. The Harris Poll reported on December 30, 1963, that Americans massively rejected political extremism and also that many had "an individual sense of guilt for not having worked more for tolerance toward others."[2] Enlisting in the national service during wartime might expiate that guilt. Before the military conflict in Vietnam called into question the patriotism of war, the administration could use war against an ancient, impersonal foe as the means by which to cater to the national need.

Not only was the declaration of war responsive to the national mood after Dallas, but it also was personally and politically valuable to the new president. When he told Walter Heller to continue planning for a program, his decision reflected his own roots: his youth in a region to which poverty had been no stranger, his memory of how poverty debilitated the young, and his knowledge that the New Deal had brought not just relief but a sense of hope. Johnson's background and convictions were not well known among the American people when he took office, however. Only 5 percent of the people thought they knew a great deal about Johnson—compared with 24 percent for Kennedy at the time of his inauguration. On the other hand, 67 percent reported that they knew very little about Johnson, as opposed to 17 percent for Kennedy. Both Republican candidates Nelson Rockefeller and Barry Goldwater had been seen or heard by twice as many people as had Johnson.[3] Clearly the new president needed to establish an identity and create a positive impression among the American people. Aside from averting chaos and panic, developing his image probably was his single greatest need in the days following the assassination.

Moreover, although he disdained such labels, Johnson often had been regarded as a southern conservative whose perspective was limited to his own region. Recent scholarship has clearly demonstrated the influence of Franklin D. Roosevelt on Johnson.[4] But that influence was felt most clearly in the Texan's early years, and the years since World War II seemed to suggest that Johnson had trimmed his liberal sails and had catered to the wishes of the new Texas wealth. Unless he could change this image to become a *national* politician, Johnson could not depend upon the support of a nationwide majority. Paradoxically, however, his heritage also counted in his favor. His advocacy of a major government program presumably would constitute reluctant testimony to its effectiveness, thereby enhancing his own credibility. This phenomenon illustrated a principle described by his speechwriter, Harry McPherson: "reasonable things could be done best by those whose heritage required that they oppose them."[5]

Other aspects of the new president's image also were important. He needed a transition between his caretaker role after the Kennedy assassination and his own presidency. He had to safeguard and nurture the Kennedy legacy, in keeping with his role as executor of the late president's political will. But as president in his own right, he also needed to define himself as a leader separate and distinct from President Kennedy. This seeming dilemma could be overcome by identifying himself with a program which Kennedy supporters might champion enthusiastically but which was not yet publicly labeled as a Kennedy effort. The new president also could distinguish himself from his predecessor if he could break the congressional logjam. By late July 1963, for example, nearly 40 percent of Kennedy's proposals had not been acted on by *either* House.[6] By initiating a major program and obtaining prompt congressional action, Johnson could restore a sense of momentum.

Poverty, then, offered Johnson immense benefits as a public issue, but only if he could arouse public and congressional support. Otherwise he could neither respond to the national mood after the assassination nor reap the personal and political dividends. It is easy in retrospect to underestimate the need to generate substantial public support, but in 1963 there existed no sense of national urgency about poverty. Douglass Cater, then national affairs editor of *The Reporter,* complained that publicists had not made it a national issue. The governor of North Carolina, Terry Sanford, testified in Congress that among the basic problems of poverty was the fact that people were unaware of it.[7] Nor were there organized strong interest groups, either among the poor or in their behalf.[8] Nor were Americans sanguine about the prospects of an antipoverty campaign: the Gallup Poll reported in 1964 that 83 percent of its sample did not believe that poverty could be ended.[9]

Although the public could be described as generally apathetic about poverty, there were occasional expressions of interest and concern from the politically marginal "new left" and from the civil rights movement. The left for some time had shown concern for the poverty problem. *Dissent* and *New America,* Lander reports, devoted far more attention to poverty than did the less radical *Commentary,* the *Nation,* and the *Progressive.* Moreover, leftist publications described the conditions of the poor in terms of moral outrage rather than romanticism.[10] Poverty also received mention in the Socialist party platforms of 1960 and 1962 (the latter contained the phrase "war on poverty") and in the 1962 Port Huron statement of Students for a Democratic Society. Probably the most significant event in making the general public aware of poverty, however, was the publication in 1962 of Michael Harrington's *The Other America.*[11]

Lacking the political leadership of lobbies or the informal political organization of the slums, Harrington argued, the poor themselves could not be expected to launch a movement for their own material improvement. They would need allies, but therein lay the paradox. Because so many Americans enjoyed the luxuries of affluence, they were indifferent or blind to poverty, and would remain that way "until there is a vast social movement, a new period of political creativity."[12]

Harrington's book, however, hardly was received with instant acclaim. But it attracted the attention of Dwight Macdonald, who reviewed the book (and several others) in the January 19, 1963, issue of the *New Yorker.* Theodore Sorensen reportedly urged President Kennedy to read the Macdonald article; Walter Heller gave the president a copy of *The Other America,* "although it is not known whether the President read it."[13] The civil rights movement, at about the same time, came to see that widespread social reform would be needed in order to achieve its objectives and that poverty was the issue which would expose this need. Once the nonviolent demonstrations of the early 1960s had kindled what Bayard Rustin called "the resurgence of social conscience,"[14] it was easier to see economic deprivation as part of an overall pattern. Once racial discrimination was shown to be national rather than peculiarly southern, it was easier to argue that civil rights laws would be of no avail to those without means. Once the problem of the black was defined as inequality, it was easier to maintain that redistributional policies were necessary.

The experience of its own social programs, the "new

left," and the civil rights movement led members of the Kennedy administration in 1963 to redefine poverty as a generic condition underlying many specific social problems. But these efforts failed to incite any significant public interest, and most Americans remained unaware of the problem of poverty at the time that Lyndon Johnson took office.

President Johnson engaged in a persuasive campaign to change this public judgment. He followed the State of the Union address with a series of speeches in the spring of 1964 to informal gatherings, university audiences, conventions, and civic groups, ranging, according to Doris Kearns, "from the Daughters of the American Revolution to the Socialist Party, from the Business Council to the AFL-CIO."[15] By his own account, the president chose to emphasize the goals rather than the contents of the poverty program. His basic message to the nation was that "the War on Poverty was not a partisan effort. It was a moral obligation and its success rested on every one of us."[16] These memorable, though vague, statements of objectives answered a vital need, by conveying a sense of Johnson's ability quickly to cope with the problems of the presidency.[17] In addition to his speeches, the president made personal visits to poverty-stricken areas. He also enlisted the support of influential businessmen who spoke in behalf of the program. They, too, frequently spoke only of the program's goals. They had been convinced that antipoverty legislation was essential as a matter of principle, and they were not very familiar with the legislative details. Also aiding the campaign were a number of articles and books aimed at convincing the layman of the scope of the problem.[18] Unlike the more technical literature, these books had as their goal the mobilization of attitudes rather than the presentation of data. They provided the general reader with basic information and arguments which could cultivate a favorable attitude toward the antipoverty program.

Another force aiding Johnson's national campaign was the speaking of Sargent Shriver. Shriver was talented as a lobbyist, as was evident from his successes in inspiring the nation to support the Peace Corps and in securing ample appropriations from an economy-minded Congress. He also had a special talent for identifying his message with the needs of his audience. Murray Kempton described Shriver's abilities in this regard by writing, "Sargent Shriver is a man who, at one and the same moment, manages to remind the dedicated that they can achieve the American vision only by intense personal sacrifice and to assure the indifferent that the American vision is theirs on a payment plan so easy that they will barely feel it."[19] Although Shriver's capacities as a salesman and lobbyist would not always be regarded as strengths, they definitely were assets in eliciting public support for an antipoverty program.

One particular aspect of the appeal for public support deserves mention. The Democrats had won the 1960 election by the slimmest of margins, and it appeared that the urban black vote was crucial to this success. Especially with the disappearance of traditional urban ethnic political machines, it became important that the Democrats solidify the loyalty of urban blacks. One obvious way to try to do so was by making them the beneficiaries of federal largesse. It also was important, however, that whites not be alienated, lest the Democrats gain one source of support only by losing another. Therefore, programs in aid of the poor must mute the question of race, translating it into terms which would command biracial support.

It is unclear to what degree this political situation functioned as a conscious motive for President Johnson and his staff. Writing retrospectively, Daniel Patrick Moynihan has claimed that administration planners were aware of the Democrats' need to solidify their political base, and that it was their intention to recreate the urban political machines. Other writers, such as Frances Fox Piven, have identified the appeal to the black vote as a function which the antipoverty program could perform, without addressing the question of whether such appeal was the administration's conscious objective.[20]

In any case, the president was successful in generating public support. Doris Kearns has written that "what had been largely the concern of a small number of liberal intellectuals and government bureaucrats became within six months the national disgrace that shattered the complacency of a people who always considered their country a land of equal opportunity for all."[21] In performing this feat, Johnson was aided greatly by the language in which he cast his program. The elements and implications of the military metaphor therefore deserve careful attention.

II

Even a casual reading should make plain the degree to which the military imagery penetrated public discourse. The war metaphor may be seen, of course, in President Johnson's State of the Union address and in his subsequent speeches. It may be found in the call made by Congressman Phil Landrum of Georgia for total mobilization of all the nation's resources, "moral, spiritual, intellectual, and financial, to challenge a condition."[22] It may be found as well in numerous corollary metaphors. Walter Reuther testified that the labor movement had "made it clear to the President that we enlist with him in the war against poverty for the duration." Mayor Raymond Tucker of St. Louis said that "to wheel up weapons and ammunition together for the first time for a coordinated, concerted, multifront offensive" was the aim of the Economic Opportunity Act, the plan of battle for a war in which the U.S. Conference of Mayors was one of the first recruits. Describing the Volunteers in Service to America (VISTA) program, the president rhapsodized in his message to Congress that dedicated Americans would be given "the opportunity to enlist as volunteers in the war against poverty." The normally staid Council of Economic Advisers described chapter 2 of its 1964 report as "designed to provide some understanding of the enemy and to outline the main features of a strategy of attack." And Secretary of Labor Willard Wirtz told the House committee, "This war on poverty is not going to be fought in the tradition of emotional crusades. H.R. 10440 [the Economic Opportunity Act of 1964] is a carefully worked out battle plan based less on praising the Lord than on passing the ammunition." Even opponents of the pending measure indulged in military symbolism. For example, Senator John Tower of Texas referred to the preemption of local control and representative government as "the first casualty of the war on poverty."[23]

Three elements of the war metaphor particularly deserve attention. It defined the objective and encouraged enlistment in the effort, it identified the enemy against whom the campaign was directed, and it dictated the choice of weapons and tactics with which the struggle would be fought.

Defining the Objective. In declaring *unconditional* war, the president made clear that his objective was vast. Not for limited goals was this fight to be waged. It was to be a total assault on the foe, as Agriculture Secretary Orville Freeman testified, "for as long as it takes, using whatever means must be employed, until the goal is won."[24] The strategic value of declaring unconditional war was apparent. It logically demanded a nationwide program.

As vice president, Johnson had played no role in the embryonic thinking and planning about poverty during the Kennedy administration, which had built largely on the experience of the juvenile delinquency program initiated in 1961. This measure made available federal funds to support demonstration projects in the prevention and control of delinquency. Approximately fifteen cities had pilot programs designed to alter the "opportunity structure" of the inner-city ghetto, thought to be the breeding ground of delinquency.[25] In a similar vein, the antipoverty task force in December 1963 favored small-scale demonstration projects in no more than fifty poverty areas. Moreover, a project would be started only after completion of comprehensive, coordinated planning. Early news reports had stressed that the forthcoming antipoverty program would *not* be an accelerated, all-out effort.[26]

Labor Secretary Willard Wirtz attacked this assumption. An unconditional war, he contended, could not be fought with a single weapon in a small number of target areas. Shriver, who had just assumed the chairmanship of the task force, was impressed by this presentation. Accordingly, on February 4, he decided to broaden the community action concept to include the entire nation—without, however, any increase from the $500 million proposed for community action projects. Shriver's explicit justification for this expansion was that the War on Poverty should be equal in scope and glamour to the image being presented in the communications media.[27] The rhetorical stance determined the direction of the policy. It converted a geographically limited program to an effort of national scope, and it de-emphasized comprehensive planning in favor of a stress on quick action.

Moreover, to advocate *unconditional* war was to imply that additional resources would be committed to the struggle as necessary in the future. In this way the antipoverty planners could reconcile the grand objectives of their effort with the low level of funding proposed for the Economic Opportunity Act. The 1964 act was to be but a *first step* in the War on Poverty. Larger attacks would be mounted as soon as the experimental probes exposed the enemy and demonstrated the weaponry for a successful assault. Shriver and his aides reportedly believed that the successes of early poverty projects would generate a supportive constituency which would demand massive increases in funds in subsequent years.[28] The unconditional war appeal was a device by which to establish first claim upon additional future revenues.

If a total national effort were to be made to wage unconditional war, then clearly there had to be centralized command. This rationale justified the creation of the new Office of Economic Opportunity, bypassing existing departments and agencies. Secretary of Health, Education, and Welfare Anthony Celebrezze explicitly linked this administrative structure to the war metaphor. "If you are going to declare war," he said, "you have to have one general of the Army. You cannot have six generals." And Congressman Landrum described the program by saying, "in recognizing this as D-day, we are just setting up a general just like we set up General Eisenhower as commander of all the forces in World War II and had him directing all those different areas of strength."[29] More-over, a separate agency would dramatize the administration's commitment to its program and would secure maximum publicity.

The war metaphor enlisted participation in the unconditional struggle. To begin with, it substantially reduced the administration's burden of proof. In any controversy, one side ultimately must prove its case; the other side enjoys presumption. The defendant in a criminal trial enjoys presumption because it is the prosecution's burden to establish guilt. Acquittal need not signify that the accused definitely has proved himself innocent; it means that the state has failed to prove guilt. Likewise, in disputes over public policy, presumption normally rests with the status quo, on the theory that present policies will continue unless alternatives are shown to be better. The classic treatment of presumption and burden of proof was written in the early nineteenth century by Richard Whately, who assigned presumption to the status quo. "There is a Presumption," he wrote, "in favour of every *existing* institution. Many of these (we will suppose, the majority) may be susceptible of alteration for the better, but still the 'Burden of Proof' lies with him who proposes an alteration; simply, on the ground that since a change is not a good in itself, he who demands a change should show cause for it."[30] Recourse to the presumption is, in Whately's view, one of the advocate's strongest arguments, since it enables him to avoid defending his position until it has been attacked.

Applied to the situation of 1964, Whately's presumption normally would rest with the existing antipoverty programs. To justify the adoption of the Economic Opportunity Act, the Johnson administration would have been required to identify substantial problems which those policies could not solve. Such an attempt would have been time-consuming and unlikely to succeed, given the predispositions of Congress and the nation. A far more expedient course would be for the proponents of the act to offer a counterpresumption which would have enabled *them* to claim preoccupation of the ground. This function the military symbolism accomplished. When a nation is at war, by definition, it has acknowledged the existence of a foe sufficiently threatening to warrant attack. A crisis is at hand, the need for action is assumed, and the persistent challenge of the enemy becomes prima facie evidence of the insufficiency of existing measures.[31] Hence, the Shriver group could stress getting programs started quickly because of the urgency of the problem and then making changes in the law later if need be.

While the war metaphor made it easier for the American people to enlist, it also made it harder for anyone to oppose the campaign. The president was able to identify the contending armies so as to isolate his opposition. A war, of course, implies the existence of an enemy. The enemy was an impersonal force, but it was aided by certain "neutrals" who did not enlist in the struggle. In a speech to the Communications Workers of America in June, the president attempted to describe these neutralists. The contest, he declared, was between the concerned and the indifferent, between the farsighted and those without vision, between "those who know that their future is tied to the future of all and those who ignore this great lesson of history."[32] This definition of the competing forces placed Republicans and dubious Democrats in a difficult position. They felt compelled to endorse the *objectives* of the bill, in order to rescue themselves from Johnson's characterization. On what other grounds, though, could they justify their opposition?

Some opponents charged that the symbolism of war was eulogistic covering for a bad bill. Senator Millard Simpson of Wyoming likened "War on Poverty" to "truth in lending": "an appealing phrase which is used in an attempt to make the bad seem good, the deceitful seem honest, and the fraudulent seem trustworthy." Senator A. Willis Robertson of Virginia decried symbolism which called upon him to vote for a bill "primarily because of the name it carries and the purposes it seeks to achieve, rather than upon testimony that the measure is actually needed and soundly conceived."[33]

Opponents of the Economic Opportunity Act also tried to capture the military symbolism for themselves, by claiming the *prior* existence of a war against poverty. The minority report of the House Education and Labor Committee claimed that America had already succeeded in its war against poverty, largely because of "a free and unregimented society, marked by a labor force and an industrial community untrammeled by the harsh hand of statism."[34]

Opponents also made several retorts to the proposed mobilization of resources and commitment to total victory. They taunted the administration for proclaiming this goal with respect to poverty when it seemingly was unwilling to do so in foreign affairs.[35] They argued that the programs would raise the expectations of the poor without providing the means to satisfy them; for this reason, former vice president Richard Nixon proclaimed the effort a "cruel hoax."[36] They argued that the commitment to use any resources necessary, while expressing the generous instincts of the American people, did not absolve legislators of the obligation to examine closely the propriety of the methods proposed.[37]

Republicans especially objected to the image of Sargent Shriver as commander in chief. During the House hear-

ings, Congressman Frelinghuysen of New Jersey mused,
"Maybe this is a good figure of speech to use and maybe it
is not." By the time of the floor debate, he had decided
the question. "The label of 'anti-poverty' on this poisonous concoction does not alter its content," he charged.
"Every power-struck totalitarian regime in modern history has promised to eliminate poverty through the complete centralization of power. Such nonsense has been the
lowest common denominator of totalitarianism of both
the right and of the left."[38]

For the most part, these tactics of opposition were
unsuccessful. Having chosen to focus the issue on the
poverty problem rather than a proposed solution, the
administration doggedly maintained its position, reinter-
preting opposing arguments as denials of the need for
action. President Johnson referred obliquely to several
objections raised by Frelinghuysen and then dismissed
them, saying, "Why anyone should hate an antipoverty
program, I don't know."[39] Once the attacks had been
redefined in terms of the administration's chosen focus, it
was easy to derogate them as partisan, trivial, and perni-
cious.

Not only did it reduce the burden of proof and isolate
the opposition, but the war metaphor also sustained national interest and participation. It was an effective unifying device. It is an item in the national folklore that war
subsumes all partisan strife in united effort for victory,
and pre-Vietnam history offers enough examples to make
the folklore credible. Appealing to the same spirit would
have maximum power in arousing an indifferent nation,
and would also help to stifle opposition (on the theory
that criticizing the government during wartime gives aid
and comfort to the enemy). In his congressional testimony, Mayor Daley of Chicago stated, "One characteris-

tic of the American people when a war is declared is that all sides come together, and this is a war."[40] This same appeal, it was hoped, would evoke an idealistic fervor which would prevent later backsliding or erosion of support. Interior Secretary Stewart Udall spoke to this theme in suggesting that the antipoverty effort might serve as William James's desired moral equivalent of war—more than self-defense, retaliation, or even vendetta, it was to be a crusade. President Johnson shared the same sentiments with the Advertising Council: "It is almost insulting to urge you to enlist in this war for just economic motivations. This is a moral challenge that goes to the very root of our civilization."[41]

In sum, the metaphor of war profoundly influenced the objectives of the poverty program. It made them vast; nothing less than the complete conquest of the foe would do. It made them national in scope and called for a centralized command. It captured presumption and thereby reduced the administration's burden of proof in appealing for recruits. It isolated the opposition and made opponents seem almost treasonous. And it served as a unifying device, rallying the nation behind a moral challenge.

It was assumed, of course, that the challenge could be met if only the will were there. Sometimes this assumption was made explicit. For the first time in history, the president believed, it was possible for a nation to eliminate poverty, and the government knew how to do it. He sounded this theme in his 1964 economic report and again in June in an address to the Communications Workers of America.[42] Both Robert Kennedy and Hubert Humphrey argued that, if America could launch a program of foreign aid for other peoples of the world, surely she could do as much for her own.[43] Others declared that a nation which could send a man to the moon certainly could relieve distress on earth. President Johnson acknowledged the potency of this comparison, noting in his memoirs that "space was the platform from which the social revolution of the 1960s was launched."[44]

Strictly speaking, of course, this claim to capacity and expertise was invalid. Statements about the nation's economic ability referred to the ability to fill the poverty-income gap—the difference between the income of the poor and the official "poverty line." Inasmuch as the poverty planners had *rejected* a definition of poverty as income deficiency, however, these statements were irrelevant. No evidence was introduced, nor could any have been, that the administration fully understood or knew how to deal with the cycle-of-poverty theory which it espoused. Similarly, the administration's presentation of its program as carefully conceived and designed was at variance with the facts, as the above review of the task force's decision-making processes should indicate. Finally, the analogies suggested by the *a fortiori* arguments were more apparent than real. The programs selected for comparison involved the technical capacity to implement agreed-upon objectives, such as the shipping of food or the assembling of rockets, rather than the selection of the objectives themselves. Competence in the former did not imply ability in the latter.

Largely because of the lack of expertise within the Congress, however, the administration's claims of adequate knowledge and technology did not receive serious challenge. Poverty was a new issue, and the Economic Opportunity Act cut across the jurisdictions of several congressional committees. Few members, therefore, were competent concerning all its provisions, and the prevailing disposition was to trust the executive.

Identifying the Enemy. No less substantial was the influence of the war metaphor on the identification of the enemy. It was not so much a precise statistical definition or a census of the poor that was needed, since by *any* acceptable definition the Economic Opportunity Act could help only a fraction of those in need. What *was* needed, though, was a working theory of the nature of poverty, so that a direction for the new program could be determined and appropriate targets selected.

This characterization drew on the American past. From the colonial period onward, the dominant belief was that poverty was an individual, not a social, problem. The working or self-supporting poor were paid scant heed; public policy concentrated on the control of pauperism. Paupers, those unable or unwilling to work, were seen in the same light as were criminals. They were characterized by reference to their drunkenness, vice, and moral depravity, conditions which in turn were asserted to be the causes of their plight. The mid-nineteenth-century humanitarian reform movements reinforced this approach, since their emphasis was on *individual* actions to improve one's life. Later, both the frontier West and the urbanizing East offered apparent access to economic opportunity. The seeming ease with which one could enjoy prosperity strengthened the belief that poverty was caused by individual defects. The individualist conception of poverty was given further support by the application to society of Charles Darwin's theory of evolution. Although thoroughly rooted in the nineteenth century, this point of view remained dominant well into the twentieth.

Between 1900 and 1960, however, this traditional view of poverty was challenged by a second perspective. The Progressive movement contributed the argument that poverty was a social phenomenon, not an imperfection of the individual, and that powerful social groups had an economic stake in its perpetuation. This argument placed special-interest groups on the defensive and led social reformers to become more tolerant of the personal derelictions of the poor. If poverty had its origin in circumstances too powerful for the individual to alter, then personal vices were more likely to be mechanisms for coping with the environment than the root causes of the individual's woe.

For those for whom relief was justified by this new perspective, private, voluntary measures were thought in principle to be superior to public aid. But increasing legitimacy was given to the use of the state's police power to compel behavior which would improve the individual's chance to escape poverty. It was assumed for some time, though, that local government should be responsible. Proponents of federal action suffered a major setback in 1854 when President Franklin Pierce vetoed a bill appropriating land to the states for the establishment of hospitals for the insane, on the grounds that charitable activities were a state function. Pierce's strict constructionism dominated most of the next century. Congressional moves to gain federal aid for the unemployed in 1893–94, 1914, and 1921 all failed. Federal child-labor laws were declared unconstitutional although similar state statutes were upheld. In 1932, President Hoover opposed direct federal relief for the unemployed because local communities could not be allowed to abandon their "precious possession of local initiative and responsibility."

It was Franklin Roosevelt's New Deal which established the place of the federal government in antipoverty policy. Roosevelt responded to the depression's severity by establishing the Federal Emergency Relief Administration, under the charge of Harry Hopkins. For the first time, the federal government assumed substantial responsibility for the administration and finance of relief. For the first time, aid was given as a right to which a citizen was entitled rather than as a charity bestowed upon particular groups. For the first time, relief was comprehensive, including not only the cost of food but other necessities such as rent, clothing, and medical care. Even so, Roosevelt soon wished to eliminate relief entirely, believing it to be destructive of individual initiative and spirit. In its place, he proposed a massive program of public employment and the adoption of the Social Security Act. Both measures departed from previous policy by recognizing a national interest in the economic security of families and individuals. Both public employment and Social Security, however, were addressed more to the problem of temporary unemployment than to the problem of recurrent poverty. Many of the poor were not even covered.

The individualist theory of poverty was the dominant view; the theory that poverty was a social phenomenon, the recessive. The Johnson War on Poverty identified the enemy so as to assimilate the social into the individualist theory, offering a unified perspective.

Rejecting the belief that poverty was the necessary outcome of a mismanaged economy, the program's planners took the traditional view, that people were poor as a result of their own inability to succeed within the economic system. Monetary relief could deal, at best, with the manifestations of poverty. Only a program concerned with the individual roots of poverty could offer a permanent solution. In the sense that the antipoverty program was aimed at changing individuals, it was fundamentally conservative, consistent with Social Darwinism.

But the program's designers modified the traditional view. They did not maintain that individual deficits were the result of drunkenness, indolence, or sin. Instead they believed that poverty was an entire style of life, sustained by its isolation from the dominant economic and social system. The Senate Committee on Labor and Public Welfare, following its hearings, reported its conviction that " 'the other America' is a world apart, inhabited by people isolated from the mainstream of American life, unfamiliar with its values and unprepared for its opportunities."[45] Therefore, the poor must be provided with the skills and opportunities which would enable them to adopt a new style of life.

The factors causing poverty were thought to exist not in isolation but together. Lack of requisite skills and abilities led to low income, which required living in slums and ghettos, in which was generated a lower-class life-style, which prevented the development in the next generation of the requisite skills and abilities to break the cycle. This cycle, a self-perpetuating vicious circle, was the key image in the program planners' thinking. They proposed to break it with a coordinated approach addressing itself to all the influences perpetuating the cycle. In his 1964 budget message, for instance, President Johnson described his plans "to break that cycle by raising the educational, skill, and health levels of the younger generation, increasing their job opportunities, and helping their families to provide a better home life."[46]

The cycle-of-poverty theory comported well with public opinion. In the spring of 1964, a Gallup poll revealed that 54 percent of its sample still believed that, when a person is poor, the cause is "lack of effort on his own part," whereas 46 percent attributed the cause to factors beyond the individual's control.[47] By stressing individual deficits as the explanation of poverty, the program's designers could appeal to those who believed that poverty primarily was a matter of personal indolence. By stressing cultural, rather than personal, explanations for the deficits, they also could appeal to those who believed that the poor were not to blame for their plight.

The cycle-of-poverty theory also offered the administration a possible defense against the charge that its programs were too limited to accomplish their objectives. Since the causes of poverty were circular, intervention at any point on the cycle would affect, at least indirectly, the entire chain. Therefore, any antipoverty measure would be desirable; intervention at any point would have effects throughout the cycle.

Although the image of the cycle logically justified intervention to break it at any point, remedial measures were most likely to succeed if they were focused on certain pivotal points. For example, the program concentrated on youth, in the belief that improvements in habits and skills could make good job opportunities available to youths, interrupting the poverty cycle before it affected another generation. For this reason, the Shriver task force stressed the role of the Job Corps in developing motivation and skills. Once the poor had acquired training and work habits, jobs surely would be available.

Since the cycle-of-poverty image made the selection of battlegrounds flexible, the administration also could mute considerations of race, implying that the Economic Opportunity Act was not another civil rights program. (The Civil Rights Act of 1964 had not yet passed Congress, and race was the most explosive issue in American politics.) This distinction was hard to maintain. Although 78 percent of all poor families were white, nearly half the nation's black population was poor. Moreover, the heaviest concentrations of poverty, in the slums of the major cities, were predominantly black. Nevertheless, the War on Poverty did not focus on race. The only black involved in establishing the program was Adam Clayton Powell. The anticipated benefits of the program for the northern ghettos were not discussed. Instead, early literature and publicity about the program concentrated heavily on rural poverty and used Appalachia as the prototype. President Johnson's tour of poverty areas in the spring of 1964, for example, was confined mainly to Appalachia.

To the degree that the War on Poverty *would* concentrate on blacks, moreover, it attempted to redefine a *racial* crisis as an *economic* problem. The riots of 1964, for instance, were interpreted widely as protests against generalized deprivation, rather than as racial revolts. Elinor Graham has suggested that the redefinition was a crucial feature of the 1964 antipoverty debates. It allowed the monetary costs of fighting poverty to substitute for the high emotional costs involved in combating racial prejudice. The white liberal, the urban public official, and the southern politician all benefited from the exchange.[48]

Even in 1964, however, there were signs that this disjunction would be hard to sustain. To assure blacks that the poverty program was not a cover for abandoning the commitment to civil rights, administration officials were forced to link both programs. Shriver, for example, told a symposium on integration that the struggles against poverty and for civil rights "are all part of the same battle."[49] In his testimony in Congress, Whitney Young of the National Urban League expressed the hope that the community action program would be "a way of shoring up responsible Negro leadership in the community, . . . planning with Negroes rather than for Negroes."[50] Finally, in the congressional floor debates, the Economic Oppor-

tunity Act sometimes was regarded as but the logical
counterpart of the Civil Rights Act which had just been
passed in June.[51]

Selecting the Weapons. If the nation is to engage in
unconditional war, it must not only define the enemy but
also select the weapons and tactics which will best achieve
its strategic objective. A primary weapon in the War on
Poverty was to be local community action, which was
talked about as conservative, tested by experience, and a
reflection of the values of grass-roots democracy. The
Senate Labor and Public Welfare Committee, for example, found the community action program to be based
upon "the traditional and time-tested American methods
of organized local community action to help individuals,
families, and whole communities to help themselves."[52]
That local citizens were in a position to know the needs of
their communities better than the more remote federal
officials was argued by several witnesses, including Jack
Conway of the United Auto Workers (who would become
Shriver's deputy after the scuttling of Adam Yarmolinsky), Attorney General Kennedy, and Senators Pat
McNamara of Michigan and Warren Magnuson of Washington. These sources took their cue from President Johnson, whose March 16 message to Congress included the
argument that each community knows its needs best and
should not have plans imposed upon it from Washington.[53] Shriver offered one of the clearest elaborations of
this traditionally conservative point of view. In a speech
to the Advertising Council on May 5, 1964, he declared,
"What will work in Cleveland will not work in Los Angeles, and a program which Chicago might use to fight
urban slum poverty will not take root in the rocky soil of

Appalachia. That is why the heart of poverty legislation is *local* community action and *voluntary* participation."[54]

Locally oriented community action also would be likely to involve local citizens, a goal encouraged by a phrase in the act calling for the "maximum feasible participation" of residents of the areas and members of the groups served by the legislation. The precise history of the phrase is unknown. Precedents can be found in draft bills prepared early in February by the Departments of Labor and Health, Education, and Welfare. The draft of February 24 was the first to refer specifically to "maximum feasible participation."[55] Most likely, the phrase was authored by Richard W. Boone of the President's Committee on Juvenile Delinquency, although credit also was claimed by Congressman Adam Clayton Powell.[56] It soon was apparent that "maximum feasible participation," like "community action" itself, was an ambiguous term. Psychologists Kenneth Clark and Jeannette Hopkins even argued that the term was inherently vague, because the legislation did not specify the nature, extent, level, goals, consequences, or standards of participation.[57]

This very vagueness, however, allowed the administration to combine *different* justifications for the choice of this weapon. While there are many shadings of difference, the basic conflict was between participation as individual therapy—the most successful way of changing individuals—and participation as a means to organize the poor into an interest group in search of political power. The former view derived from group-dynamics research which concluded, as Gordon Allport expressed in his "law of active participation," that, when the individual is involved actively in a learning situation, he acquires the desired response more rapidly and the response is likely to be more stable than when learning is passive. This view was supported by social-welfare professionals who argued that active participation was a necessary condition for therapy. As social-welfare professional Charles Schottland testified, "in 1 to 1 personal services we recognize that a helping service does not begin until the individual wants it and participates in the helping process."[58]

The view that participating in community action was a path to political power for the poor began with the observation that poor communities frequently were characterized by weak social organization. With the exception of a few articulate leaders, who often moved from the community or took little interest in its development, residents could not make their voices heard in any meaningful way. Participation in community action was the means by which these people could be organized and their concerns represented.[59] A slight variation on this theme was the argument that participation was a means to take advantage of the presumed expertise of the poor about matters concerning them. This argument contrasted participation with the paternalistic administration of many social programs, in which individuals had little voice in decisions affecting them. It was a fortuitous move to take over the favored symbol, "democracy," and to align it with a particular *procedure* for achieving that value.

The administration was not forced either to reconcile these justifications or to choose between them, particularly because the specific "maximum feasible participation" language received little public attention. Robert F. Kennedy was the only administration witness to refer to the phrase in his congressional testimony; even Sargent Shriver, in his description of the operations of community action programs, omitted any reference to "maximum feasible participation."[60] Although the Republican members of the House Education and Labor Committee generally were skeptical about community action, they directed no specific challenges to the "participation" clause. Anne Murphy characterized the image of participation presented in the House committee report as "reminiscent of barn-raisings and husking bees where everyone collaborated on a community task."[61] The same pattern of neglect persisted in both Houses during the floor debates in 1964.

By default, then, the proponents of antipoverty legislation were able to defend "maximum feasible participation" as a natural concomitant of community action. In turn, community action was justified as being consistent with traditions of grass-roots democracy and therefore conservative. It could be a means of coordinating existing programs for greater efficiency—a rationale strongly championed by the Budget Bureau and endorsed by the president. "Community participation," he wrote, "would give focus to our efforts."[62] Although Johnson referred to the need for "shaking up" existing institutions, the context of his memoirs suggests that he had in mind a reorganization of resources to avoid duplication and waste, not that he envisioned social or political activism.

Participation also was justified as a way to counter impersonal forces. During the 1960s, a general reaction began to set in against the increasingly impersonal large bureaucracies, from the workings of which many individuals felt alienated. Miller and Roby have suggested that the emphasis during the decade on "participatory democracy," of which the Economic Opportunity Act's "participation" clause was a part, was an attempt to reverse this trend. A similar explanation is offered by Goldman, who claims to have suggested that the 1964 State of the Union address emphasize participation as opposed to a "spectator society."[63]

Community action was not the only weapon in the War on Poverty. Manpower programs would also figure prominently. These programs of job training, vocational education, and work experience would attack the cycle of poverty at one of its vulnerable points, as has been noted already. They also permitted the administration to distinguish its new program from public welfare, which was politically unpopular. Relief agencies were anathema to those seeking lower taxes and convinced that welfare subsidizes indolence and illegitimacy. Particularly when Aid to Families with Dependent Children (AFDC), rather than Old Age Assistance, became the most substantial relief program, hostility grew. Gilbert Steiner thought the image conjured up by AFDC was "an uneducated, unmarried Negro mother and her offspring," and therefore that it was politically vulnerable.[64]

There is abundant evidence of efforts to define the poverty program as entirely different from traditional public welfare. In his opening statement before the House Committee on Education and Labor, Walter Heller specifically rejected an "income" strategy for the War on Poverty, claiming that it would touch only the symptoms and not the roots of the problem. Congressman Roman Pucinski of Chicago asserted that the underlying purpose of the new legislation, far from sustaining welfare, was to get people off relief and to reduce the welfare state. Senators Pat McNamara of Michigan and Ralph Yarborough of Texas argued that economic opportunity was the very antithesis of the dole.[65] These disjunctions were encouraged by President Johnson. To the convention of the United Auto Workers, to a group of Argentine senators, to the American Society of Newspaper Editors, the president contrasted the War on Poverty with traditional welfare programs, insisting that the new effort's aim was "making taxpayers out of taxeaters." The same theme was repeated twice in the president's remarks upon signing the Economic Opportunity Act in August, at which time he declared, "We want to offer the forgotten fifth of our people opportunity and not doles," and again in October at the swearing-in of Shriver as director of the Office of Economic Opportunity.[66]

The final major tactical choice was to emphasize that the war would be frugally administered and accountable to the Congress. It would not be marked by profiteering or cost overruns which might erode public trust and support, and it was not to be a grant of unlimited authority to the commander in chief that would permit a "poverty czar" to operate in dictatorial fashion.

By early January 1964, even before the outline of the poverty program had been conceived, President Johnson had decided that its net cost would not exceed $500 million. This low initial cost enabled Congressman Phil Landrum to champion the measure, asserting, "This will not be an expensive program. This will be the most conservative social program I have ever seen presented to any legislative body. There is not anything but conservatism in it."[67] Furthermore, it was expected that future increases in cost would be offset by savings elsewhere in the federal budget. The main source of these savings, ironically, was expected to be the Defense Department, whose budget already had been reduced by Secretary McNamara as an economy move.[68]

In the long run, furthermore, the program would save more money than it would cost. Supporters of the legislation argued that the costs of inaction were greater than the costs of the bill. Senator Humphrey cited lost production, lack of purchasing power for the poor, and welfare payments as costs of continued poverty.[69] By contrast, it was argued that tax revenues gained and welfare payments saved by making citizens productive would justify the cost of the new program.

This emphasis on cost-consciousness came directly from the president. In a cabinet meeting in the fall of 1964, he insisted that the public would support social programs "*only* if we take positive steps to show that we are spending what we legitimately need to spend."[70] In a similar vein, Shriver tried to answer congressmen who had reservations because the scope of the 1964 bill was limited. He stated, "We propose to do this first year only so much as we are sure we can carry out efficiently, with a dollar's value for a dollar spent."[71] Moreover, supporters argued that the limited resources could be extended farther than might be expected, because the bill's emphasis on coordination would prevent duplication of programs.

Not only did the program planners insist that the war would be frugally administered, but they also emphasized their accountability to Congress. Sargent Shriver made frequent reference to the fact that the Economic Opportunity Act would require an annual appropriation. As a result, he told the legislators, his office would have to come back in a year and justify itself; "you are not buying a pig in a poke."[72] In several respects, the administration catered to the legislative branch's desire for accountability. President Johnson recalled that, when Shriver was appointed to head the planning of the poverty program, he was told that "he would have to work fast. Not only did I want to propel a program through the Congress immediately but I wanted the plan to produce visible results, so that there would be no question about Congress' continuing the effort with adequate funding in the years ahead."[73]

The selection of the military metaphor, then, significantly influenced both the design of the poverty program and the public discourse surrounding it. The image of war affected the objective, the enemy, and the weapons. These choices, in turn, proved quite helpful to the president in 1964. Some helped to define his image as a liberal humanitarian; some, to quiet opponents and rally public support; some, to enable Johnson to avoid clear-cut selections among alternatives; and some, to persuade the Congress.

III

In March of 1964, Congress received the proposed Economic Opportunity Act. It was an omnibus bill which members of the Shriver task force could support, each for his own reasons. Title I, including employment and training programs, was authored by Daniel P. Moynihan. Richard W. Boone of the juvenile-delinquency staff drafted the community action section, which became Title II. The remaining titles were written by James Sundquist (agricultural loans and grants); Harold Gallaway of the Small Business Administration (SBA loans); James Adler of Health, Education, and Welfare (work-experience programs for welfare recipients); and William Cannon of the Budget Bureau (administration and coordination).[74] Much of the bill was not new. Similarities could be found, for example, between the Job Corps and the New Deal's Civilian Conservation Corps, between work-study and the National Youth Administration, between VISTA and the

Peace Corps.[75] What was new, though, was the combination of these elements under a single rubric.

No one could be sure that the 88th Congress would support the program, and there was not yet tangible evidence of public pressure. Congress would need to be convinced. By persuading Congressman Phil Landrum of Georgia to sponsor the bill, the White House hoped that votes could be garnered from southern Democrats. In combination with administration loyalists, their numbers would be sufficient to obtain passage. Then if Republicans wished to take the partisan stance of opposing an antipoverty bill, the administration would not object.[76] Opponents would be placed in a position of maximum discomfort, however, because of the way in which the bill's supporters set the terms of debate. They insisted upon focusing on the problem of poverty, not on the merits of the specific legislation or the alleged deficiencies of existing programs. In this way, the very existence of poverty would serve as a reason for the program. Opposition attempts to shift the focus of discussion could be ignored.

The administration strategy can be perceived by examining the hearings in the House. The bill promptly was referred to the Committee on Education and Labor, of which Adam Clayton Powell was chairman. A phalanx of administration witnesses testified in support of the measure: twenty-nine of the seventy-six supporting witnesses were from the administration or were consultants in planning the legislation.[77] Congressman Pucinski, a Johnson stalwart on the Education and Labor Committee, was moved to remark, "As far as I know, this is the first time in the history of this country that all of the Cabinet members, except the Secretary of State, have testified in support of an important measure. The President certainly has assigned this as one of the most important measures of his administration."[78] The advocacy of administration spokesmen, however, was of a very general sort, stressing the need for antipoverty action, assuring the committee that the bill would be compatible with ongoing programs, and occasionally discussing matters at best tangentially related to the legislation. The same pattern of emphasis may be found in the testimony of other supporting witnesses, representing social-welfare, civic, and religious organizations, state and local government, technical advisers, educators, businessmen, and members of Congress. Anne Murphy has characterized the function of these hearings as generating phrases for the expression of the official philosophy about the poverty program and the proposed legislation.[79]

Opposition to the bill was ineffectual. Of the nine opposition witnesses in the House hearings, five opposed the measure on ideological grounds, but none of them represented organizations with vital interests at stake. The other four opponents were two Republican congressmen and two educators, who maintained that the program was misdirected or unnecessary. Among the objections raised against the bill were its unique administrative structure, which was alleged to duplicate programs already in existence, the challenge posed by the bill to states' rights, and the fear that the measure would hasten the pace of racial integration. The latter two objections, especially, would have been appealing to some southern Democrats who otherwise might have supported the bill.

By far the most persistent objection raised during the hearings, however, was the charge of unfair partisanship in their conduct. This charge was not without foundation. Chairman Powell selectively enforced a five-minute time limit on the cross-examination of witnesses, becoming especially strict when Republicans were questioning. The minority party was not allowed to question a witness until six Democrats had done so, although the committee's custom was to alternate between majority and minority members. Republicans further complained that they were not given sufficient advance notice of the committee's meetings. Powell defended these departures from normal practice with the boasts, "The chairman has the right to use the procedure he desires," and, "I am the chairman. I will run this committee as I desire."[80] Republicans also were excluded from the final "markup" session in which the bill was revised. Every major amendment they proposed was rejected, often by straight party vote and frequently without time being allotted for the Republicans to explain the nature or purpose of their amendments.

Predictably, Republicans became enraged at this treatment. But, since the Democrats had chosen to focus only on the need for action, they were able to subordinate the Republicans' attack on their partisanship. They could argue that the opposition, unwilling to challenge directly the need for the legislation, could only engage in carping, dilatory tactics. The Education and Labor Committee reported the bill on a straight party-line vote.

Believing that the Democratic majority was more reliable in the Senate than in the House, though, the administration attempted to obtain the bill's passage from the upper body first. Brief hearings before the Senate Labor and Public Welfare Committee repeated the essential pattern of the House hearings. In the committee report, the minority charged that the administration had rushed the bill through "with such haste that the record is practically nonexistent,"[81] but Senator Warren Magnuson of Washington insisted that the modern critics were "just as hard pressed today to find real sources of criticism as the critics of [the New Deal] 30 years ago."[82] Senator Goldwater denounced the bill as a "Madison Avenue stunt" by Lyndon Johnson.[83] The measure passed the Senate in midsummer by a vote of sixty-one to thirty-four. Twelve Democrats and twenty-two Republicans opposed it.

Still, there was no assurance that the bill would pass the House. Many northern Democrats became hesitant over the summer, owing perhaps to reports of a "white backlash" among their constituents. Many southern Democrats followed the Rules Committee chairman, Howard W. Smith, and became confirmed opponents, owing to their belief that the proposed legislation would quicken the pace of racial integration. The head count kept by congressional strategist Lawrence O'Brien showed the House deadlocked by July 31, with approximately thirty southerners undecided.[84] Accordingly, once the Rules Committee reported out the bill by an eight to seven vote, these undecided congressmen became the target for special appeals from the White House.

By early August, these efforts centered on a group of uncommitted Democratic congressmen from North and South Carolina, whose support was believed to be essential. It was obtained in return for a presidential pledge that Adam Yarmolinsky (then in the Defense Department but widely thought to be slated as Shriver's deputy) would not be involved in the program's administration.[85] The bill passed the House by a vote of 226 to 185, and on August 20, 1964, the Economic Opportunity Act became the law of the land.

The president had obtained his legislative victory, but the bill's passage did not necessarily suggest that there was a broad congressional antipoverty consensus. The House, in particular, was deeply split. Whether support for the program could be retained was an open question: would a prosperous majority permanently support programs to benefit a poor minority? And there were other unsettling questions posed by the administration's rhetoric. Did a declaration of "unconditional war" raise expectations that could not possibly be satisfied? What if the cycle-of-poverty theory did not fit the facts? What did community action really mean? Could meaningful results be obtained for such a relatively small expenditure? Pehaps most important, how would one *know* whether or not the war had been victorious? And without such knowledge, was the War on Poverty destined to be a war without end?

Rhetorical choices are not static entities. People understand and interpret the world through symbols on which they bestow meaning. A change in the symbolic "map" leads to changes in interpretation and expectation. Even as they contributed to the passage of the 1964 law and made the inception of the antipoverty campaign a success, the administration's choices modified the whole frame of reference for thinking and speaking about poverty. These modifications, most of them unintended, were harmful to the effective operation of the poverty program—even though, ironically, they were outgrowths of decisions very helpful in securing the program's adoption in the first place. How this irony came about is the concern in subsequent chapters, in which the transformation of each of the basic rhetorical choices during a period of rhetorical crisis is explored.

3

Rhetorical Crisis
The Transformation of the Military
Objective

Kenneth Burke has written that "a given frame tends to develop by-products. In aiming at one thing, we incidentally bring about something else."[1] The by-products of the call for unconditional war were attacks on both the specific policies and the general credibility of the Office of Economic Opportunity. Against these attacks, the agency could mount only a weak defense.

These events were set in motion by the unresolved rhetorical problems of 1964, which caused the call for unconditional war to lose its symbolic force quickly. The enemy was ill-defined; the attack was not massive nor the mobilization total; the program was not concerted, comprehensive, or carefully planned. In the inception phase, the administration had been able to ignore these gaps by defining poverty as a crisis, thereby capturing presumption. Objections to specific features of the legislation were countered with the plea that *something* must be done. But with the adoption of the program, this presumption was moot. The real issue became one of *cure:* was the program effective in achieving its objectives?

As the poverty program got under way, further gaps between symbol and act became evident. The work-training, work-study, and work-experience programs were only incremental departures from earlier efforts, not a new front in an unconditional war. And without the assurance of employment or income, these measures by themselves could do little to eliminate poverty. Likewise, few of the local community action programs sought the abolition of poverty itself, although that was the stated purpose for community action. Also, community action funds were used to mount numerous small-scale demonstration programs, which seemed blatantly inconsistent with the concept of unconditional war. One witness, the president of the Metropolitan Citizens Advisory Council of Washington, sketched the contrast for the Senate Labor and Public Welfare Committee: "We don't fight wars on a demonstration basis, suggesting to the opponent that a target area be selected, control groups be established, make a basic decision on which branch of the service is going to be responsible for the war, and then attempt to coordinate the attack by putting 10 federal generals in charge of 86 programs."[2]

Perhaps the most obvious discrepancy was between the "unconditional war" goals and the funds appropriated for prosecution of the campaign. Most programs were not budgeted beyond the pilot-project level. The OEO's own figures convinced the Senate Labor and Public Welfare Committee in 1966 that only a small percentage of the poor even had been "reached" or "affected" by the program.[3] The gap between the vast objectives of the War on Poverty and what could be achieved with the funds at hand led one critic to speak of OEO's "ballyhoo problem" and led another to assert that the war was "more rhetoric than combat."[4]

I

The widening gap between the goals of the war and the achievements of the poverty program imperiled the administration; somehow it must be closed. Three possible strategies for closing the gap were available. The poverty warriors could deflate their original objectives in retrospect, so that the goals were brought into line with the actual results. They could exaggerate the actual results, to justify the original level of expectations. Or they could try to buy more time, claiming that the future effectiveness of their programs would justify the past rhetoric. The first of these reactions was unacceptable to the administration, since it would admit the inappropriateness of the rhetoric of 1964. Each of the others, however, was employed.

Exaggeration of Results. Exaggeration, of course, was unique neither to the poverty program nor to Lyndon Johnson. "Since Kennedy had promised to get us moving again," speechwriter Harry McPherson explained, "Democratic writers had forced the pace of everything their Presidents said. Nothing was too small to be termed 'urgent.' The consequences of inaction were never less than drastic; action would always bring redemption, prosperity, or civil peace." Similarly, John Kenneth Galbraith, in a critique of the Democratic party, has argued that its general oratorical style since 1960 has been affected adversely by what he calls "Dawnism": the hope "that some new leader, some new victory, some new policy will bring the dawn of a new day."[5]

The Office of Economic Opportunity was especially vulnerable to overselling itself. It conducted a public relations campaign which, even its partisans later admitted, offered an unrealistic, purely visionary presentation of the agency's accomplishments.[6] OEO received far greater exposure to mass media than did most similar federal agencies. In part, the flair for publicity reflected Shriver's personal style, which bordered on the messianic. Reportedly, he took great interest in the promotional details of OEO, including such matters as the selection of names and emblems for each of the agency's component programs.[7] Shriver's agency also developed a public affairs department which aggressively promoted its program in local communities and to the relevant congressional committees. In the statement of purpose in the department's handbook, it was explained that "if a CAA [local community action agency] operates in the dark, unmindful of the need to share news of the activities with the public, it can expect misunderstanding and a general lack of sympathy for its objectives on the part of the uninformed." OEO advised word-of-mouth publicity, newsletters from local community action agencies, and press releases to local media as means by which activities could be publicized.[8]

The program's deliberate promotional campaign did get the desired publicity. Assessing OEO's public relations, Edwin Knoll and Jules Witcover wrote that its promotional activities exceeded those conducted in behalf of any relatively small program since the New Deal.[9] Even the program's critics noted that the public relations effort was the most effective administrative operation of OEO, whose budget was "utilized in a furious churning out of beautiful brochures and tons of press releases which tell what a grand and glorious job OEO is doing to lift the poverty stricken up by the boot straps."[10] The resulting publicity, hovever, was not entirely to the office's benefit. Once the media were sensitized to the newsworthy nature of OEO's activities, they focused attention on its failures as well as its successes.[11] News of the failures, of course, supplied ammunition to the program's opponents. Moreover, the virulence of OEO's own press releases, distributed to refute the program's critics, called more attention to the criticisms and gave the critics added reason for antagonism.[12]

Abundant evidence exists of OEO's exaggeration. For example, in a letter of transmittal to the president of the Senate and the Speaker of the House of Representatives in February 1965, President Johnson contended, "It is now clear that the war against poverty has touched the hearts and the sense of duty of the American people. This cause has truly become their cause."[13] In his 1965 congressional testimony, Shriver claimed that OEO "has been successful in launching every new program authored by Congress," although no criteria for success were specified. Shriver reportedly also offered the guess "that no federal government program in peacetime has ever gone so far so fast, nor ever zeroed in so well."[14] In a speech to the National Conference on Social Welfare in 1965, Shriver ticked off a list of six prophecies of the "cliché experts"which OEO had refuted, ranging from the belief that the poor were lazy to the belief that VISTA would lack recruits.[15] In its 1966 Annual Report, OEO alleged that its early critics had been converted to staunch supporters. The report added, "In all parts of the country, from all types of institutions and all types of people, there is a sudden recognition that the poverty program is accomplishing great things for America, that its echo is being heard with far greater volume than its original sound."[16]

Several methods of exaggeration were used. Means were transformed into ends. Arousal of the poor, which originally had been regarded as one of the means by which poverty was to be reduced, came to be defended as a goal in its own right. In OEO's first annual report, it is stated that "the most significant results of our first year of operation are *not* measurable in terms of expenditures, projects begun, or people helped [factors which were related to the original goals]. . . . Throughout this affluent nation, there has sprung up a new and growing concern for a minority who might otherwise be doomed to a life of poverty."[17] A year later, Shriver cited alerting "the conscience of the country to the problem of poverty and [focusing] the attention of our citizens on what can be done about it" as the major success of the war.[18] Lacking tangible results, he chose to elevate *methods* to the level of results.

Also, the part was elevated to the status of the whole. As OEO programs evolved, there appeared individual case studies of success in relieving distress. The annual reports of OEO, in part, are compendia of these anecdotal data, which served to support an argument by example. If specific programs are meeting the needs of specific individuals, so the argument ran, then the program as a whole probably is meeting the needs of the poor. From a logical standpoint, of course, an overwhelming number of such examples would have been needed to establish the claim with probative force. The use of specific examples, therefore, served not to justify a proposition in the strict sense of the term, but to evoke positive affect toward the program. Helping some individuals would seem equivalent to meeting the program's national objectives. As the OEO's *Public Affairs Handbook* explained the rationale, "Americans soon grow weary of social problems. What keeps them enthusiastic about needed change is that something is 'working.' "[19]

Spokesmen for OEO also sought to transform the past

into the present, by harking back to the obstacles to the act's adoption in 1964 and claiming that surmounting those obstacles was by itself enough to prove the program's accomplishment. In 1966, for example, Congressman Pucinski warned his colleagues, "But let us not obfuscate the real issue. The real issue is that this program has been a massive effort for the first time in recorded history to do something about poverty." Senator Robert Kennedy similarly defended OEO programs, arguing,"the war on poverty is unique. The war on poverty, like it or not, is the single outstanding commitment this Nation has made to the principle that poverty must be abolished."[20] Great hurdles *had* been overcome in 1964, but that fact did not necessarily mean that the programs were working effectively in 1966.

Buying More Time. In addition to magnifying the results of the present, OEO chose to place great stress upon the prospects for the future, insisting that the level of success would be commensurate with the earlier rhetoric. Johnson reaffirmed his faith that all men could have an equal chance to share in life's blessings. To achieve that end, early in 1965 he also reaffirmed "our solemn commitment to prosecute the war against poverty to a successful conclusion. For that struggle," he added, "is not only for the liberation of those imprisoned in poverty, but for the conscience and the values of a prosperous and free nation." In a message to Congress in mid-1967, the president returned to his metaphor of technical mastery: "As disease can be conquered, as space can be mastered, so too can poverty yield to our determined efforts to bring it to an end."[21]

By far the clearest example of overselling the program's potential, however, was a statement made by Shriver to

the Senate Labor and Public Welfare Committee on June
21, 1966. Near the end of his prepared testimony, Shriver
posed and answered two questions which he said he
frequently was asked: "Can the War on Poverty really be
won?" and "How long will it take?" The answer to the
first question, Shriver maintained, was yes; the answer to
the second, "about 10 years."[22] The original source for
Shriver's win-the-war-by-1976 statement was a study done
by OEO's Office of Research, Plans, Programs, and Evaluation. That office had attempted to prepare a comprehensive five-year antipoverty plan for the period of
1967–72, assuming both that appropriate increases in the
OEO budget would be forthcoming and that a negative
income tax and other measures beyond the purview of
OEO would be adopted. The report concluded that adoption of this plan could reduce the number of poor persons
to 10.9 million by 1972 and to zero by 1976.[23] Shriver
neglected to inform the Congress of the additional yearly
cost of this plan, estimated by Levitan at $20 billion.[24]

Before long, Shriver's exaggeration would be evident.
Later in 1966, in response to a question asked by Senator
Robert Kennedy, Shriver denied that the 1976 victory
date was possible at the current rate of effort.[25] Even more
pessimistic was the prediction of Robert A. Levine, who
in 1966 became head of Research, Plans, Programs, and
Evaluation. On June 22, 1967, almost a year to the day
after Shriver's original statement, Levine told the Senate
Labor and Public Welfare Committee that the War on
Poverty *never* could be won without "certain changes in
programs not now foreseen."[26]

In discussing the 1976 target date, the *New York Times*
editorialized that there seemed to be a direct relationship
between the difficulties OEO encountered and the assurances given by its officials that a final solution was at

hand.[27] Shriver's extravagance reflected a desperate move for time. As it became apparent that the achievements of the program were not yet sufficient to generate the desired national consensus, attention to the future was a possible way to deflect concern away from the present.

II

By redefining "results"—transforming means into ends, part into whole, and past into present—OEO supporters seemingly closed the gap between promise and prospect. But asserting a definition of the situation is not enough to make that definition persuasive to one's audience. In the case of OEO, each of its means for closing the gap invited a vigorous counterattack. Exaggerating current results led to charges that OEO lacked credibility; stressing future potential, to charges that OEO aroused false expectations. Both attacks began to be heard during 1965 and rose to a crescendo during 1966 and 1967. Their implication was that the War on Poverty was not being won after all.

The Attack on Credibility. If the standard for results were material gains by the poor, then OEO had failed to measure up, notwithstanding its glowing reports. If the agency's rhetoric was not justified by its performance, then its reporting and advocacy would be thought unreliable. In a phrase later to be applied to the entire Johnson administration, OEO suffered from a "credibility gap." The assault on the poverty program's credibility took several forms. In some quarters, there was a general feeling of distrust about OEO publications. For example, California's Senator George Murphy complained, "It is true that OEO presses have cranked out endless press releases singing the praises of the poverty program. However, when one cuts away the camouflage and when one removes the emotional rhetoric, the cold record reveals not only confusing information but also frequently conflicting statements."[28] As a result, he complained, Congress lacked the data which it needed to make an intelligent judgment of OEO's effectiveness. This distrust was not displayed only by Shriver's usual adversaries. During the 1966 House hearings, for instance, Congressman Pucinski lectured one witness, "You have an impressive list of programs. As a matter of fact, I can't even keep up with all the programs you have going here but this is tokenism. . . . You have a very lovely report over here which has a lot of agencies getting a lot of money but when we look behind the facade, . . . how many people are you helping?"[29] Oregon's Congresswoman Edith Green also admitted at one point that she was "a bit leery when I get a snow job that everything is great."[30] Distrust of OEO's publications extended even to their appearance. There were frequent complaints of excessive costs for pictures, expensive paper, colored ink, and other such frills. One witness, claiming an inverse correlation between the pretentiousness of an agency's publications and the agency's success in receiving appropriations, advised, "Something a little less expensive and on cheaper looking paper would be more appropriate, even if there were little or no actual savings."[31]

The feeling that OEO publications generally were not to be trusted had a poisonous effect: the charge could not be answered effectively. Failure to deny it would admit it implicitly. But a denial would be tainted by the same lack of credibility which had prompted the attack in the first place—particularly when error or deception *was* exposed occasionally in specific OEO reports. For example, at one point Shriver demonstrated the success of Project Upward Bound by observing that 80 percent of its graduates went to college, reportedly neglecting to note that 50 percent of them subsequently were failing.[32] Congressman Goodell of New York referred to the OEO statistic that there was in 1967 a 53 percent placement rate of Job Corps trainees. Before the Job Corps was initiated, Goodell stated, the placement rate for trainees in traditional programs had been 58 percent. It hardly was fair, he concluded, to cite the Job Corps figure as evidence of a successful program, although that was the purpose for which OEO had used the figure.[33] The agency's statistical reports contained such inexact terms as "reached," "affected," and "served," so that it was virtually impossible to know how meaningful were the millions of "contacts" that had been made. These problems did not seem to be isolated cases. Their cumulative impact was to induce distrust in OEO's statistical reports. Chicago's Congressman Roman Pucinski, for example, lectured one witness, saying, "I am not persuaded by the statistics of this dialog simply because I think these statistics in many instances, wittingly or unwittingly, are inflated or misrepresented."[34]

In effect, members of Congress began to discount OEO statistics for their incredulity. This discounting thrust the agency into a seemingly unsolvable problem. If it failed to produce statistics establishing the results of its programs, it was assailable for being unable to justify specific operations. If, however, the agency did produce the desired statistics, they were suspected of being misleadingly favorable toward the program.

Not just for its statistics, however, was OEO's credibility suspect. It stood accused of using the congressional hearing, not as a device to present information about its programs and plans, but as a means to whitewash its conduct of the antipoverty campaign. Congressman Ayres of Ohio asserted that committee hearings in 1965 had been brought to an abrupt close only because the administration's image as champion of the poor was being tarnished seriously; House Republicans in 1966 similarly charged that committee hearings that year were "an 8-day parade of administration spokesmen and apologists for the poverty program who spent hours relating self-serving statistics and stressing debatable accomplishments." Republicans also charged that OEO tried to discredit claims of abuses by accusing Republicans of the "big lie" technique without controverting the facts alleged in their charges.[35]

There was even suspicion that representatives of the poor who appeared at congressional hearings were "showcase exhibits" who had been selected and briefed by OEO so that their testimony would reflect favorably on the agency. Senator Murphy of California pointedly questioned one such group, although its members denied vociferously that OEO had influenced their testimony. Senator Prouty of Vermont made the same charge with respect to witnesses heard on one- or two-day field trips to antipoverty projects around the country. When Adam Clayton Powell criticized Shriver's effectiveness, there was inserted in the *Congressional Record* a long series of telegrams from program administrators supporting Shriver. Congressman Dave Martin of Nebraska charged that the telegrams not only were solicited by OEO but also were financed with federal funds.[36]

To the degree that these charges struck a responsive chord in Congress, they damaged OEO greatly. The agency's one real strength in its legislative relationships was its ability to use the hearing procedure to provide information about its program and to inspire confidence in its leadership. If the opposition could succeed in defining the hearings as a whitewash, this strength would be lost. A "discount for incredulity" similar to that applied to OEO's statistical presentations would be applied to the agency in general. That there was a slackening of confidence in OEO's presentation in committee hearings can be inferred from the increasing calls for an independent study and thorough investigation of the agency.

The Charge of False Expectations. If critics found OEO's exaggeration of past accomplishments to be unbelievable, they found the agency's promises for the future to be harmful: they aroused expectations which could not be satisfied. Those who argued in this vein took at face value OEO's unrealistic standards for performance and alleged that the impossibility of attaining these standards resulted in disappointment and frustration among the poor. During 1966, this theme was sounded by Mayor A.V. Sorensen of Omaha and Congressmen Charles Goodell and Paul Fino of New York, among others. The same argument was made during 1967 by A. Philip Randolph, Mayor John Lindsay, Congressman Augustus Hawkins of California, and Senators Hugh Scott of Pennsylvania, George Murphy of California, and Winston Prouty of Vermont.[37]

As one example of the frustration and disappointment, these sources referred to the effort of OEO to promote enrollment in the Job Corps. Apparently concerned that not enough youths would be attracted, and convinced that underregistration would be a personal and political hazard, Shriver approved a national advertising campaign to attract the interest of the potential clientele. The response was overwhelming. Even before its first center was opened, the Job Corps had received several times as many applications as it possibly could accept. Its critics charged that the effect on applicants of being rejected from the corps was psychologically debilitating, the last in a long chain of failures which dampened the hope and enthusiasm of the youths.[38]

To argue that the poor were discouraged by the impossibility of OEO's achieving the levels of performance implicit in its promises, one would need some reason to believe that the poor took seriously the standards for performance and trusted the promises. Two reasons were offered. Some writers claimed that the plight of the poor was so serious that they were desperate for hope and willing to trust any promises of a bright future. This explanation was offered, for example, by Kenneth B. Clark, Robert Levine, and S. M. Miller and Pamela Roby.[39] Others argued that the poor raised their aspirations because of their relative deprivation. The War on Poverty caused the poor to focus more intently on the gap separating them from the rest of the population, to feel more acutely deprived, and therefore to respond positively to suggestions that the poverty program would integrate them into the economic and social mainstream. Furthermore, they would measure their gains not against their point of origin but against the distance yet to be traveled.

For the most part, arguments about the psychological effect of promises upon the poor did not derive from information supplied by the poor themselves. As was typical of the War on Poverty, the poor were an issue about which others spoke. There is only limited evidence of the actual effect of the promises upon the poor. For example, the Los Angeles Riot Study, following the Watts riot, indicated that 42 percent of the blacks in the Watts area thought that the poverty program would "help a lot" and another 45 percent believed that it would help "a little."[40] Data of this sort were scanty and unclear as to their meaning; this fact, however, did not deter speakers.

How was the frustration resulting from unfulfilled expectations thought to be manifested? Some observers maintained that disappointment led to a general cynicism or alienation from the political process. Both Housing and Urban Development Secretary Robert Weaver and Herbert J. Gans, a prominent urban scholar, argued that the frequent announcement of new programs which could not equal the claims made for them produced a cynicism which potentially was volatile. William Haddad, Shriver's first inspector general, himself admitted that poverty-war failures made the poor distrustful of government generally.[41]

As racial turmoil came to the nation with the regularity of the summer solstice, OEO's harshest critics began to see the causes of the riots in the frustration and disillusionment resulting from the false expectations which the agency raised. House Minority Leader Gerald Ford in 1966 ventured the opinion that the administration's promising far more than it could deliver might have been a factor in the disorders of that year. Congressman Quie of Minnesota and Mayor Sorensen of Omaha expressed similar opinions. In 1968, the Republican Coordinating Committee saw little doubt "that the repetition of irresponsible promises and political slogans by the Administration in 1964 and 1965 contributed to the violence of the succeeding two summers," because "the rhetoric of the war on poverty and the Great Society created the impression among the disadvantaged of the cities that their living conditions would be dramatically and rapidly improved."[42]

This argument, too, was developed without much recourse to empirical data. Researchers typically could not offer evidence about possible causes until long after a riot had occurred, whereas the need to assign blame was immediate. Moreover, empirical data were inconclusive. For example, the Lemberg Center for the Study of Violence, at Brandeis University, conducted a survey asking whether broken promises by the antipoverty planners had contributed to the ensuing riots. Only 13 percent of low socioeconomic status blacks (compared with 42 percent of the whites of similar status) minimized the importance of this factor. Hence far more blacks than whites did attribute the riots to broken promises. On the other hand, supplemental studies prepared in 1968 for the National Commission on Civil Disorders concluded that blacks ranked "broken promises" relatively *low* among the causes of riots.[43] In any case, though, the attack was a strong challenge to OEO and placed the agency on the defensive.

A dramatic episode illustrating the attack on false expectations aroused by OEO occurred in April 1966 at a conference sponsored by the Citizens' Crusade Against Poverty, a private group formed as a lobby to support antipoverty programs. To the two-day conference came approximately one thousand delegates from Watts, Harlem, Appalachia, the Mississippi Delta, and other impoverished areas. Unexpectedly, on the first day, a "mutinous" mood developed among many delegates, who expressed not their thanks to the administration but their outrage at how little was being done to help them, especially by the OEO.[44] Shriver, scheduled as the luncheon speaker for the second day, reportedly had prepared a speech candidly admitting many of his agency's shortcomings. Apparently stung by the first day's protests, however, he insisted that his speechwriters prepare a sterner speech, which was almost totally defensive of the OEO record.[45] During the speech, members of the audience began to heckle Shriver, interrupting him with shouts of "You're lying!" and "He hasn't done anything for us!" and preventing him from completing his remarks. The heckling prompted Shriver to reply that he was "not a bit ashamed of what has been done by the war on poverty; I don't apologize to anybody in or out of this room about the results." He refused, however, to remain to answer questions, saying that he would "not participate in a riot."[46]

Later, Shriver asserted that the demonstration was not spontaneous but had been organized for the purpose of embarrassing him. Both Jack Conway and Richard Boone, former Shriver aides, disagreed. They explained the incident by saying that the audience members, impressed with the goals to which OEO was dedicated, were anxious to see results. They came to the meeting with what Boone described as "great tension, great unrest, a great sense of frustration" about OEO's apparent lack of impact in their own communities. When Shriver chose not to relate to those concerns but to attempt to overwhelm the auditors with success stories and promises, this collective tension was manifest in hostility and disruptive behavior.[47] Shriver's dilemma, however, as one writer put it, was that his attackers "were the very activists his rhetoric had spawned"[48]—people who had been moved to commit themselves to attacking poverty and then let down by the failure of Shriver's agency to achieve what had been promised.

III

Compounding Shriver's dilemma was the fact that the administration was severely restricted in its ability to defend itself against these attacks. In his monograph on community conflict, James S. Coleman refers to what he labels "one-sided" issues.[49] This term refers to controversies which can be argued successfully on only one side, because the world view implied by an argument precludes the possibility of refutation. The original argument can envelop the attempt to challenge it. Conspiracy rhetoric offers perhaps the clearest illustration of one-sided issues. To an advocate alleging the existence of conspiracy, refutation is impossible. Denial of the charge serves only to offer further proof of how sinister the conspiracy really is.

In the attack on false promises and the attack on the credibility of the Office of Economic Opportunity, opponents of the poverty program had "one-sided" issues. By their nature, the attacks on OEO tainted the ability of the agency to defend its record. The charge of excessive expectations was a universally applicable explanation for disappointing results. Those who believed the charge could always apply it to subsequent events. By contrast, agency spokesmen could not deny that their record included *some* disappointments. Nor could they deny that OEO's promises had aroused the poor, unless they were to concede their own failure at what they regarded as their primary mission. Nor could they dispute, at a common-sense level, the logic that people led to expect the impossible will be frustrated. Similarly, if one believes that OEO information is not credible, the agency has virtually no convincing response. Its attempt to defend itself would suffer from the very same lack of credibility. So it was extremely difficult for the agency to answer its critics.

Moreover, suspicions of the administration's credibility increased its burden of proof. It was not enough to show that, on balance, OEO programs were working successfully and therefore should be strengthened. Even if acceptable criteria for "success" existed, the data and statistics OEO would use in making its argument would be discounted because of the widespread belief that they were misleading and self-serving. Accordingly, it was not enough to point to the benefits of the program. Those benefits must be shown to be great enough to withstand the discount for incredulity. Congressman Goodell challenged the OEO: "You spend $486 million and you are going to do some good. That is not the issue. The issue: Is it doing as much good or substantially as much good as it should be?"[50] To recover the support of skeptics in Congress, it no longer would be enough for OEO to claim that its programs were *productive*. To offset the discount for incredulity, they must be shown to be *optimal*. Since the agency already had admitted the existence of some defects in the program, this was an impossible burden. Moreover, if OEO had tried to claim that its programs were optimal, the claim would be so far from the perceptions even of its supporters as to strain the agency's credibility beyond the breaking point. In short, the critics of OEO's administration had the agency in a rhetorical quagmire from which it could not maneuver.

One attempted response by the administration was to dismiss criticisms of OEO as politically motivated, or, if not to disregard them entirely, to reduce their significance. With regard to the charge of arousing false expectations, for example, Shriver implied that this criticism was ritually invoked by those opposed to progress. In 1967, he told a House committee, "some people felt the Declaration of Independence was an incendiary document, that it raised false hopes, and the Constitution of the United States when it was written, that it raised false hopes that never would be fulfilled."[51] Clearly, the intended implication was that the charge was no more valid with respect to OEO programs than with respect to the historic documents Shriver cited.

The suggestion that external conditions *required* that OEO oversell its programs was another line of defense. Herbert Kramer, the OEO director of public affairs, implied that the program could not otherwise have been initiated. As Kramer explained, "the techniques of mass communication had to be used almost with a bludgeon effect. . . . We had to create a market."[52] Similarly, it was alleged that the only way to *sustain* the program was through a dramatic publicity campaign. Kramer argued that such a campaign was needed lest the public's attention be diverted to the war in Vietnam; Arthur Shostak likewise alluded to the nation's record "of assuming that social problems that leave the headlines are either solved or contained."[53]

Finally, defenders of the administration sometimes admitted that errors had occurred in the program but insisted that they were unavoidable because the severity of the problem required that *something* be done. In his 1967 message to Congress concerning poverty, for example, the president maintained that errors were inevitable because "the need was for action. America could not wait for a decade of studies which might not even show precisely what should be attempted." The next year, he told OEO assistant and regional directors, "You hear a lot about the mistakes. God knows we have made them and made plenty of them, because we were unafraid to break new ground."[54]

In discussing one-sided issues, Coleman indicates that,

lacking an effective direct reply to them, the most one can do is to hope that they will go away. Each of these three defenses reflected an attempt to help the one-sided issue to disappear by directing attention elsewhere. Dismissing criticisms as partisan sniping directed attention to the opponent's motive. Arguing the inevitability of oversell directed attention to overall social conditions. Maintaining that *something* had to be done redirected attention to the severity of the original problem.

But the deflections were not likely to succeed. A steady stream of specific incidents could be drawn upon to support the charge of exaggerated expectations or the charge of a credibility gap. The constant availability of anecdotal evidence made it possible for adversaries of OEO to *renew* attacks against the agency, refocusing attention on the one-sided issues by offering new cases. Moreover, OEO's repeated use of its themes of defense permitted the agency's opponents to attack *these*. Charles Goodell, for example, in 1966 said that legislators "get a little tired of the reply constantly that we have to expect these things, and we do not do anything differently to perhaps improve the program."[55] By maneuvers such as these, critics were able to strengthen the advantage of their position. Not only did they have possession of one-sided issues, but the administration's repeated invocation of its defenses, rather than deflecting attention, could reinforce the critics' position. Necessarily, then, only a feeble defense could be mustered.

The administration's defense was further enfeebled by the implication that it did not, after all, know how to solve the problem of poverty in America—for that was the only alternative to the inference that it was inept. The self-confidence of 1964 had been shattered by the criticism. The fact was that the administration did *not* know, in that it lacked the means to test its working hypotheses against reality or to evaluate its efforts.

The theories guiding the program, such as the view attributing poverty to the opportunity structure or the view of poverty as a vicious circle, were so cosmic in their scope that they could not be tested, because no poverty program could control all possible sources of error variance. A term such as "poverty culture" could not be defined operationally in sufficiently small scope to be tested in the program. Consequently, one had no basis for inferring, for example, that a particular community center enhanced the "opportunity structure" of the ghetto.

Evaluation of the poverty program also was stymied by the lack of reliable measurements. What could be measured statistically was income, but the goal of the poverty program was not simply to increase the incomes of the poor. The criteria for a satisfactory solution to poverty typically stressed reductions in inequalities of justice, education, and power, for which no statistical measures were available.

Another cluster of obstacles to evaluation befell virtually *all* social programs. For example, programs frequently did not permit the control which is characteristic of experimental design, holding constant all possible sources of error variance and then manipulating the independent variable. In his discussion of juvenile-delinquency programs in Boston, Thernstrom observed that strict experimentation was not possible because of the need to convince the public of the program's worth. The electorate, imposing regular deadlines for results, forbade the luxury of negative findings. A project which failed to produce the intended results would be terminated rather than redirected.[56] Furthermore, antipoverty projects depended on the goodwill of the poor, who might regard research as a dodge for postponing action and hardly could be expected "to appreciate the scientific investigation of social policy as grounds for denying or limiting services" to those in immediate need.[57]

These difficulties placed OEO in a dilemma. On the basis of assumed knowledge and expertise, the agency had promised Congress an evaluation and accounting. But deficiencies in the conception of social programs generally and the poverty program particularly made systematic evaluation impossible. OEO was unable to do what it had promised to do. Moreover, the nation was impatient to see quick results, and the administration, with its misbegotten claims to expertise, had encouraged impatience.

The agency's dilemma could be circumvented only by rhetorical maneuver. In the absence of accepted criteria and measures of success, satisfying the Congress was a matter of convincing its members that the poverty program indeed was successful. Belief was proof; if Congress judged the program to be a success, then a success it was. The relevant question for the administration, then, was, "By what means could the Congress be convinced that the War on Poverty was being won?"

OEO had emphasized moving quickly and visibly, magnifying its results to make them commensurate with its goals, and buying time. But these approaches could not offset characteristic congressional budgetary reviews, the force of which was intensified by the partisanship surrounding the War on Poverty. Legislating the federal budget is difficult, because the scope of concern is so vast and the variables so numerous. In the absence of complete understanding, the legislator must simplify the task so that it can be performed meaningfully and not capriciously. Several simplifying procedures are especially significant for the War on Poverty. One, the importance attached to legislative hearings, generally worked to the administration's advantage. Others, however, such as the tendency to judge complex programs by reference to specific incidents, the tendency to vary budgets only incrementally from the previous year's allocation, and the presumption that agency budgets should be cut, did not.

In his discussion of the politics of the appropriations process, Richard Fenno speaks of the importance of committee hearings. These hearings represent an opportunity for an agency head to provide information about the programs he administers and also to convey an image of himself as a competent, dedicated executive who is deserving of the committee's confidence. In fact, Fenno argues, the reaction to the agency head and his presentation may be the single most important specific item from which generalized congressional reactions are formed. Among the clues to the administrator's competence are the proportion of questions he answers himself rather than delegating to a phalanx of subordinates, and the impression he creates of being fair and frank.[58] In short, the hearings are valuable for what they symbolize about an agency's operation.

As a witness at hearings, Sargent Shriver excelled. He always was ingratiating and deferential, even when he disagreed strongly with his congressional interlocutors. Although many of his subordinates accompanied him to the hearings, Shriver attempted to answer most questions himself. He continued to keep congressmen informed of the course of the War on Poverty, especially when the news was good.

But other norms of the congressional budgetary process did not augur well for Shriver. For example, incrementalism hurt the administration. An agency's budget for one year ordinarily is taken as the base point for considering its budget for the next, and adjustments in the total allocation from year to year are minor. Incremental budgeting gives little emphasis to fundamental values; sometimes, the analysis of values is omitted altogether. As Braybrooke and Lindblom explain in their treatise on incrementalism, "both because values sometimes conflict and because they sometimes complement each other, those actually relevant to policy choices are values of increment or decrement, that is, marginal values—rather than abstractions such as defense, full employment, liberty, or better highways."[59] The greatest rhetorical strength of the administration, however, was its commitment to the value judgment that poverty in modern America was an intolerable, unnecessary evil. But once the programs were initiated, these values would not help the OEO in its quest for larger budgets.

Conversely, the marginal values which *were* important to the legislators could not be addressed by the antipoverty agency, because it lacked the means to measure or to evaluate its programs. It could not predict, for example, how many more people would be brought out of poverty in return for a given increase in funds for a work and training program. Without information of this type, it was unlikely that Congress would approve more than marginal increases, even for the programs which OEO instinctively regarded as its most successful. But without the realistic probability of major expansion, the administration would not be able to capitalize on its gains and advance its programs beyond the pilot stage.

Finally, the administration was placed at a disadvantage by the congressional role of guardian of the public fisc, and by the concomitant expectations that agency budgets should be scrutinized and, usually, that they should be

cut. Although agency executives will defend their proposed budgets as the minimum amount necessary to implement their programs, the appropriations committees
believe that there is "padding" in the budget and that
virtually all agencies can survive satisfactorily with less
money than they request.[60] This orientation toward economy presumably reflects the American public's traditional
resistance to increased government expenditures.

To be sure, there were exceptions to this general belief
that budget requests should be cut. Typically, agencies
receiving budget increases from the House Appropriations Committee were popular with the public, performing services which were universally appreciated, or
were accepted as performing necessary tasks, or had the
type of workload which permitted them to relate specific
expenditures directly to the performance of noncontroversial functions.[61] The Office of Economic Opportunity
did not fit any of these patterns. In fact, it fit the description of the agency most likely to receive *cuts* in its budget:
the agency which was engaged in open-ended activities
carrying unlimited potential for growth in federal spending and influence. Of course, belief that the poverty
program's budget was ripe for cuts was exactly counter to
the administration's original assumption that dramatic
increases in funding would be forthcoming once the program had taken hold.

These characteristics of the congressional decisionmaking process probably would have hurt the administration even if, in all other respects, congressional predispositions were in its favor. But discontent was augmented by
the partisan atmosphere in which Congress had considered the Economic Opportunity Act. Probably to
strengthen the political affiliation of the poverty program's intended beneficiaries, the Democratic congressio-

nal leadership had chosen in 1964 to identify the new measure with their political party rather than with bipartisan national objectives. Even if this partisan orientation could have been justified with reference to the 1964 election, it is difficult to justify its persistence during 1965 and 1966.

Numerous examples could be cited of the partisan orientation of which the Republicans complained. Having accepted the basic goals of the poverty program and having been prevented from making constructive suggestions, they had few options other than partisan attack. The hearing record for 1966 includes a number of testy, partisan exchanges between Republicans and the House committee chairman. Witnesses requested by the minority were not called; Congressman Quie of Minnesota complained that the most hostile witness of 1966 was the director of the program, Sargent Shriver![62] The imperiousness with which Adam Clayton Powell presided over the House hearings no doubt contributed to the belief that they had been unfairly conducted, as did his arbitrary decision to terminate them "because I am the chairman." The opening of floor debate in the House in 1966 was marked with slurs about Powell and his handling of the committee chairmanship, without a single congressman rising to speak in his defense.[63]

One might expect that the Republican opposition would inspire congressional Democrats to support the poverty program more strongly. But that did not happen. By 1966, the president had stopped exerting himself to secure the votes of individual legislators. Although Johnson was increasingly preoccupied with Vietnam, his tendency to lose interest in programs was an enduring trait throughout his career.[64] In any event, for congressional Democrats there was little political gain in identifying

themselves with the administration on a measure in which
the president appeared to have lost interest. In fact,
Democrats may have gained by stressing their independence from the executive branch. Congressman Sam Gibbons of Florida opened floor debate on the Economic
Opportunity Amendments of 1966 by stating, "This is not
an administration bill. This is not the same bill which
came to us from the agencies. This is a bill which is the
work of Congress and the work of a committee."[65] When
the partisan tone of congressional hearings and debates
antagonized Republicans without uniting Democrats in
support of the administration, the fate of the poverty
program seemed sealed. This tone, though, only added
impulse to what already was the likely congressional
response.

IV

Belief that funds for the War on Poverty would increase
dramatically was shaken—abruptly, according to OEO's
research director, Robert A. Levine, who cites September 1965 as the time when the presidential commitment to
the program's expansion was abandoned. The change in
policy, Levine believes, was caused partly by the increasing fiscal demands of the war in Vietnam but also by the
fact that "the political fruits had fallen off the tree of
administrative chaos and program excess with dull
squashy thuds."[66] As early as May 1965, OEO had received instructions from the Budget Bureau to "bear
down hard" on its forthcoming budget request. Similar
communications were sent in June, July, and August.
Shriver was told, for example, "There is no question but
that it will be necessary to find savings in existing pro-

grams of each agency to help finance increased spending for higher-priority programs." Shriver initially balked at these instructions, maintaining that they implied that his program had failed, although "no one can demonstrate failure, because there has been little failure."[67] By the following year, however, his office acknowledged that funds would be finite and would remain limited.

A justification was needed for this change in budgeting. The administration could not acknowledge that it had lost congressional support, so it justified its limited requests by claiming that the program must not outstrip the administrative capacities of its managers, and it insisted that OEO was requesting the maximum sum that would assure that all funds were spent properly. For fiscal year 1966, President Johnson proposed to double OEO's budget, from $750 million to $1.5 billion. In congressional testimony, Shriver labeled the proposed new budget conservative and argued that the request was small because "we are determined to keep a careful control over all of these activities." Shriver objected to a proposal by Adam Clayton Powell to appropriate $3 billion. The president's request was sufficient, the OEO director said, because "we will be able to spend it more intelligently and more efficiently."[68] The administration also believed that its limitations would not significantly impair the poverty program. Defending the cuts for 1967, for example, Charles Schultze wrote the president, "As you can see, none of these cuts really reduces the level of the OEO program. The only thing that might be said is that we might be delaying by two to four months the start of some new projects."[69]

If the president limited his requests in the name of limited administrative expertise, the Congress limited its appropriations in the name of economy. Senator Prouty of Vermont argued that any nonincremental increase in poverty spending actually would hurt the poor. Government spending would add to the inflationary pressures in the economy, he reasoned, and the poor were the chief victims of inflation.[70] Using a similar line of reasoning, in 1967 the Senate adopted an amendment, initiated by Everett Dirksen but reportedly with the blessings of the administration, to reduce the authorization for the War on Poverty from the $2.496 billion proposed by the Senate Labor and Public Welfare Committee to the $1.75 billion originally requested by the president.[71]

Both the alleged limitation of managerial expertise and the alleged need for economy probably were pretexts rather than reasons for reducing antipoverty appropriations. They were undermined by the revelation that OEO originally had requested a substantially higher figure than the president's budget provided but had been told by the Budget Bureau to cut back on its requests so that President Johnson could propose a budget whose total overall spending did not reflect a large increase.[72] The comment that the agency was not requesting more money than it could spend wisely was also intended to spark confidence in its accountability. Read another way, however, the statement that the agency could spend only such a relatively small sum wisely would hardly inspire support.

Congressional claims that the budget must be reduced in the name of economy also probably represented a sham argument. Even if it were true that inflation required budgetary restraint, this argument would call only for a limit on the total of federal spending. It would not automatically follow that cuts should be made specifically in the poverty program. Shriver fumed about the judgment of priorities implicit in the 1966 cuts in the OEO program. "The poor will feel they have been shortchanged," he said. "They will feel they have been double-crossed. The poor will feel that democracy is only for the rich."[73] Several members of Congress in fact had argued for larger authorizations; during 1965, it was the president who had requested only modest funding. Refusing to reduce authorizations to the level the president had requested, Senator Morse of Oregon insisted, "I do not intend to pull the trigger of the President's torpedoing of his own Great Society program."[74]

Although the reasons given by the executive and the Congress for limiting funds probably were bogus, they had catastrophic consequences for the antipoverty program. Expansion of existing programs was stymied. New programs could be added only at the expense of ongoing ones which had begun to develop a supportive constituency. Local governments, uncertain about the prospects of receiving federal funds, were reluctant to commit themselves to innovative programs. Scarce funds meant that groups among the poor were competing with each other for the allocation of resources, rather than cooperating in an effort toward a common goal. If the poor had participated actively in the planning and design of a program only to learn that there were insufficient funds for its implementation, the results might well be frustration and rage. And if funds for the program were cut, then efforts which had been made by local communities in planning programs and requesting funds were wasted.

Not least among the effects of funding limitations was that they were inconsistent with a major aspect of the administration's rhetorical stance. In invoking the military metaphor, the president had implied that a total mobilization of all the nation's resources would be necessary to fight poverty. Obviously, to tighten the reins on antipoverty programs in response to budget pressures was

to betray a less than total mobilization. Mayor Lindsay of
New York, in his 1966 testimony to the Senate Labor and
Public Welfare Committee, put the issue directly. "In
essence," the mayor said, "we are finally faced with a
question of intent—whether we really mean our rhetoric
when we use the label 'war on poverty.' The level of
current operations is not that of a war in which every
available resource is turned to the single task of winning
the war."[75] Charles Schultze of the Budget Bureau also
was worried about the inconsistency in the administration's position. In a lengthy memorandum to the president, he stated that the major problem with the fiscal 1968
budget was that "*we are not able to fund adequately the
new Great Society programs.* At the same time, States,
cities, depressed areas, and individuals have been led to
expect immediate delivery of benefits from Great Society
programs to a degree that is not realistic" (emphasis in
original). Schultze predicted that frustration, loss of credibility, and deterioration of state and local services would
be the results of this dilemma and warned, "This sets us
up for some real punishment by the opposition in 1968."[76]

By demonstrating the inconsistency between one aspect
of the administration's rhetorical stance (the military objective) and another (the promise of accountability), advocates of higher funding might have been able to muster
support. Here, as elsewhere, rhetorical choices led to
symbolic contradictions. No one had intended that "accountability" would be an excuse for de-escalating the
proposed war, yet this is what had happened. If proponents of higher funding had been able to show how
trimming the program's sails was inconsistent with the
"unconditional war" objective, they conceivably might
have been able to prevail. But the administration publicly
avoided the appearance of any inconsistency by being less

than candid about the funding of the antipoverty program. It magnified the scope of its program and minimized the impact of the funding limitations. For example, President Johnson on several occasions referred to his request for $1.5 billion for the 1966 fiscal year as a "doubling" of the appropriation from the first to the second year. Since the approximately $750 million appropriated for the first year was not spent until halfway into the year, the projected increase really was no increase at all, and the administration knew it. In a letter recommending that the president sign the 1965 act, Sargent Shriver commented, "The measure provides authorizations which are sufficient to carry out programs under the Act *at their currently budgeted levels*" (emphasis added).[77] In fact, the appropriation for fiscal 1966 actually represented a cutback, because it was not possible to maintain the rate of spending that existed at the end of the year. It was instead necessary to revert to the *average* rate of spending for the preceding year.

Just as the administration magnified the scope of its activities, it minimized the impact of funding limitations. This effect was achieved through a transformation of the meaning of the term "War on Poverty." Originally, the term had been roughly equivalent to the scope of activities authorized by the Economic Opportunity Act. As funds grew tight, however, the term was conveniently enlarged to include many older programs and make the war effort seem larger. In his Economic Report of January 1967, the president referred to "many fronts in the War on Poverty," and listed them as including full employment, health and guidance services, education and training, income maintenance, and programs to break the cycle of poverty. In June 1968, Johnson included measures ranging "from increased social security benefits to

financial aid for slum schools; from medical care for the
poor and aged to a higher minimum wage for the Nation's
workers."[78] By this maneuver, the administration could
make the limitations on OEO's funding seem less ominous. If one program was stagnating, what did it matter;
total antipoverty spending (as redefined) was substantial
and increasing. The president justifiably could say, as he
did in 1967, "More money will be spent on poverty in the
United States in trying to do something about it this year
by the Federal Government than we spend in Vietnam."
Indeed, the president's budget message of January 1967
had identified a total of $25.6 billion in antipoverty spend-
ing, of which the programs of the Office of Economic
Opportunity represented only about 8 percent.[79]

Although it may have blunted the charge of apparent
hypocrisy, however, the administration's stance did not
engender support for its broader conception of the War
on Poverty. The difficulty was that the phrase "War on
Poverty" had become identified in the public mind with a
component even *smaller* than the Office of Economic
Opportunity: local community action. Other antipoverty
projects such as health, education, and legal services had
achieved separate identities. Both for this reason and
because of the number, newness, and visibility of local
community action agencies, this one portion of the poverty program often came to symbolize the whole.[80] But
community action programs had become the *least* popular
of the OEO activities.

So the Johnson administration faced a trade-off. En-
larging the apparent scope of the term "War on Poverty"
would attach to other programs the onus which many
Americans had come to place on community action. Al-
ternatively, however, the poverty warriors would need to

acknowledge that the "unconditional war" had been aborted almost as soon as it had begun.

The "unconditional war" objective implied a far more intensive and concerted effort than the actual scale of the poverty program warranted. But this discrepancy could not be acknowledged, lest the choices of 1964 seem in retrospect deceitful or disingenuous. So OEO's supporters described "results" in a way that made them compatible with the goals implicit in the military metaphor. To do so, they exaggerated the significance of tangible accomplishments to date, while offering great promises for the future. But each of these methods invited a strong attack. Exaggeration opened the agency to the charge that it generally was not credible; great promises, to the charge that OEO aroused impossible expectations, leading to frustration and violence.

By 1967, the rhetorical tactic which once had aided the administration led to consequences which strengthened its adversaries. The military metaphor was not the only tactic to suffer this fate.

4

Rhetorical Crisis

The Transformation of the Enemy

Like the "unconditional war" objective, the image of poverty as a vicious circle was useful for the administration in 1964. It located the problem within the individual, not the macroeconomic system; yet it did so without the moral stigma implicit in traditional beliefs about the poor. Moreover, it allowed administrators to mask their aid to blacks, by defining racial problems as really economic in nature.

Yet a program to aid the poor would have to be large enough, and potent enough, to have a real impact at the point to which it was addressed, much less throughout the cycle. Diffusion of efforts in order to attack the cycle superficially at many points would have been wasteful, and even a far larger budget than OEO received would not have allowed a concentrated effort everywhere. It was necessary, therefore, to make decisions and to set priorities. Unfortunately, though, this exercise actually inverted the value of the vicious-circle image, so that it became an argument against rather than for the program.

The image of the poverty cycle dictated no rationale for setting priorities; so, to claim primacy for attacking poverty at any point, it was necessary for OEO supporters to convince Congress and the public that they had selected important targets and were attacking them with the right weapons. As with the military objective, proof was equated with belief, and inducing belief was a matter of persuasion. But convincing the congressional and public audiences was difficult with respect to each point of concentration which the OEO had selected. In fact, the ultimate consequence of the vicious-circle image of poverty was to entrap OEO supporters in a destructive web of discourse. Opponents could call upon the very same image to justify abandoning the poverty program and reaffirming the older view that if a person was poor it was his or her own fault.

I

Children and Youth. The first concentration was on programs for children and youth. These were thought to be a wise investment which would be repaid by the permanent breaking of the poverty cycle. Congressman B. F. Sisk of California, for instance, believed "that the cycle of poverty can be broken by beginning first with young children" and accordingly proposed in 1966 "to take maximum advantage of those programs offering the greatest opportunity for success."[1] The "investment" theme justified giving lower priority to the current generation of adult poor, for whom suffering might be relieved but for whom the underlying causes of poverty could not be removed. And it offered the promise of a higher rate of return from the initial expenditure, thereby making programs for children and youth financially sound.

Moreover, the motivation which OEO instilled in youths would become a self-propelling force; continued personal growth and development could be anticipated. The Neighborhood Youth Corps frequently was defended on the basis that the income which it provided to its enrollees allowed and motivated them to remain in school to acquire needed basic education and specific skills.[2] The impact of the program on the rate of school dropouts often was cited as an index of its success in instilling motivation.

Third, youth programs were thought to contribute to reduction of juvenile delinquency and youth crime. In its first annual report, OEO credited the Neighborhood Youth Corps with the decline in juvenile crime in Berkeley and Oakland; in 1966, a similar claim was made for Newark. Robert Kennedy generalized the argument in a Senate speech on October 3, 1966, in which he attributed to the secretary of labor a statement that, in some cities, the rate of delinquency dropped by 80 percent when poverty programs were begun.[3]

These defenses of youth-oriented programs found such wide acceptance that the popularity of the programs preceded proof of their effectiveness. When the results were later found to be uncertain, both the wisdom of the poverty planners' judgment and the extent of their knowledge were called into question. Evidence began to accumulate, for example, that the effects of educational programs were short-lived. Reviewing this evidence several years later, Robert A. Levine, director of OEO's Office of Research, Plans, Programs, and Evaluation, would declare, "we know virtually nothing about what techniques of education, compensatory or otherwise, work to improve the education of the poor." Levine counseled that OEO should not make a major effort in the field of education, because there were too many ways in which the effects of a program like Project Head Start could be lost.[4] No such counsel was offered, however, in 1965 and 1966.

Evidence also accumulated that the training programs geared to youth had little long-term impact. Reviews of antipoverty programs made by the General Accounting Office in 1968 recognized that developing good work habits was not sufficient to enhance the employment potential of Neighborhood Youth Corps enrollees. As the comptroller general summarized these findings in his report to the Congress, "The great majority of youths who have been enrolled in the NYC Program in-school and summer components would probably have remained in or dropped out of school irrespective of their enrollment in the NYC program."[5] It also became apparent that, in the absence of meaningful job opportunities, instilling motivation only planted seeds of frustration.

These criticisms challenged both the investment potential and the motivational value of youth-oriented programs. Once these two defenses were compromised, only the third remained: that such efforts reduced the incidence of youth crime and delinquency. This defense received increasing emphasis. Both Levine and Kershaw spoke of the service performed by the Neighborhood Youth Corps in "keeping kids off the streets"; President Johnson advocated supplemental appropriations for summer programs "to take care of idle youth in our teeming cities."[6] For the most part, the nation found this defense reassuring, at least initially.

Treating youth-oriented programs as an "aging vat" meant that their effect was to buy time rather than to combat crucial social problems. Congressman Erlenborn of Illinois was concerned that the original purpose of these youth programs had been subverted and replaced by "that of keeping youngsters off the street—a sort of

babysitting program for older babies."[7] Black leaders,
ranging from Kenneth Clark to Stokely Carmichael,
viewed the programs disapprovingly as being aimed at
pacifying the ghettos rather than preventing poverty.[8]
Some social workers, Kershaw reports, also began to
dissociate themselves from programs which seemed designed to provide "the illusion that the young people of
the slums and ghetto are being helped." They believed, as
social work theorists Richard Cloward and Robert Ontell
put it, that "It says something about a society that it can
generate so much enthusiasm and consensus about programs that avoid the problems they are designed to
solve."[9]

Perhaps the strongest challenge to the emphasis on
children and youth, however, derived from the logical
corollary that such an emphasis neglected the problems of
the current generation. The cycle of poverty could be
broken only in the distant future. As the benefits of a
focus on children and youth became more equivocal, the
problems unanswered by such an approach became more
apparent, and OEO moved progressively toward concentrating on a different point of the poverty cycle.

Job Training. During 1966, it became apparent that the
primary focus of the War on Poverty had shifted to
programs of job training. To some degree, this shift was
prompted by Congress. According to Shriver, 46 percent
of the OEO budget for the 1967 fiscal year would be
devoted to programs of job creation or training, a sharp
increase from the previous year.[10] And other training
programs, such as the Manpower Development and
Training Act, were also redirected to focus primarily on
the poor.

Officially, it was claimed that this shift in focus resulted from a decision to concentrate on programs which offered the best chance of success. If unemployment were viewed as the primary cause of poverty, then efforts to deal with this problem would produce effects throughout the poverty cycle. Secretary of Labor Willard Wirtz contended in 1966, "The most direct answer to poverty is jobs"; Republican Congressman William Ayres of Ohio advocated that the War on Poverty "should be an honest effort to help people caught in poverty . . . to regain the independence and the dignity that is lost through unemployment"; A. Philip Randolph listed full employment as the top priority in his proposed "Freedom Budget."[11] By 1967, the House Committee on Education and Labor— and, by 1968, OEO itself—would declare that jobs were the primary means to achieve economic independence and thereby to eliminate poverty.[12]

Redirection of the War on Poverty toward job training seemed useful for the program's designers. Training programs recommended themselves on grounds of economy, since the costs of training could be recouped quickly. Secretary Wirtz asserted that the cost of on-the-job training was recovered in two years in savings from welfare expenditures; a similar statement was made by Secretary John Gardner of Health, Education, and Welfare.[13] Perhaps more important, training and employment programs were thought to be noncontroversial in nature. As a result, they could rescue OEO from the maelstrom into which it had been thrust by critics of the educational and community action programs. James Ridgeway of the *New Republic* predicted that stressing employment would "shunt to one side the controversy over 'maximum feasible participation of the poor' in the anti-poverty war."[14]

But the emphasis on training programs, like the emphasis on children and youth, soon played into the hands of OEO's adversaries. These programs also became controversial and fell far short of their intended purpose. Administrative problems abounded. Because of the haste to fill places in the Job Corps, Senator George Murphy charged, screening was inadequate and the results were disciplinary problems in Job Corps centers.[15] Several congressional spokesmen complained about violence in Job Corps centers, arguing that it contributed to a high withdrawal rate and deterred prospective enrollees. As a remedy for these problems, Congressman Paul Fino of New York proposed that "we ought to draft our Nation's punks and hoods instead of coddling and paying them in the Job Corps."[16] The high dropout rate, regardless of its cause, meant that funds were being spent on persons who did not remain in the corps long enough to benefit from the experience. The high cost of training also was seen as a major defect in the program. Although the costs might be recouped eventually, the initial outlay was considerable: the Job Corps was alleged to be so badly mismanaged that the cost of training an enrollee was greater than the cost of a Harvard education.[17]

OEO attempted to rebut each of these charges. Referring to hostility at Job Corps centers, Sargent Shriver tried to make the reported friction into a virtue, arguing that it proved that the program really was reaching its intended targets. "I personally feel," he said, "that if the Job Corps was composed of nothing but kids who had very good records and very good possibilities of success, we would not be dealing with the very population for whom the Job Corps was created."[18] He also attempted to minimize the significance of friction, however, asserting that there had been hostility at no more than ten or twenty Job Corps centers, despite the fact that riots had occurred "in some of the fanciest high schools in the country."[19]

The retention rate of the Job Corps also was seen by OEO as proof of success rather than failure. In its second annual report, the agency emphasized the challenges implicit in the corps. The report said, "It is not a Summer camp; it is not a free ride. . . . Given these conditions, the Corpsmen's previous history of failure, and the demands of the program, the Job Corps retention rate (above 70 percent) is impressive."[20] Moreover, it was argued that this rate had increased since the earliest days of the program.

Several answers were offered by OEO to the charge of excessive cost. The high costs were said to reflect initial capital outlays and could be expected quickly to decline. Shriver replied that the comparison between the Job Corps and a Harvard education was misleading. When the total cost of Harvard was considered, rather than only the cost paid by the student, it was substantially more expensive than the Job Corps. Besides, Shriver asserted in a letter to the editor of the *Washington Post,* "the *real* question for taxpayers to decide is *not* whether the Job Corps costs more or less than a Harvard education, but whether it is worth investing tax revenues in education and training to keep these young men and women off tomorrow's relief rolls and out of tomorrow's courts, and get them into tomorrow's ranks of productive citizens and taxpayers."[21] In general, Shriver compared the administration of the Job Corps to a commercial enterprise, telling the House Appropriations Committee, "Of course, we have had trouble. If you tried to open up 107 Sears Roebuck stores in 18 months, you would have had a hard time getting 107 good store managers in a hurry."[22]

Eventually, these defenses would attract more supporters of the Job Corps, but only after steps had been taken within the program which implicitly conceded the force of the attacks. The corps became increasingly selective by accepting only those most likely to benefit, thereby increasing the retention rate and cutting costs.

OEO might be able to explain the administrative problems in its training programs, but some critics posed a far more serious and fundamental challenge to concentrating on this point of the poverty cycle. They maintained that training without the promise of subsequent employment was not only useless but counterproductive.

Originally, the link between training and employment was not viewed as a problem by the poverty warriors, who assumed that an expanding economy would naturally generate enough new jobs to absorb the graduates of manpower programs if only these people were properly trained. This assumption was crucial. If graduates could not find jobs, their loss of morale and motivation would undermine the benefits of training, which would not have offered an exit from poverty in any case. The vast opportunity offered by the training program would be exposed as bankrupt, and general distrust of the government would ensue. Adam Clayton Powell rebuked Willard Wirtz for the limited achievements of manpower programs, saying, "To train and to educate without guaranteeing job placement is to create a Molotov cocktail of frustration." Shriver himself conceded, "Without jobs, programs to increase capabilities would create hopes without creating a chance for their fulfillment."[23]

During 1966 and 1967 it became apparent that the War on Poverty included neither the direct provision of jobs nor the guarantee of eventual employment. Robert Kennedy was accurate in his conclusion, "No Government program now operating gives any substantial promise of meeting the unemployment crisis affecting the Negro of the cities."[24] The comptroller general later reported to Congress that post–Job Corps employment experience since the beginning of the program had been "disappointing," and advised, "In light of the costly training provided by the Job Corps program, we doubt that the resources now being applied to this program can be fully justified." The employment record was especially discouraging for graduates of the conservation center portion of the Job Corps.[25]

This criticism of the training emphasis, if allowed to stand, exposed the program as insufficient at best and fraudulent at worst. The antipoverty planners had stressed a program which could not achieve its objectives without the guarantee of employment, which it failed to provide. It was almost as though the OEO chose to create its own vicious circle: supporting only those programs which it knew would not work. To place the attack within this frame was to indict the judgment, if not the wisdom, of OEO, yet it was a difficult charge for the agency's defenders to answer. Shriver dismissed as "pure idealism" the suggestion that any manpower programs could be planned so that there always were jobs waiting upon its completion; the normal flux within the economy prevented such an outcome.[26]

Shriver, then, made his defense of the training emphasis contingent on general economic growth. In fact, the 1968 and 1969 annual reports of the Council of Economic Advisers found economic growth to be the most significant factor in reducing poverty during the previous decade, since the most impressive reductions occurred among households headed by a working male. Shriver agreed: "Obviously we cannot take the credit for all or even most of the improvement—the greatest part of it has been due to general economic progress and decreased unemployment."[27]

This criticism, of course, had a potentially devastating effect. OEO programs seemed unrelated to the reduction in poverty; at best the agency seemed superfluous. To avert this problem, OEO advocates sought a middle ground, defending economic growth yet arguing that it was *insufficient* as a remedy for poverty. Social programs were needed too. General stimulation of the economy, it was argued, would not help those who were outside the labor force, particularly the unemployable and the "hard-core" poor, a category in which the President's Commission on Income Maintenance Programs would place "the aged, the disabled, female-headed families, and those whose limited skills seem unlikely to be demanded by an increasingly complex industrial system."[28] But this argument contained a trap. If the War on Poverty was fought in behalf of *these* groups, then its emphasis on job training made little sense. Even with training, the "hard-core" poor were the least likely to find jobs. Therefore, it seemed unlikely that focusing on training programs would produce effects throughout the poverty cycle. OEO claimed in 1967 that many of the poor who got the jobs which economic growth yielded were trained for them through its own and related programs.[29] But there was no way to prove that OEO's training had made the difference, and accumulating contrary evidence made the causal connection seem tenuous.

Aid for the Ghetto. OEO programs also were concentrated in urban ghettos, in an attempt to combat the culture of poverty in the place where it was thought to be transmitted. This view of the enemy was quite different from that in 1964, when every effort was made to portray economic deprivation and race as two distinct fates. During the spring of 1964, as Douglass Cater has observed, the prominent image of the poor man was not the northern ghetto black but the rural Appalachian white.[30] Quickly, however, this perception changed.

Demography offered the clearest explanation for the metamorphosis. In 1964, 70 percent of the poor were white, and nearly half the poor lived in rural areas. It was in the central cities of the nation's metropolitan areas, though, that the greatest *concentration* of poor people was to be found. Here, too, were the largest concentrations of blacks. In metropolitan areas with populations in excess of one million, 71 percent of the poor in the slums were black. It was logical that urban ghettos be the primary targets for OEO's intervention. Limited resources could be spent best in areas in which large numbers of the poor could be reached. Community action programs most easily could be mounted when the community was geographically compact. Training programs most profitably could be addressed to a large pool of the unemployed. The culture-of-poverty theory could be tested best in an environment in which virtually all of the cultural characteristics were present.

In their operation, therefore, most OEO programs focused on the ghetto. Walker examined early community action programs and found that the selection of poverty target areas, the attempt to attract minority group professionals, and the emphasis on nonprofessional neighborhood workers all exemplified the program's concern with racial and ethnic minorities. Similarly, the official study of the Los Angeles riots contained the statement that federal antipoverty programs "were expressly designed for the urban Negro."[31]

Public discourse in 1964 had made the antipoverty effort a matter of economics *rather than* race. But in their haste to open fronts against the enemy where he was vulnerable, the poverty warriors could not sustain the distinction. And the focus on the ghetto, like the foci on youths and job training, proved to be harmful—not only because it failed to conquer the enemy but also because it alienated whites whose support for the war was crucial.

OEO programs, seen as designed for blacks, were rejected by the white poor. The Harris Poll revealed that, although black people favored the War on Poverty by a five-to-one margin, Americans generally were critical of the program by a margin of five to four. The Harris Poll also revealed that the most negative reactions against the War on Poverty came from poor whites, 70 percent of whom believed "that the War on Poverty is a black program and does not deal with their needs because their skins are not black."[32] That this difference in the rates of approval developed over the life of the poverty program can be seen by comparing these later data with the results of a Gallup poll taken in 1966. In that poll, 65 percent of the black poor and 60 percent of the white poor expressed favorable judgments of the antipoverty program's first year.[33] Walker explained the most likely reason for the erosion: "If the War on Poverty is actually seen by the white poor, as well as by those who have written about it, as a program that was born in the Black Revolution, then the different level of identification . . . is easy to understand. Urban poor whites have rejected the Black Revolution."[34]

Kenneth Clark has described the psychological processes involved. If the problems of the urban slum are viewed in terms of race, he wrote, that perception calls forth defensive attitudes which historically have characterized American racial crises. The power of the poor will be restricted, and the problem of poverty will be redefined as the need to contain an incipient racial revolt rather than as the need to end economic deprivation.[35] Clark judged the poverty program a failure, at least in part because of its growing identification with the Negro. A similar conclusion was drawn by Sargent Shriver, who told an audience on the National Educational Television network in January 1968 that his agency's program had not received sustained national support because it had been identified in the public mind as a program for blacks.[36]

Perhaps the unkindest cut to Shriver's agency was that the equation of poverty and race came at a time when the civil rights movement was overtaken by a new surge of militancy. In an atmosphere of urgency, anything short of absolute commitment was suspect. For example, Soskin alluded to editorials in Harlem's *Amsterdam News* which suggested that government projects in Harlem were no more than schemes by local groups to pay their members large salaries. The editorials assailed groups receiving federal funds as having been "bought off" by the white power structure.[37] Charles Hale, political chairman of Brooklyn's chapter of the Congress on Racial Equality, charged in 1967 that "fascistic thinking" characterized the antipoverty programs. The federal government, Hale believed, had recruited members of the "black bourgeoisie" to "corral the niggers."[38] More generally, Tucker observed that by 1967 and 1968 the announcement of new government programs for the ghetto no longer was met with excitement among local residents. By this time, they had denounced all conventional programs as insufficient.[39] This stance, suggesting both ingratitude and an insatiable appetite for resources, hardly would cause whites to think favorably about measures to benefit blacks. Instead, as black militancy became more common, each race saw the other as a threat. Blacks saw whites as threatening the chances for racial justice; whites saw blacks as threatening social stability.

So each point selected for special emphasis was vulnerable. The stress on children and youth offered no chance of improvement to the adult poor. The stress on job-training programs ignored the "hard-core" poor, precisely those who OEO said could not benefit from economic growth. The stress on the ghetto aroused the antagonism of much of white America. More generally, attempts at concentration at one point along the poverty cycle were weakened by the fact that the effects did *not* extend throughout the cycle.

This problem did not result simply from the choice of poor places at which to intervene. Indeed, the same criticism applies with respect to *any* concentration at one specific point of the cycle. There always would be some groups among the poor who would be unaffected. Seemingly, the dilemma was inescapable. The logic behind the image of the vicious circle was incompatible with the programmatic concentration at specific points along the circle. Carried to its logical conclusion, the defense of OEO's specific activities undermined the agency's general rationale of an emphasis on services and training. Conversely, the defense of its rationale undermined its activities.

II

The damage to the administration was greater still, because a different reading could be given to the theory of the "vicious circle"—an interpretation which would avoid the administration's dilemmas but which would damage the poverty program severely. The various points of concentration chosen by OEO would appeal to different publics, but all reinforced moderate or traditional values. As problems emerged with each defense, then, the natural recourse of the target audiences was to traditionally dominant American ideology with its view of a separate "culture of poverty."

It was possible to view the poor as a culture lacking commitment to middle-class values. What made the circle vicious, in this view, was that the entire culture seemed impervious to modification. Although the term "culture of poverty" was used loosely, sometimes as only a euphemism for the life-style of the ghetto, it did have a more precise meaning. Several scholars have maintained that the poor were characterized by patterns of conduct, habits and values, and general world views quite distinct from those of the larger society. Among the often-cited differences were the poor's inability to delay gratification; their fatalism; their linguistic habits, including incompetence in patterns of middle-class interpersonal communication; and their low levels of aspiration.[40] Living for the present, believing that one's destiny is controlled by external forces, lacking "social acceptability" in language, and apathy were thought to set the poor apart, as a distinct culture.

Each item in this culture-of-poverty theory was open to serious question. The studies on deferred gratification were inconclusive and may have been affected by the presence or absence of a real chance for later gain.[41] Fatalism could be offset by involvement in social action and the experience of leadership roles.[42] Linguistic differences among the poor need not be regarded as deficits.[43] Aspiration levels might be increased, given realistic goal setting and the possibility of achieving the goal.[44] The specific claim that the poor were not inclined to work was easily refuted.[45] In addition to these empirical challenges to the theory, it was attacked on conceptual and method-ological grounds as well.[46]

Although the theory of the poverty culture was not established unequivocally by research, in its popularized form it was attractive to critics of OEO. A reason fre-quently cited for the long-run difficulties of education and training was that participants returned to the same culture from which they had come. If *that* environment reflected the culture of poverty, the participants really could not be aided until the whole culture was transformed. But such an undertaking obviously was infeasible and prohibitively costly. In its absence, however, extensive spending on antipoverty programs would be unproductive, so those programs should be curtailed.

The cycle-of-poverty theory could be used to justify ending OEO programs as well as expanding them. In effect, as Kenneth Clark noted, this series of arguments made recitation of the problems of poverty a substitute for action to correct them.[47] Action at any one point on the poverty cycle would be useless without action at every point, to break the hold of an entire way of life. Since the latter was not possible, the former was not fruitful.

Still, relatively few people were ready to abandon all hope of overcoming poverty. More effort therefore was required, but of what kind? One could maintain that programs of massive social reform, redistributing power and influence, were necessary to alter the entire social environment of the poor. But, with the exception of radical social critics, this interpretation attracted few ad-herents. Far more widespread was the second possible interpretation: in order to eliminate poverty, it would be necessary to change the *individuals* in the poverty culture. This interpretation strongly fit the War on Poverty within the traditional ideology.

This view invited danger. Modifying the habits and behavior of the poor could be portrayed as a shift from a war on poverty to a war on the poor—a change in status of the enemy. Moreover, believing that personal changes were necessary for the poor was but a short step from believing that the poor were poor because something was wrong with *them*.

Important elements of the traditionally dominant ideology still persisted in the 1960s. Chief among them, perhaps, was an attitude of condescension toward the poor, manifested even in programs designed for their aid. Often, excessive checking was done to determine eligibility; aid was extended only grudgingly. These practices implied that the poor were disreputable. By equating poverty and disrepute, one could justify a posture of condescension.

The persistent function of the traditional ideology that poverty is a defect of the individual has been to promote social cohesion through victimage. The middle class reaffirms the ideals of equal opportunity by victimizing the poor, attributing their plight to personal failure. Members of the middle class thereby need not feel responsible for the persistence of poverty. At the same time, the larger society supports those traditional social welfare programs which represent corporate acts of philanthropy and which do not threaten middle-class status. William Ryan, in a critique of this ideology, maintains that the generic process of "blaming the victim" is applied to virtually every American social problem.[48]

Since the historic poverty ideology still was functional for many Americans, one should not be surprised at its

persistence through the 1960s. In his informal account of
the decade, William O'Neill offers the judgment that "the
Protestant Ethic never really died among Middle Americans, who continued to think their prosperity, however
slight, the reward of virtue, and other's poverty, however
great, the penalty of vice."[49] In the spring of 1964, the
Gallup Poll found 54 percent of its respondents believing
that poverty was caused by lack of individual effort; in the
fall of 1971, Robert Lauer reported the results of a survey
which asked the nonpoor for their opinions as to the
causes of poverty. The factor named most often was
"motivation," by 43 percent of the sample. Lauer concluded, "In spite of the amount of material written about
America's poor over the last decade, *America's vast Middle Class views the poor as a culpable rather than a
victimized group*" (emphasis in original).[50]

An even stronger testimony to the durability of the
poverty ideology was the fact that it had taken hold
among the poor. Scott Briar found that most welfare
recipients viewed the welfare department as a "benevo-
lent autocracy" which legitimately was entitled to know
how they spent their money, to terminate aid if funds
were not spent properly, and—according to two-thirds of
his respondents—to conduct nighttime searches of their
homes. In Pittsburgh, Gilbert and Eaton discovered that
the poor expressed "apparent satisfaction with neighborhood conditions which professional planners and citizen
activists clearly view as substandard." In Wisconsin,
Handler and Hollingsworth revealed that recipients of aid
were able to internalize the poverty ideology by distin-
guishing themselves from other welfare recipients. Defining *themselves* as "deserving" but *others* as "unde-
serving," they were willing to condone restrictive welfare
practices which, they assumed, would be applied not to

themselves but to others.[51] Likewise, Briar found that his interviewees referred to recipients of welfare as "they" rather then "we."

Of course, it is possible to exaggerate the degree to which the poor accepted the traditional ideology. Cloward and Elman have hypothesized that, although *in public* the poor may support the traditional position, in private they express more specific and immediate grievances directed at welfare administration.[52] And Gilbert and Eaton do refer to the development of a minority of activists among the poor. It appears, however, that only this minority was repelled by an emphasis on individual improvement.

III

The theory of the "vicious circle," when applied to OEO's practice, led to self-defeating results. In particular, the belief that OEO was a program for blacks was almost fatal to the War on Poverty as white America groped for an explanation for the riots which swept the nation between 1964 and 1967. The riots had great symbolic significance; they were viewed by many whites as the "telling sign" that antipoverty efforts were misdirected.

Whites tended to believe, a priori, that riots were unconscionable and to express surprise when they occurred. The sociologist T. M. Tomlinson theorizes that the dominant white reaction, that "riots cannot be tolerated," reflected the widespread belief that no just cause could be advanced by such an unjust means.[53] Whites also believed that only a small minority of blacks were involved in the riots and that this minority represented disreputable elements of the black population, or "riff-

raff." After the Watts riots, for example, whites estimated that no more than 2 to 5 percent of the area's
blacks participated in the riots.[54] This belief was reassuring to whites; it made the riots less ominous than they
appeared.

Frequently, whites attributed to "outside agitators" the
inspiration for the riots. The study of six cities by the
Lemberg Center for the Study of Violence, at Brandeis
University, found that "outsiders coming into a city and
stirring up trouble" was the only possible cause for riots
accepted as true by a large percentage of whites; Rossi
and his colleagues found that this judgment was shared by
each of five occupational groups serving the ghetto.[55]
Mayor Locher of Cleveland, in response to a question by
Senator Robert Kennedy, alleged that the riots in his city
in 1966 would not have occurred had it not been for the
involvement of Communists.[56]

The stereotype of a "riffraff" of "outside agitators"
inciting a gullible black population to riot was not supported by the facts. Indeed, one could interpret the riots
as a form of symbolic communication, much like mass
demonstrations or protest marches. Robert M. Fogelson,
in his examination of the 1960s riots, concludes that the
incidents can best be understood as forms of "symbolic
speech." They were, he wrote, "attempts to alert
America, not overturn it, to denounce its practices, not
renounce its principles."[57]

This interpretation of violence as protest, however,
found few adherents among white politicians, as can be
seen in the results of a poll taken by *Congressional
Quarterly* of 268 congressmen, 16 governors, and 130
mayors. Asked to evaluate reasons for the riots, many
congressmen identified such factors as joblessness, idle-
ness, or whites' indifference to blacks' needs. In addition,

though, 47 percent of the congressmen thought that black irresponsibility was an important cause of riots; 46 percent so evaluated black separatist agitation; 33 percent, recent decisions of the Supreme Court; and 10 percent, Communist influence. When they were asked to evaluate antiriot proposals, large numbers of the congressmen advocated state, local, or private activity. Only 26 percent attached great importance to a federally financed "Marshall Plan" for the cities, as would be proposed by Vice President Humphrey in 1968. Seventy-three percent, however, emphasized traditional and family values; 61 percent, the need to stiffen penalties for agitators and rioters; and 54 percent, larger and better paid police departments. Fogelson characterized the response of the governors as "similar, if somewhat more perceptive" and the opinions of the mayors as "if anything, less sophisticated."[58]

Just as blacks' self-assertion led to their distrust and disdain for whites, so had whites' perception of black aggressiveness led to distrust and disdain for blacks. It was an unfortunate coincidence for OEO that these developments occurred just as community action programs became operational. Since the War on Poverty was thought to be for blacks, the coincidence tempted some spokesmen to argue causality—to claim that the War on Poverty had inspired the militancy and disorders.

On July 18, 1967, Senator Prouty of Vermont read into the hearing record of the Subcommittee on Employment, Manpower, and Poverty of the Senate Labor and Public Welfare Committee, a telegram to Sargent Shriver from the Newark police director. The director complained that employees of a local community action agency had been threatened with the loss of their jobs if they did not participate in picketing and demonstrations against local government agencies. He predicted that the continued escalation of such activities would lead to rioting and anarchy. The telegram requested an immediate reply from Shriver, but no reply was forthcoming.[59] Within the next three weeks, the riots predicted by the police chief occurred. The House Education and Labor Committee, which had virtually completed its hearings on the Economic Opportunity Amendments of 1967, reconvened on August 1 to hear testimony from several Newark officials. City Councilmen Frank Addonizio and Leo Bernstein charged that Newark's community action programs "have definitely played an important part in setting off the riots in the city of Newark." This effect allegedly was achieved by community action workers who made inflammatory remarks at public hearings, jumped up and down, and agitated the audience. Upon being questioned by the committee members, both councilmen repeated that poverty workers had contributed significantly to the Newark riots.[60]

The charge that OEO had instigated the riots was easy to deny. In a statement following the Newark and Detroit riots, Shriver asserted that in twenty-seven riot cities only six poverty workers had been arrested and none had been convicted. In fifteen cities, by contrast, local community action agencies defused volatile situations which otherwise might have exploded into riots.[61] A spot-check of forty-three cities made by OEO's Office of Inspection found that the agency's summer programs usually had helped to forestall violence and that, where riots had occurred, program participants had exercised a calming influence.[62] In Newark, the photographs of public meetings, alleged to prove provocation to riot, actually had been taken many months before. For these reasons, Shriver concluded that attempts to create doubt or fear about OEO in the aftermath of the riots were "unworthy of any public official or private citizen."[63]

If it was easy to rebut the charge that OEO had instigated the riots, though, it was far harder to reply to a more sophisticated charge that the agency at least indirectly had influenced the disorders. This charge was an amalgam of several assertions, to each of which there was a kernel of truth. It was alleged that OEO had supported the activities of black militants, allowing them to grow in strength to the point that they could precipitate riot. Congressman Fino of New York asserted that "troublemakers and malcontents have been bankrolled and payrolled in incredible numbers." Another Republican, Congressman Gardner of North Carolina, agreed with Shriver that OEO employees were not involved in the actual riots. But, he added, "the important thing is that you people are agitating the poor sections of our cities, Newark for a prime example, . . . to go out and demonstrate against the authorized authority in that city, and what happens, it gets out of hand."[64] Moreover, it was true that OEO had funded some black militant activities, such as the Black Arts Theatre in New York and a "liberation school" in Nashville, Tennessee.[65] In each case, funds had been withdrawn once the nature of the project was discovered, but the memory lingered.

Furthermore, it was reasonable to argue that OEO, by using its programs to quell volatile situations, had provided an implicit incentive for those seeking funds to instigate or threaten disturbances. The Watts riot of 1965, which "so disturbed OEO officials that comparatively vast sums of money were allocated to the city,"[66] served as a precedent. Increasingly, blacks thought that "it is necessary to have a civil disturbance in order to get necessary attention to local problems and services."[67]

Rather than respond to each of the specific connections alleged to exist between the poverty agency and the riots, the administration challenged the underlying assumption, arguing that there could not possibly be *any* connection between OEO and the riots. In support of this position, they offered an empirical and a theoretical defense.

Empirically, it was argued that most of the serious riots had occurred in cities without substantial poverty populations and hence, presumably, without substantial OEO funds. Most of the major riot cities ranked toward the bottom in a listing of the one hundred cities with the greatest incidence of poverty. In other riot cities, such as Detroit, Newark, and New Haven, the number of persons assisted by federal social programs constituted only a small fraction of the need.[68] It was unlikely, therefore, that such a minuscule program could have triggered such a major disturbance. If anything, the *absence* of the poverty program was more likely to be responsible.

Theoretically, it was argued that the activities of the Office of Economic Opportunity never had been designed as antiriot programs. To attack them for failing to solve a problem which they had not been intended to solve was to create a "straw man." This theory was advanced explicitly in testimony by the OEO research director, Robert Levine, in June of 1967. "I have no objection," Levine said, "to keeping [youth] off the streets. The point I make is the one Mr. Shriver has made frequently, that the objective of OEO is not to avoid trouble in the streets. The objective of OEO is to get rid of poverty."[69] Among the more basic causes for riots, according to supporters of OEO, were inadequate housing, employment, and education, and the general alienation and frustration of the ghetto.

The problem with Levine's rejoinder was that its theoretical premise was impure. When officials maintained in 1967 that OEO had not been designed as an antiriot program, they referred back to the *original* formulation of the Economic Opportunity Act of 1964. But when the agency had appealed to Congress for increased funds in 1965, 1966, and 1967, the budget justification frequently included the claim that OEO programs indeed *had* been effective in preventing riots. The administration had portrayed OEO programs for blacks as the successful *alternative* to urban riots. In the absence of riots, the administration had claimed success. Must not the presence of riots therefore imply failure?

Abundant evidence could be found to suggest that, in good times, OEO *was* regarded as an antiriot program. In 1966, Congressman Jake Pickle of Texas attributed the lack of riots in his state to "the outstanding progress of the war on poverty."[70] In a statement to OEO regional directors in 1967, Shriver declared, "The over-all anti-poverty program has turned out to be probably the best anti-riot weapon ever devised."[71] In a press conference in 1967, President Johnson answered a question about the administration's efforts to prevent urban violence by referring to his request of May 2 for supplemental *antipoverty* funds.[72]

Unfortunately, however, the success of OEO as an antiriot program was quite uncertain. In fact, several riot studies concluded that, since riots had erupted in cities of virtually all types and with a wide range of social problems and policies, it was impossible to predict the circumstances under which a riot would occur.[73]

In claiming for OEO the credit for tranquil times, the agency's supporters had done more than engage in promotion for their program. They were offering a criterion

for judgment. If supporters of OEO claimed the program
to be an antiriot measure, then by that standard it could
be judged. By demonstrating that the program defaulted
on its self-proclaimed objectives, opponents cast serious
doubt upon its value. Following the riots of 1967, George
Mahon, chairman of the House Appropriations Committee, mused, "The more we have appropriated for these
[urban] programs the more violence we have." Mahon
suggested that it might be more appropriate for the government to stress "discipline, self-respect, and law and
order enforced at the local level."[74] Seeing that the
ghettos had not been pacified by the War on Poverty, a
result which earlier claims of success had led the nation to
expect, the middle class grew progressively more disenchanted with the poverty program. The War on Poverty
had acquired the negative connotations of a program to
aid blacks at a time when black militancy and racial riots
made this goal unacceptable to increasing numbers of
whites.

In the aftermath of the riots, it was no longer clear who
the enemy was. The war had been launched against a
cultural phenomenon transmitted across generations in a
vicious circle. But each attempt to find a point at which to
break the circle seemingly had led only to frustration. The
theory did not seem to work—unless one took it to mean
that the circle must be broken by changing the individual
personalities of the poor. Sargent Shriver was probably
correct in saying that "this country has really resisted the
idea of giving aid to the poor just because they're poor."[75]
That view was in keeping with the traditionally dominant
antipoverty ideology, but it effectively turned the campaign into a war against the poor. Whites who thought
OEO responsible for the riots did not always find a
struggle against the poor to be unattractive.

Like the designation of the military objective, the choice of the enemy had led to consequences that seriously hurt the War on Poverty. By 1967 the whole question of the program's future was in doubt.

5

Rhetorical Crisis
The Transformation of Weapons and Tactics

To fight the War on Poverty, the Johnson administration in its public discourse emphasized three primary weapons and tactics: local community action, which was explained as being consistent with grass-roots democracy and hence conservative; manpower programs to expand opportunity, rather than welfare; and frugal and careful administration, to assure that the war was waged efficiently without embarrassing cost overruns. Each of these weapons was useful in launching the war but harmful in its prosecution. And the difficulties lay primarily in the symbolic realm. The ambiguities surrounding community action could not be resolved and proved to be counterproductive. The attempt to distinguish the anti-poverty effort from welfare did not hold up in practice. And the pledge of sound and prudent management was undermined by a series of embarrassing incidents which symbolized lack of control over the War on Poverty. The transformation of these key symbols explains in large part the political difficulties in which the program soon found itself.

I

The ambiguity surrounding community action was fundamental. If it was a device for therapy, then the poor were
seen as deficient in personal skills and traits which the
dominant society benignly desired that they acquire; community action was a means to this end. But if it was the
path to political power for the poor, then the view was
that, while the poor could act as experts with regard to
diagnosing their problems, established agencies and governments would not act voluntarily to solve them. The
underlying assumptions of these two approaches were
incompatible with respect to the competence attributed to
the poor and the motives attributed to the dominant
society. OEO sought a rationale for community action
which would transcend these conflicts, reducing ambiguity
enough to permit programs to operate but not so much
that support for the agency would be fragmented. The
rhetorical history of community action is the story of
successive failures to formulate a public rationale which
would achieve this goal.

Democracy. One approach was to ground community
action solidly in democratic theory. Sargent Shriver insisted that "democracy" was the most important ingre-
dient in the War on Poverty, and likened the community
action programs to "the approach our country started off
with." His draft for the president's 1967 message to
Congress expressed the same theme, calling community
action "the modern equivalent of the New England town
meeting and the common school board of the 1870's."[1]
The director of community action programs, Theodore
M. Berry, denied that involvement of the poor was a

novel idea, claiming instead that it was "completely
within the mainstream of American democracy."[2] In
OEO's second annual report, community action was described as "a merger of our past town meetings and
citizens assemblies with the latest thinking of social scien-
tists." It was claimed to be a "quiet revolution," "in the
best traditions of American democracy."[3]

Democratic theory offered themes to which adherents
of both sociotherapy and institutional change could sub-
scribe. As an added benefit, it was able to attract the
support, or at least to quiet the opposition, of some
congressional conservatives. Theodore Sorensen aptly observed that the philosophy of community control would
have few opponents "so long as it is confined to appealing
Jeffersonian slogans that sound like conservative Republican doctrine."[4] The democratic rationale also permitted
Shriver to account for the existence of controversy and
dissension. He told the American Public Welfare Association in December 1965, "Criticism, experimentation, and
even mistakes are recognized as part of the learning
process. That's democracy."[5]

When OEO spokesmen referred to democracy, they
meant widespread involvement in decisionmaking; they
contrasted this approach to administrative edicts of an
unrepresentative body. But local public officials, not surprisingly, took democracy to mean control by those accountable to the people, namely themselves. To them,
not "widespread participation" but "accountability" was
the essence of democracy.

This conflict had been foreshadowed in 1964. Mayor
Wagner of New York felt "very strongly that the sover-
eign government of each locality in which such a community action program is proposed, should have the power of

approval." Mayor Daley of Chicago believed "that any program of this kind, in order to succeed, must be administered by the duly constituted elected officials of the areas with the cooperation of the private agencies." Mayor Tucker of St. Louis expressed similar feelings. Mayor Briley of Nashville argued that the local government should in all cases be the grantee of funds, to achieve the highest degree of coordination and efficiency as well as to avoid administrative problems. Mayor Walsh of Syracuse was the most explicit, saying, "If we could not have direct control of the program we did not want it."[6] The mayors' concerns were shared by several members of the House Education and Labor Committee, notably Congresswoman Green of Oregon and Congressmen Pucinski of Illinois and Frelinghuysen of New Jersey.

This concern was finessed in the passage of the Economic Opportunity Act. But as the program was implemented, the mayors' clamor increased. Mayor Shelley of San Francisco charged that OEO was "undermining the integrity of local government"; Mayor Wagner of New York urged that Congress require closer coordination between community action agencies and public officials; Mayor Yorty of Los Angeles wanted control because "mayors all over the United States are being harassed by agitation promoted by Sargent Shriver's speeches urging those he calls the poor, in quotes, to insist upon control of local poverty programs."[7]

By far the clearest instance of the mayors' concern came at the June 1965 meeting of the U.S. Conference of Mayors. Shelley and Yorty introduced a resolution accusing the Office of Economic Opportunity of "fostering class struggle" in the cities and "creating tensions" between the poor and existing agencies. The Shelley-Yorty

resolution attracted wide support. It was likely, in fact,
that it would have been passed, had it not been for the
last-minute involvement of Vice President Hubert
Humphrey, who, according to the executive director of
the conference, concurred with the belief that "it is absolutely essential that the mayors take the leadership in the
anti-poverty program."[8]

Since most of the protesting mayors were big-city Democrats, the problem was particularly sensitive for a Democratic administration. But Shriver could not capitulate to
the mayors, since the local electorate underrepresented
the poor, who were less likely to participate in politics or
to be convinced of its efficacy, and who felt excluded from
the political process.[9] The fear was that local officials
would not be attentive to the needs of the poor, whose
active involvement was thought essential for the success
of the program. Traditional politics was, as Michael
Lipsky put it, "a bargaining arena from which the poor
are excluded because they have nothing to trade."[10]

But if OEO were not to yield to the mayors, it must
make its view of democracy more persuasive than theirs.
Shriver attempted this task in 1966 testimony before a
Senate subcommittee. "Democracy," he said, "means
more than giving every man a vote, because many of the
problems we face today will never appear on a ballot:
welfare regulations; code enforcement; garbage collection; police brutality." Shriver then proceeded to expli-
cate his own position, saying, "Beyond the formal ballot
comes the larger mandate of democracy—to give the poor
an effective voice in the reshaping of our cities. To give
the poor a role, an opportunity to contribute to the
rebuilding of our society."[11] In requesting special voices
for the poor, above and beyond the ballot, Shriver was
arguing implicitly that the only way to eliminate poverty

within a "democratic" context was to assure political power for the poor. Community action programs therefore must prod the political system to make it more responsive to the needs of the poor.

Even though he recognized that this approach to community action might well produce local conflict, Shriver gave it his endorsement. In 1965, he told the House Education and Labor Committee, "When we see disputes at the local level, then we think we are getting exactly what Congress asked us to encourage."[12] To the National Conference on Social Welfare, Shriver said that he had anticipated controversy: "I said to Congress that if our activities did not stir up a community, then Congress should investigate it."[13] And in his speech to the American Public Welfare Association, he took pride in the fact that OEO was funding the activities of social critics, including those who chose to criticize OEO.[14] Some of the agency's supporters were even more fervent in celebrating social conflict. Congressman Scheuer of New York prophesied in 1966, "I am sure we will continue to see chaos and clash and conflict as voices that were heretofore stilled, finally have been given voice."[15] The following year, when the same view attracted far less support, Congressman Holland admonished his colleagues, "If keeping the promises of the Constitution and spreading the good news of human equality was revolutionary, then I would say hooray for the revolution."[16]

But Shriver's defense of participation-as-power was not viable, as the administration's reaction to the Conference of Mayors should have made clear. Competition among interest groups for possession of the term "democracy" was self-defeating; support was needed from *all* groups in the fray. So the "democracy" rationale for community action would not do.

Flexibility. A second approach to finding an acceptable meaning for community action reaffirmed the importance of participation by the poor but conceded that it could be achieved by a variety of methods, ranging from representation of the poor on policymaking bodies to the formation of block clubs and the publication of neighborhood newspapers.[17] What constituted the "maximum" feasible participation was also variable; Shriver refused to specify any numerical criteria such as the requirement that a specific percentage of the members of community action boards be poor.[18]

Conceivably, the posture of flexibility might have permitted community action to circumvent the need for any unifying rationale. But as OEO responded in ad hoc fashion to the needs and pressures of individual localities, disparities in administration were inevitable. Similar circumstances were treated differently, and the differences seemed unjust. Congressional critics ranging from Adam Clayton Powell to Albert H. Quie charged that, in some cities, OEO pressured for the selection of a certain percentage of agency board members from among the poor, while in others—chiefly Los Angeles and Chicago—local officials were allowed to act as they pleased.[19]

The defense offered by OEO for its apparent inconsistency was pure pragmatism. Bernard Boutin, selected by President Johnson to be Shriver's deputy after the departure of Jack Conway, defended the Chicago program: "I have been guided all my life by the value of success. The Chicago program is one of the most successful that we had anywhere in the country. Mayor Daley has kept it free from politics. . . . Mayor Daley has really run an outstanding program to aid the poor."[20] Once the agency opted for flexibility, however, there was no generally accepted definition of "success" by which programs could be judged. To Boutin, the Chicago program might be judged a success because it involved large numbers of the poor; to Quie, it might be thought a failure because it involved them only as nonprofessional employees and not as policymakers. Because *no* set of interests was likely to be fully satisfied by any position taken by OEO, antagonism toward the agency was likely to increase. Adam Clayton Powell, Seligman wrote, was disappointed with the Chicago program and thought that OEO had "sold out" to Mayor Daley. A pro-Daley congressman, however, was equally convinced that OEO was being run by the militant disciples of Saul Alinsky.[21] The Chicago situation was typical.

Johnson and Shriver soon came under fire from both directions. Militant poor and some members of Congress alleged that the poverty program had been taken over by local political establishments, in the pattern of regulatory agencies which ultimately serve the interests of those whom they are supposed to regulate. The first public sign of this dissatisfaction was a flareup between Shriver and Adam Clayton Powell in 1965. In his statement opening the hearings of his committee, Powell declared, "In far too many communities, giant fiestas of political patronage have been encouraged on both the local and the State levels of the war on poverty administrative mechanisms, having been seduced by politicians who have used the reservoir of poverty funds to feed their political hacks at the trough of mediocrity."[22] Charges similar to Powell's soon were heard across the land.[23]

Johnson and Shriver initially responded to the accusations of "sellout" by dismissing the charge. At his news conference on April 27, 1965, the president placed activist critics in the same category with those who *initially* had opposed the Economic Opportunity Act. Ducking the reporter's direct question, Johnson said, "I think there has been unjust criticism and unfair criticism and uninformed criticism of the poverty program even before Congress passed it. Some people opposed it every step of the way. Some people oppose it now."[24] Shriver, in an interview on the television program *Face the Nation* on April 18, 1965, asserted that Powell's "fiesta of patronage" was an exaggeration. "I would suspect," Shriver said, "that there are 10 times as many private citizens, philanthropists, social workers, welfare workers, and so on, involved in this war already as anybody who would be identifiable as a politician."[25] The integrity of this denial, though, was compromised substantially by the disclosure early in 1966 that OEO had given the mayors of about fifteen selected cities an informal veto power over programs for their cities. The agency would not approve an application for a community action program to which the mayor objected. So the mayors did have control over OEO programs after all. "Flexibility" was not a device to match programs to local needs but a means to avoid local political conflict.

It now was easy for militants to portray the mayoral veto as a "sellout" by OEO. Clear evidence of their disenchantment could be found in the People's War Council Against Poverty, held in Syracuse, New York, on January 15 and 16, 1966. This meeting attracted approximately six hundred representatives from grass-roots organizations in twenty states. Although OEO officials and political leaders were invited, none came to the conference. At the meeting, speaker after speaker condemned the War on Poverty as currently administered, and demanded "total participation" by the poor.

Although the militant poor may have thought that OEO had sold out to local politicians, many political leaders at the same time thought that OEO was financing social revolution. Critics of this latter stripe charged that the stresses on "community action" and "participation" were masking a struggle in which insurgent groups used these terms as weapons to oust the incumbents and to assume control of what Silberman labeled the "welfare industry."[26] Kenneth Hahn, a county supervisor in Los Angeles, expressed a similar view: "There is a great struggle for political power. There is a great undercurrent of who is going to really run it. There is a great tension that I feel, behind closed doors, who is going to control this billion dollar program in America." Describing The Woodlawn Organization, a Chicago neighborhood organization based on the Alinsky approach to change, Congressman Pucinski alluded to "the fantastic power struggle that is going on all over America between the duly elected officials . . . and the private organizations."[27] Mayors Sorensen of Omaha, Addonizio of Newark, Yorty of Los Angeles, and Shelley of San Francisco, among others, expressed doubt about the ability of the community action groups to accomplish anything meaningful. Mayor Shelley, for example, described insistence on "maximum feasible participation" as a "mandate so broad and with guidelines so vague as to make every attempt at local implementation a new object of distrust."[28]

This controversy led to caution within the federal government itself. The Bureau of the Budget, according to a "high government source" quoted in the *New York Times,* instructed OEO to give less emphasis to policy-making by the poor in community action programs. According to the report, the Budget Bureau interpreted participation to require involvement of the poor in implementing poverty programs but not in their design. Shriver

denied receiving any such instructions and further denied
that there would be any shift in his agency's perspective
toward community action. Two days later, the Budget
Bureau denied having given the instruction to OEO.[29]
These denials were disingenuous, however, since the
Budget Bureau had indeed offered strong advice along
the lines reported in the *Times,* and the president had
accepted it. The "instructions" were contained in a memorandum from the budget director, Charles L. Schultze,
to the president, suggesting that "this last concept—involving the poor in the program—got the wrong emphasis
from the start." Involvement, Schultze wrote, ought to
mean hiring the poor, getting volunteers from poor neigh-
borhoods, and talking to poor people about what their
problems are. "In other words," he concluded, "we ought
not to be in the business of organizing the poor politically.
We ought to involve them at the actual working level in
the poverty program." In the margin, Johnson penciled,
"O.K. I agree. L."[30]

Within the Congress, too, once-stalwart supporters of
the poverty program had become disturbed by the evolution of community action. One journalist reported early
in 1966 that a clear majority of the Democrats on the
House Education and Labor Committee wished to rewrite
the community action provisions of the Economic Opportunity Act to reduce OEO's discretion.[31] In the end, the
committee decided against such a course, although its
decision would be reversed on the House floor.

Although OEO officials opposed any restraints on their
flexibility, they, too, actually were reverting to a more
moderate pose. Jonathan Spivak reported the belief of
"many OEO officials" that they had overstressed the idea
of indigenous leadership and that more attention should
be given to training the poor for positions of responsibility.[32] And OEO came increasingly to interpret "maximum

feasible participation" as requiring that one-third of the representatives on community action boards be representatives of the poor, although it objected to writing that standard into law lest its necessary flexibility be impaired. "Flexibility," however, had fared no better than "democracy" as an overarching rationale for community action.

Specificity. Since vagueness and inconsistency themselves were cited as reasons for OEO's political difficulties, attempts were made to specify the goals of community action more carefully. Two major specifications were attempted during 1966. The first, requiring that one-third of the members of community action boards be representatives of the poor, was initiated by congressional Republicans and was a potential embarrassment to big-city Democratic mayors. The second, creating national emphasis community action projects and earmarking funds for them, was initiated by congressional Democrats and was a potential catalyst for public support for the War on Poverty. Both specifications initially were opposed, though effectively implemented, by OEO.

In the very early community action projects, participation by the poor was interpreted to mean their employment in the program. Soon, however, policymaking came to be seen as the most important component of participation, and involvement of the poor was defined as their inclusion on the governing boards of community action agencies. Pressure from congressional Republicans led to the adoption in 1966 of the Quie amendment, stipulating that one-third of the members of community action boards be representatives of the poor. Although the Republicans no doubt saw in this proposal a means to embarrass big-city Democratic mayors, it is unlikely that Quie was engaging in idle talk when he urged his amendment because "the poor are keenly interested in playing a part in this. They know that they can develop, in a democratic process, a sense of representation, of belonging."[33] The administration, which initially had opposed the Quie amendment, moved rapidly to implement it. In March of 1967, OEO reported that only about 5 percent of local agencies, predominantly in the Northeast, were delinquent in compliance. Shriver testified that only eight programs had not been brought into compliance with the regulations by July.[34]

But how were the board members to be selected? If the mayor appointed them, he would be attacked for paternalism. But at first there was no alternative process for selecting these representatives in an orderly way. So OEO began to encourage neighborhood elections, which not only could short-circuit this dilemma but also could be explained as the natural corollary of grass-roots democracy.

But very few of the eligible voters participated in the elections; in one of the most successful, in Philadelphia, the turnout was only 3 percent.[35] In retrospect, these results could be explained by factors ranging from the absence of any tradition of civic participation by the poor to the fact that many of the elections required proof of one's poverty. Mayor Daley used the "pauper's oath" as his explanation for the absence of poverty elections in Chicago. He told the Senate Labor and Public Welfare Committee, "This is the most disgraceful thing that is facing our Nation. I would hate to have my mother and dad stand before that desk and be identified as the poor participating in an election. I think it is contrary to all our thinking in America."[36]

Actually, the entire effort to define "participation" as "board membership" probably was misdirected. OEO encouraged that definition in the belief that it would offer the poor a meaningful policymaking role; congressional Republicans saw in it a way to reduce the power of big-city Democratic mayors. Implicit in their encouragement was the belief that board membership was an appropriate way for the poor to participate. But that belief was open to serious doubt. Board membership was a realistic opportunity only for those among the poor who were relatively the best in education, upward mobility, and leadership abilities. Accordingly, selection for membership became a "creaming" process, in which the natural leaders were drawn into an establishment-dominated board. They thereby lost the opportunity to exert independent leadership, and the poverty board meanwhile made no dent in the hard-core problem.[37]

In the absence of tangible powers resulting from board membership, participation was of mainly symbolic value. It reassured supporters of grass-roots democracy that the interests of the poor were being taken into account, without providing a forum in which those interests could lead to meaningful results. Kenneth B. Clark described the ritualistic component of participation: "the poor serving on community action boards have proved vulnerable to blandishments and have been easily absorbed or controlled, or flattered. They are permitted to blow off steam; a proportion of agenda time is, as it were, allocated to group therapy, permitting the poor to speak out. . . . But it seldom affects the outcome of policy." Elsewhere Clark theorized that catharsis and pride associated with involvement of the poor served as a substitute for actual social change.[38]

It might seem that the symbolic and diversionary nature of participation would be to the rhetorical advantage of OEO. Exploitation of the symbolic might allow the agency to resolve the cross-pressures between the poor and the traditional urban constituencies. The former would be appeased by a change in symbols, by the trappings of social change. The latter would be placated by the fact that no meaningful social change was likely, that a change in symbols was substituting for a change in policy.[39] Even if OEO and its early staff had not been actively committed to social change, though, this hypothetical "dual-track" approach would be unlikely to succeed. The poor and the urban politicians each could "overhear" appeals transmitted to the other. Messages designed to arouse and reassure the poor simultaneously threatened the traditional urban political bloc.

In the end, a small number of the poor were participants and the nature of their participation was superficial. In general, provisions for citizen participation were implemented by asking groups, pro forma, to approve plans already devised by professionals. Yet OEO maintained that participation by the poor really was significant. In 1966 it reported to Congress, "More than 15,000 citizens are serving on the governing boards of Community Action agencies, nearly 5,000 of them from among the people who are being helped."[40] Rather than acknowledging that 5,000 persons was an infinitesimal fraction of the poor, or speaking of the possibly limited depth of participation, administration spokesmen treated all possible drawbacks as arguments simply for expansion of the antipoverty program. Meanwhile, mayors remained fearful of the consequences of placing poor people on the agency boards, and militants among the poor viewed the low rate of participation as evidence of OEO's tokenism or worse. Defining participation as board membership fared no better than had flexibility in attracting the support of multiple constituencies.

A second attempt at specifying what community action was about was the designation, beginning in 1965, of national emphasis programs. Lacking experience in the design and execution of projects such as those envisioned in the Economic Opportunity Act, many communities understandably were slow to develop operational programs. Aware of congressional pressure for a quick demonstration of results, OEO attempted to expedite the planning process with prepackaged designs which communities could adopt as components of their own programs. This approach might seem antithetical to "flexibility." Initially, however, local communities were free to include or omit the national emphasis projects. The first of these projects, and the most famous, was Project Head Start, a summer program for preschool children which was begun in 1965.

National emphasis projects proved far more popular than the locally designed programs. In 1966, the House Education and Labor Committee announced that the War on Poverty henceforth would give more attention to national emphasis programs by earmarking large portions of the community action funds for them.

Earmarking was justified by the claim that poverty was national in scope. "Many problems which appear to be the problems of particular cities or rural districts," the Council of Economic Advisers declared, "are not, in fact, local problems in any meaningful sense. They represent the local outcroppings of more basic national problems."[41] Moreover, earmarking offered the most efficient allocation of scarce resources. And, given the volatility of urban areas throughout the mid-1960s, it was thought wise to direct funds to the less troublesome, more innocuous aspects of poverty.

At least in the short run, the equation of community

action programs with national emphasis programs may have been a wise strategic choice. By discouraging more radical local experimentation, the national emphasis projects helped communities to avoid antagonism and divisiveness over the fate of the poverty program. Simultaneously, by offering programs with a high probability of success, administration supporters could increase the likelihood of nationwide endorsement of OEO.

In the long run, however, earmarking did not help. Local political leaders found it inconsistent with local discretion and self-determination. In its study of community action programs in the Northeast region, the Institute of Public Administration reported "almost unanimous criticism of the tendency to prepackage programs which OEO in effect imposes upon the communities." Mayor Cavanagh of Detroit, Mayor Yorty of Los Angeles, Mayor Lindsay of New York, and Deton Brooks, director of the Chicago community action agency, also testified similarly that earmarking was destructive of local initiative.[42]

These critics suggested, in sum, that earmarking was destroying community action in order to save it. To rescue local programs from controversy, OEO had chosen a procedure which undermined the justification for locally based action in the first place. Despite these defenses of local initiative, the practice of earmarking continued. By 1968, 60 percent of the funds allocated for community action had been committed to national emphasis programs. Earmarking reduced the amount of discretionary revenue for local use to a level sufficient only to refund existing projects without further expansion. Such a constraint made the issue of participation by the poor on agency boards virtually moot; the boards, after all, had a very narrow range of choice.

Even if earmarking were compatible with the goals of community action, it was a potentially dangerous move. National emphasis programs were established in haste, and an initially popular but insufficiently tested program could be included. In the short run, OEO would reap the benefits of nationwide publicity. In the long run, though, if the program ultimately were found to be unsuccessful, the failure similarly would be of national proportions.

Project Head Start offers a good case in point. It was designed carefully to be an experimental program in early childhood education. As Williams and Evans explain in their review of its effectiveness, however, "The idea . . . was too good. It was an ideal symbol for the new war on poverty. It generated immediate national support and produced few political opponents."[43] Accordingly, on August 31, 1965, President Johnson announced plans to expand the program. The president declared, "Project Head Start, which began as an experiment, is now battle tested and it has proved worthy." Two years later, he made a similar statement to the Congress. "Head Start . . . has passed its trials with flying colors," he said. "Tested in practice the past two years, it has proven worthy of its promise."[44]

Regrettably, however, the only "tests" to which the president could have referred were reports of the program's immediate popularity. Little evidence was available concerning its short- or long-term educational effects. It was known that Head Start enrollees improved their learning abilities over the life of the program, but it was not known how long these gains would last or how they compared with normal gains made by students not in the program. Gradually, evidence began to accumulate that the benefits of Head Start were only temporary.[45] These reports were disturbing; they suggested that this

"battle-tested" program really did not work, and therefore that it should be abandoned or curtailed. The popularity of Head Start's early days proved to be ephemeral.

The champions of earmarking purchased some short-
term popularity at the price of possible long-term disaster.
That national emphasis programs courted this risk while
failing to placate either the local communities (who saw
planning and control attacked) or the poor (who saw the
principle of participation attacked) suggests that they
were rhetorically unwise. Neither national emphasis programs nor defining participation as board membership
resolved the problems created by the earlier stance of
flexibility.

II

Despite each of these attempts to solve the problem,
ambiguity surrounding the meaning of community action
remained. The administration itself continued to issue
mixed signals about the extent of its support for social
activism. Following his meeting with the mayors, Vice
President Humphrey reportedly issued instructions "to
defuse the more explosive aspects of the war on poverty."[46] Shriver delivered a speech in December 1965 in
which he declared that the controversy over "maximum
feasible participation" could be resolved by viewing the
poor as one would view an architect's client, who participates in designing a house but does not himself build it.[47]
And OEO withdrew funding from controversial projects
in Mississippi and in Syracuse, New York, claiming in
each case that federal funds should go instead to "umbrella" agencies—comprehensive multipurpose agencies
which had the support of all segments of the community

and would be less likely to serve as vehicles for social change. To committed activists, these moves all signaled retreat on the part of the federal government. Concerning the last, Adam Clayton Powell threatened, "The poverty program is not going to be an umbrella-type organization under a monopolistic basis or there won't be any more poverty program."[48]

But if there were signs of retreat, there also was evidence that OEO's commitment to social change remained strong. Despite pressure from the Budget Bureau, Shriver proclaimed, "Our policy is today and will remain exactly what it has been from the very beginning."[49] To emphasize that local governments had not dominated community action programs, he testified in 1966 that 74 percent of the agencies administering programs were independent organizations.[50] He began in his speeches to de-emphasize participation of the poor and yet continued quietly to press for it and to withhold funds for noncompliance.[51] It remained hard to discern OEO's true intentions, and the ambiguity surrounding community action continued.

This persistent ambiguity denied the administration the ability to control the agenda of public discussion. First, concern for the meaning of the symbol deflected attention from the real success of many community action programs. OEO could not convince the public that the programs were working because, under the strain of constant redefinition of the terms, the genuine accomplishments were lost. Second, unable to establish a clear and consistent definition of community action in the public mind, the administration surrendered that prerogative to the more militant spokesmen for the poor.

Despite the national controversy over the meaning of community action, many local programs made real progress. Militant confrontations were few. In the thirty-

five communities studied by investigators for the Senate
Labor and Public Welfare Committee, there was discovered only one instance of misuse or abuse of funds, and
that instance already had been corrected. There were only
three instances in which agencies purposefully created
conflict and deliberately sought confrontation with established power, and these three encompassed all which were
known to exist among the more than one thousand community action agencies.[52] Far more typically, the community action agency had been set in motion by a mayor's
task force, and the agency subsequently retained its ties
with influential segments of the local community.[53] Factors limiting militancy included the absence of a common
political strategy, internal factionalism within community
action programs, and the nonideological orientation of
the poor. Kramer observed that the trend, between 1964
and 1967, to use community action programs for deliver-
ing services rather than for organizing the poor, was
nationwide.[54] The House Education and Labor Committee found that, in 1967, "the great weight of evidence . . .
indicated that these services were effectively reaching the
poor."[55] In addition to providing needed services, programs frequently succeeded in employing poor persons in
nonprofessional capacities, such as teacher aides, family
planning aides, and community health aides.

As the success of individual local programs became
clear to them, mayors also changed their tune. In contrast
to its doubts about community action a year earlier, the
1966 Conference of Mayors *opposed* a resolution to restrict the role of the poor and to increase the role of local
officials in the War on Poverty. William H. Crook, OEO
Southwest regional director, wrote in a 1966 memorandum to Bill Moyers that "the mayors of *all* our southern
cities are purring like kittens asking for another bowl of

milk." And, in a handwritten note to the president, Shriver took pride in the fact that Mayor Naftalin of Minneapolis, who in 1965 "was giving OEO h———" in a twelve-page letter to Hubert Humphrey, now had endorsed the OEO program. In a postscript, Shriver added, "And I don't think Dick Daley has uttered one word, or even a hint of complaint, in more than a year."[56] Shriver also cited support in 1966 from other local officials, community chests and health and welfare agencies, and governors, all of whom had been neutral or hostile in 1965, as evidence that the concept of community action had taken hold at the local level.[57]

Yet these successes of community action received scant attention in public discourse. Smoothly running, successful programs were not newsworthy. Conservatives who resented the fact that the president's program seemingly had been thrust upon them, found an outlet in searching for flaws rather than strengths.[58] A few of the early community action projects *had* attempted the purposeful creation of conflict with established powers. Images of this conflict formed many persons' first impressions of OEO, and these initial perceptions were highly durable even when they no longer corresponded to reality.[59] But beyond these specific problems was the overarching fact that the administration's attention was distracted by the public fervor surrounding the question of what "community action" would mean and the contest for possession of the term—a contest which would be increasingly irrelevant to the operation of community action programs.

But the Johnson administration suffered a far more serious fate than irrelevance. Despite all its efforts, it could not devise an acceptable and persuasive specification of community action. Persistent ambiguity on such a

fundamental point is uncomfortable, and, nature abhor-
ring a vacuum, the term came to be defined in the public
consciousness by the more militant spokesmen for the
poor. Increasingly, they defined poverty as the absence of
independent political power and insisted that traditional
government programs could not be trusted to yield power
to the poor. Accordingly, the goal of community action
programs was to confront the existing power structure and
force a redistribution of power.

In part, this redefinition of poverty, participation, and
community action reflected the impact of two external
forces: the quickening civil rights revolution and the radicalization of the social work profession. The civil rights
struggle had increased political awareness and consciousness among blacks. Insofar as this "awakening" had taken
place, the therapeutic goals of the poverty program were
rendered irrelevant: the civil rights movement already
had achieved them. Militant leaders hence attempted to
transform the goals of community action from self-help to
social change. Meanwhile, the opportunity for participation by civil rights leaders in "the jobs, the status, the
government sanction, and the authority over public programs" related to the War on Poverty multiplied the
strength of the civil rights movement.[60]

The radicalization of the social work profession reflected its increasing concern for community organization
practice and a weakening commitment to the more traditional one-to-one, caseworker-to-client relationship. It
also reflected a general aversion among many social workers to the impersonality of government and the unrespon-
siveness of bureaucracy. This brand of "neo-Populism" is
identified with Richard Cloward of the Columbia University School of Social Work, who maintained that the chief
contribution which the poverty program could make

would be to deliver to the poor the responsibility for controlling funds and programs.[61] Advocates of social change came increasingly to believe that they could not depend upon the normal political process to achieve their goals. Believing that society was unresponsive to the needs of the poor, militant leaders thought it necessary to mobilize the poor to confront the establishment with pressure which would force social change. For a time, they had hoped to use the community action programs as the means to prepare for this confrontation.

A deepening commitment to the tactics of confrontation aligned these militant leaders with a theory of social change articulated most notably by Saul Alinsky. Alinsky, a professional community organizer whose experience dated to the Back of the Yards organization in Chicago during the 1930s, argued that the poor would need to seize power if their needs were to be met. For this purpose, a mass organization was necessary. In the absence of such an organization, people would tend to resign themselves to their negatively privileged status. Conventional community councils and organizations, however, did not offer a base of power. They functioned only to coordinate professional agencies which played a superficial part in community life, and they appealed for support on the basis of abstract values rather than immediate and highly salient issues.[62]

In developing a broad base of support for a people's organization, it was useful to have a concrete enemy. This view, of course, contrasted with the administration's implicit theory of social change, according to which a broad consensus could be gained for incremental changes which would add up to substantial improvement in the lives of the poor. Alinsky believed that "the action is in the reaction," that the responses of the established order to a provocation would be the primary catalysts, mobilizing the previously uncommitted and thereby inducing change. Hence, a major task for the people's organization was to goad officials into making what Horwitt called "errors of social control," so that the citizenry would be polarized and the people's organization would seem more attractive.[63]

Alinsky's theories were appealing to community organizers who had become more militant, had seen the need for social reconstruction in order to solve the problems of poverty, and had been frustrated by the apparent incompatibility between this objective and the conventional instruments of politics. A theory of social change which emphasized the need for conflict would offer interest and enthusiasm to the once-apathetic poor who had been brought into an organization. It would define institutions in personalized terms and seek culprits on whom to place the blame for undesirable conditions.

Could community action programs become the basis for Alinsky-type organizations? Early organizers sometimes thought so, and precedents could be cited for government action which strengthened the bargaining position of a social interest. With the Wagner Act, government had lent its support to labor organizations. With subsidies to agriculture, it had lent its support to farmers. With tax incentives and concessions to special interests, it had encouraged the activities of these groups. Moreover, the original Economic Opportunity Act was silent with regard to the proper limits of public support for protest.

Nevertheless, the confrontational approach to community action faced a substantial problem: it was sponsored and financed by the very "Establishment" it sought to denounce. While not impossible, it was hardly likely that either government officials or taxpayers would support efforts to undermine their own legitimacy! Not surprisingly, there was a counterattack against confrontational approaches to social change. Indeed, the response could have been predicted from the 1964 controversy surrounding one of the Kennedy administration's early juvenile delinquency projects, New York City's Mobilization for Youth (MFY).

MFY lacked its own political constituency, and its support from the city weakened as it began to expose officially sanctioned injustices. In response, the agency tried to bolster its position by attracting the support of civil rights groups as a new source of countervailing power. It therefore began to espouse the tactics of confrontation and supported protests against the New York City school system. These tactics, however, aroused opposition among those who controlled the resources on which the agency depended. MFY was charged with instigating the 1964 riots in Harlem by publishing inflammatory material about the triggering incident, the killing of a black youth by a policeman. In August 1964, the *New York Daily News* carried a story in which it was charged that over 10 percent of the agency's employees had previous ties to the Communist party or to Communist-front organizations; Republican vice presidential candidate William E. Miller promised that the alleged Communist subversion of MFY would be a key issue in the 1964 campaign. Other charges against the agency included "loose and shoddy" administrative practices and "lavish and improper" spending.[64]

Lurking beneath these charges, which MFY claimed to be diversionary "smears," was the belief that the project's objectives and methods of operation were inappropriate. Following the controversy, regulations were issued to prevent the use of public funds to finance political activ-

ism. Nor was support for the militants forthcoming from
the federal government, which feared that involvement in
New York City's controversy might hurt the developing
national antipoverty program.[65]

Similar events occurred on the national stage between
1965 and 1967. The confrontation approach was portrayed as an attack on the legitimacy of government itself.
Congresswoman Edith Green, for example, voiced alarm
that poverty funds were being spent on seemingly systematic efforts to oppose local government. "I want you to
know," she added, "that I would not approve of one dime
of Federal funding being paid to anybody for the purpose
of going out to upset the democratic process."[66] Mitchell
Sviridoff, president of the National Association for Community Development, though generally quite supportive
of the poverty program, spoke to the same principle,
separating the ideology of any specific militant group from
the issue of the inappropriateness of government support.
"If a protest group favored by those who now control the
government is supported," he wondered, what would
happen ". . . when the government changes hands and
another kind of protest group seeks government funds?"[67]

As with Mobilization for Youth, the most dramatic
method of inspiring opposition to governmental support
for social protest was guilt by association. Congressman
John H. Buchanan of Alabama alluded to "mounting
evidence of involvement of subversive elements and of
left-wing extremists in the antipoverty program"; Congressman Joel T. Broyhill of Virginia complained that
"the most vicious abuse of this program was perpetrated
in many parts of our Nation by those who used Federal
funds to develop a political power block"; New York's
Congressman Fino decried "the care and feeding of

punks, rioters, and black nationalists" who, he clearly implied, were associated with the poverty program.[68]

Attacks on the confrontation strategy were sufficient to induce the government to define militant social change as inappropriate. It had been criticized as well by academics and others concerned with community action.[69] Instead, the argument ran, successful programs depended upon organized *cooperation* with the "establishment." During the 1966 and 1967 congressional hearings, Senator Clark of Pennsylvania stated almost as an aphorism, "When you get the local power structure involved in the community action program, then you have a good chance of success. However, if the local power structure turns its back on the whole program, you are in trouble."[70]

Responding to all these concerns, Congress extended the Hatch Act's prohibition against "political action" to employees of poverty projects. The Senate passed an amendment prohibiting the payment of salaries or anti-poverty benefits to any participants who belonged to subversive organizations or incited riots; a similar amendment would pass both houses in 1967. The administration, too, disavowed any support for "the Alinsky theory" of social change; in 1967 Shriver specifically denied that OEO believed in or practiced it.[71] Similar disavowals were issued by local community action agencies.

But there was the rub. For lack of any clear and consistent alternative, confrontation strategies were widely viewed as the essence of community action itself. Those involved in local organizations were not soldiers in the War on Poverty but militant radicals intent on subverting American government. When OEO, goaded by pressure, repudiated them, it seemed to be repudiating its own chosen antipoverty weapon. The persistent ambiguity surrounding community action not only made it impossible for the administration to argue convincingly that local programs were a success, it also cost it control of the war. Johnson and Shriver had surrendered the power of definition, and that proved to be the most important power of all.

III

The demise of the other two major antipoverty weapons and tactics can be more briefly told. The administration chose to stress manpower programs rather than welfare, in the belief that training programs would provide exits from the vicious circle of poverty. Problems with the theory of the vicious circle already have been noted. In addition, though, OEO was not able to maintain the strict separation in principle between its own activities and those of public welfare.

The distinction was not lost for want of efforts to sustain it. Welfare was almost universally unpopular. A study prepared for the Senate Committee on Labor and Public Welfare concluded that welfare "catches it from both sides: the affluent damn it because it pauperizes the poor at their expense; the poor damn it because it meets their needs in a minimal way and because it demands a demeaning attitude from them."[72] Not only was welfare an unwise model for the War on Poverty, then, but the new programs should be kept as far apart from the old in the public mind as possible. Accordingly, there was no end to statements that the War on Poverty was antithetical to public relief. As if to emphasize this antithesis, several spokesmen maintained that the goal of the Economic Opportunity Act was to reduce the relief rolls. Congressman Roman Pucinski insisted that taking relief clients off the welfare rolls was the War on Poverty's primary objective. President Johnson drew the same contrast. In a speech at a Democratic party dinner in 1967, he explained that the War on Poverty had been launched "not to give away the taxpayer's hard-earned treasure, but to help every citizen discover the treasure of his own ability; to help him get a job and become a taxpayer, not a taxeater."[73]

Especially in its early days, OEO also criticized as ineffectual "the welfare establishment," which included much of the social work profession, not just administrators of public welfare. While insisting on the need for professional training in order to solve the real problems of poverty, OEO maintained, social workers had bungled the job. Shriver mildly rebuked them in a 1965 speech to the National Conference on Social Welfare. He paid tribute to the dedication of social workers, many of whom worked long hours for inadequate pay. But then he added, "Yet some of them seem to think that working with the poor is their exclusive problem. They reject outsiders. They are wedded to professional opinions and ideas. And frequently those in charge of these programs resist and even resent questions about their own effectiveness, about their own cost of operation."[74] In keeping with his belief that poverty was too important a problem to be left to social workers, Shriver was especially convinced of the value of the "inspired amateur"—the citizen whose lack of professional experience was offset by the intensity of his commitment.

But neither with respect to recipients nor with regard to staff could the War on Poverty sever a link with welfare. This fact, aside from exposing the bankruptcy of the symbolic distinction, eventually transferred to the new antipoverty programs all the stigma and opprobrium associated with the old.

Paradoxically, one of the first effects of OEO programs was to *increase* the number of public assistance recipients dramatically. By 1967, according to Wilbur Cohen, the rate of increase in the population receiving Aid to Families with Dependent Children had doubled.[75] In retrospect, this paradox can be explained easily. Early community action programs, seeking easy targets for victory, organized the poor with the goal of securing rights already recognized legally. As a consequence, these organizations began to advertise the availability of public welfare.[76] But this organizing effort entailed a danger. Urging potential welfare recipients to enlarge the rolls seemingly demonstrated that the poverty program did not function independently of welfare. "Opportunities" were provided to those in need by using the poverty program to pressure welfare administrators. Rather than being functionally separate programs, both were addressed to the same population, and the two efforts validly could be described as interlocking parts of a larger system. Senator Ribicoff of Connecticut provided evidence for this linkage when he noted in 1966 that 89 percent of welfare recipients in Chicago, and 85 percent in Oakland, lived in the communities designated as targets by OEO. Ribicoff's hardly surprising conclusion was, "Welfare recipients live in slums."[77]

The distinction between the welfare professional and the "inspired amateur" also could not hold up. Many of the first community action efforts were started by local social welfare agencies. Since many of the professionals who felt themselves under siege were integral to OEO's own programs, the situation clearly was untenable. Accordingly, in his speech to the American Public Welfare

Association meeting in Chicago in December 1965, Shriver changed his course. Rather than challenging the nation's welfare workers, he courted them. He told the group, "I feel very much like a recruit when I talk to you. . . . After all, all of you have been in your own war against poverty for many, many years." He went on to say that the support of social welfare professionals was essential to the full success of the antipoverty weapons at his command, and that it must be kept in mind that the enemy was poverty, "not our neighbors, who work in the YWCA, or the settlement house, or the city hall."[78] With this speech, Shriver signaled his intention to placate the welfare professionals. But in doing so he had to acknowledge that the poverty program and older efforts were interdependent rather than distinct. Indeed, Lombard reports in his dissertation, the *poor* did not differentiate between welfare and antipoverty programs, seeing the old as part of the new.[79]

But the melding of the two programs in public discourse was harmful, since it transferred to the poverty program the preexisting, negative appraisal of public welfare. Some leftists, dedicated to the poor, now saw the chief effect of the War on Poverty as being the creation of jobs for middle-class persons yearning for social relevance;[80] some conservatives saw the poverty program as just another means to coddle the lazy and invite fraud.

At the same time, people began to argue that if OEO were basically a welfare program, then perhaps the simplest approach to welfare—giving cash to the poor— might also be the best. Martin Luther King, Jr., for one, claimed to have been convinced by the experience of indirect service programs which tried to eliminate poverty by eliminating some other condition, that a guaranteed income—the most revolutionary approach to antipov-

erty—also might be the simplest.[81] Simplicity, indeed, was
the essence of the guaranteed-income proposal. It defined
poverty as deficient income, and proposed to guarantee to
the citizen the difference between his income and the
poverty line. Success was assured by definition.

Although he cautioned that guaranteed-income proposals were "almost surely beyond our means at this time,"
President Johnson announced in 1967 his intention to
appoint a commission to examine income maintenance
proposals. The commission submitted its report in November 1969. Its contents, and the results of congressional hearings begun in 1968, laid the groundwork for later
discussion of President Nixon's proposed Family Assistance Plan. For the present, however, the significance of
the guaranteed-income concept is that the search for some
new antithesis to welfare programs made plain the failure
of the War on Poverty to perform that role. The antipoverty effort had fallen victim to the popular hostility toward welfare, from which it had sought a clear separation.

IV

The Johnson administration had promised in 1964 that the
War on Poverty would be managed prudently and fought
cost-effectively. This promise, together with the fact that
the initial costs were low, did much to allay fears of a giant
boondoggle of wasteful expenditures and excess profits.
But it, too, was a promise mired in ambiguity. Applied to
the poverty program, nobody really knew what such
terms as "frugal," "prudent," or "cost-effective" *meant,*
and the image of the enemy as a vicious circle virtually
precluded the possibility of specification. And yet the

rhetors of 1964 had created an expectation against which later results would be judged.

Here, too, in the absence of comprehensive guidelines or definitions, Congress employed simplifying devices to make accountability and evaluation at all possible. And once again these devices made it difficult for OEO to argue convincingly that its program was cost-effective and well managed. Probably the most important of these devices is the legislative tendency to focus on specific cases in which the performance of an administrative agency is open to question and then to generalize to a judgment of the agency's program as a whole. This focus on specific statistics, examples, and case studies minimizes the congressman's disadvantage with regard to the amount of information he has about a program and thereby makes complex programs comprehensible.[82]

An agency's success depends upon its ability to manage impressions by controlling and reducing the number of instances in which its performance might be questioned. But, perhaps because it was so decentralized, the War on Poverty generated a steady stream of embarrassing incidents. Among them were an alleged scandal over the leasing of the Kanawha Hotel in Charleston, West Virginia; the 57 percent pay increases given to the staff at Camp Gary, a Job Corps center at San Marcos, Texas, violence at a Job Corps camp in Mountain Home, Idaho; the ordering of too many Li'l Abner comic books, which were used to promote the Job Corps; the granting of community action funds to the Black Arts Theatre of LeRoi Jones; the presence of ineligible youths in Neighborhood Youth Corps programs in Chicago and elsewhere; the erroneous determination that Danville, Illinois, and Danville, Indiana, were eligible for OEO funds; the faulty location of a Women's Job Corps center in St. Petersburg, Florida; the delays in establishing a national literacy program which was to have been organized by James Farmer; the attendance records of board members of the community action agency in Washington, D.C.; leaks to the *New York Times* and the *Washington Post* of internal disagreements within the OEO; and the difficulties of obtaining a telephone book for the national OEO headquarters until the text of the directory was printed in the *Congressional Record.*[83] Almost inevitably, new cases of alleged abuse could be discovered faster than OEO could investigate its program and defend its action. And just a small number of such instances could do much to shape one's perception of the poverty program. Shriver himself acknowledged that the characteristics of specific local programs often were projected onto Washington, causing OEO to receive undue credit for well-administered programs and undue blame for those which were managed badly. "That," Shriver concluded, "is one of the vicissitudes of community action."[84] But it made persuading the Congress difficult.

The congressional penchant for examining specific instances, and the OEO's inability to supply evaluative information in the form desired, led naturally to attacks upon the agency's administration and discrediting of its image. Republicans on the House Education and Labor Committee charged in 1965 that the Office of Economic Opportunity, administered by a part-time director, was uncoordinated.[85] The charges grew in intensity with time. In 1966, Senator George Murphy of California, although he could not "say for certain that the Office of Economic Opportunity is the worst run agency in Washington," stated, "I have not come across an agency where such administrative chaos and inefficiency reigned." Congressman William H. Ayres of Ohio was less coy. The administration of OEO, he declared, was "the worst in living memory."[86]

Some complaints were more specific. OEO stood accused of establishing a costly bureaucracy, wallowing in apparent indecision while performing shoddy work, and causing needless waste and expenditure. Congressman Ayres declaimed that over seven thousand permanent employees were required to administer the program, to say nothing of the large number of persons employed by local community action agencies. "This is the fastest growing bureaucracy in the history of American Government," concluded Ayres, "and it is swallowing up these funds as fast as we can shovel them down its giant maw."[87] It became an easy rallying point for congressmen who were opposed to the program to object that funds were being spent on high-salaried bureaucrats rather than going to the poor. Conveniently forgotten was the fact that Congress originally had not *wanted* funds to go directly to the poor, lest the poverty program resemble the handouts of traditional welfare. Instead, congressmen were able to characterize the "setting up a group of bureaucrats at high salaries, with expensive offices, and so forth," as sabotage.[88] To place controls on a wayward bureaucracy, the House in 1966 passed an amendment, authored by Congressman Ashbrook of Ohio, to limit the number of "supergrades"—top-salaried officials—to a ratio of one-hundredth of the total employment in the program.

A frequent complaint against OEO was that its administrative procedures were irregular, needlessly cumbersome, and dilatory. Although Shriver continued to defend flexible procedures as the best way to assure that needs were being met, many in Congress argued that flexibility meant whimsy and caprice. Congressman Goodell of New York was especially bitter in saying, "We can't get answers from [OEO]. One moment they indicate you are going to get so much money and then it is changed. They do it by telephone. They don't have an administrative procedure that anybody can understand. There is conflict in the agency."[89] When haste resulted in bad judgment or needless confusion, it was easy to cite those results as evidence of maladministration. The more such cases could be cited, the less confident would Congress be of OEO.

Republicans also charged that the agency was susceptible to undue political influence. Congressman Ayres judged the poverty program to have been "mired in politics ever since [1964], providing the richest lode of political patronage ever mined by political gold diggers." Ayres added, in a conspiratorial interpretation of events, "Now, this should come as no surprise to anyone, because it was planned that way." Using even more colorful imagery, Congressman Andrews of Alabama described the War on Poverty as "a political extravaganza, a political carnival—filled with barkers, shell game artists, cupie dolls, and cotton candy."[90]

It was not always clear to what specific instances these charges referred. But no matter what referents were evoked, the persistence of the charge hurt OEO deeply. One of the strongest virtues of the military metaphor had been its ability to unite the nation, to transcend partisan or political disputes by the need to conquer a common threat. The charge of political influence challenged this appeal directly. It depicted the War on Poverty as being not above the struggles of partisan politics but a part of them, and it thereby also helped to undermine the military metaphor. "In the bourgeois body politic," Kenneth Burke wrote, "even *politicians* damn an opponent's motive by calling it *political;* and professional politicians like to advocate their measures as transcending factional antitheses."[91] As the assertion that OEO was mired in politics gained currency, the agency's ability to transcend factionalism was impaired.

Another sign of the agency's fading credibility was the change in attitudes about the director, Sargent Shriver. In the early days, Shriver had been regarded as a charismatic figure who had been successful in mobilizing the Peace Corps and who would duplicate that success at the Office of Economic Opportunity. Indeed, during 1964 and 1965, he received strong personal approval and support from Democrats and Republicans alike. Increasingly, however, there were attacks on his administrative ability and even demands for his resignation. On August 29, 1966, Adam Clayton Powell asked that Shriver resign, because "he is the greatest salesman in Washington but probably one of the poorest administrators."[92] The following month, Congressman Quie of Minnesota proposed that "the first order of business to meet the faltering war on poverty and to get on the road to victory would be to replace the Director, Sargent Shriver." House Republicans called for Shriver's resignation because of inadequate management of the agency, employment of too many high-salaried consultants, and "profiteering" by two Job Corps contractors. In 1967, following a report on the activities of VISTA volunteers in Appalachia, Congressman James H. Quillen of Tennessee called for the abolition of OEO and for Shriver's dismissal. Even the National Prohibition party called for Shriver's ouster, on the basis of alleged political scandal within the program.[93] The increasing attack on an administrator once thought to be unassailable was a sign of the point to which OEO's congressional relations had deteriorated.

To be sure, the administration tried to defend the management of the War on Poverty. A 1967 OEO publication described efforts to operate the programs on a "business-like" basis. For example, the average request for antipoverty funds was reduced by 20 percent before approval by OEO, a fact which testified to the agency's "fiscal sternness" and made more money available for other programs. The pamphlet also noted with approval that only 3 percent of the OEO budget was spent on administration.[94] Finally, OEO argued that there had been remarkably little scandal and corruption in the administration of its programs and agencies. Investigations by the news media during 1966 resulted in findings of very slight misuse of funds, political patronage, or maladministration.[95] Specific abuses were atypical, exceptions which could be explained by the need to develop operational programs quickly and by the magnitude of the problem the agency attempted to tackle.

These defenses by the administration did relatively little to reassure those who were dubious about the program's worth. Although the congressional penchant was for specifics, administration spokesmen often did not answer the specific charges brought by their opponents. They contended that instances of mismanagement were exceptions, but they were unable to defend that claim by comparative analysis of other specific situations or by supporting contrary generalizations. Frequently, the charges of opponents were not even acknowledged.

In reviewing the unintended symbolic consequences of the military metaphor—whether with respect to the objective, the enemy, or the weapons and tactics—one is led to similar conclusions. Originally the symbols had been quite useful, and ambiguity was not a serious problem. Over time, however, the administration's inability to specify meanings meant that opposition would be aroused from all sides, as people *assumed* one or another meaning to be guiding the program and then concluded that the actual program did not measure up to their assumptions. OEO was unable to set the agenda for public discussion of its programs, because it was unable consistently to espouse a meaning which would satisfy the competing interests. The agenda-setting function of definition hence was assumed by others, and the meanings which framed public discourse typically worked to the disadvantage of the administration. Choices that had been helpful in gaining the adoption of the poverty program proved to be hindrances to its implementation. The struggle among competing groups for the prerogative to define was the essence of the Johnson administration's rhetorical crisis. Matters came to a head in 1967, when the country was increasingly preoccupied with the war in Vietnam, when the president's popularity had declined and his relations with Congress were far less secure. Things did not bode well for the future of the War on Poverty.

6

Consummation

The Stalemated War

Without doubt, 1967 was the year in which the rhetorical crisis of the War on Poverty came to a head. The decision to call the effort an unconditional war had profoundly affected the public discourse, influencing the way officials talked about the objective, the enemy, and the weapons and tactics. The symbols and images developed in 1964 had helped the adoption of the program, but their internal dynamics also helped to erode public support. City governments saw their power being challenged by the poor; militants objected that any compromise was hypocritical; Republicans chafed at the poverty program's partisan identification; and conservatives found it to be an inappropriate exercise of government power.

These troubles had been brewing for some time. What made 1967 the critical year was the political situation. Forty-five sympathizers of the Office of Economic Opportunity were defeated in the 1966 midterm elections; forty-five of the newly elected Republicans were known to oppose any increase in antipoverty spending.[1] Of 160 members of Congress surveyed by United Press International, two-thirds favored cuts in domestic programs either to pay for the war or to curb the developing

160

inflation.[2] Rainwater and Yancey, analyzing controversy sparked by the program, prophesied in November 1966 that OEO would be a likely casualty of the "turn to the right" evident in the election returns,[3] and many others thought the war was doomed.

Indeed, its prospects were dim. Supporters would need to enlist the help of influential constituencies and convince a skeptical Congress. But it was not possible simply to employ the same tactics as in 1964. Measured against the discourse of that year, the record had been one of disillusionment. Legislators were influenced by that record; three years earlier they had written law on a blank slate. Now it was OEO, not poverty, which was under scrutiny.

The Johnson administration adapted its public discourse to this new exigence. Each of its major rhetorical decisions was akin to one of the tactics of 1964, modifying it as required by changes in circumstance. The modifications, however, involved substantial concessions from the original vision. The idea of the War on Poverty remained, but the goals, enemy, and tactics all were reinterpreted. The result was to stalemate the war.

I

In seeking to conciliate Congress, the administration made major changes in the way it defined the objective, identified the enemy, and chose its weapons and tactics. Instead of a declaration of unconditional war, it settled for the preservation of OEO as a symbol of a national commitment. Instead of a manpower program to break the cycle of poverty, it settled for a more selective Job Corps and an acknowledgment that programs primarily benefited blacks. Instead of a flexible community action program, it settled for extensive involvement of local politicians and an even more fervent pledge of prudent management.

Defining the Objective. Sargent Shriver apparently had decided early in 1967 that his agency as a whole was less popular than were some of its specific programs. Accordingly, testimony before Congress emphasized the individual component programs of OEO and praised their accomplishments in the hope that support for the parts would generalize to support for the whole. This approach, however, was dangerous. Congress might decide to continue popular programs but to fragment them, placing them under the aegis of less controversial agencies and abolishing OEO.

To avert such a possibility, administration supporters defended the continued existence of OEO as a symbol of the nation's antipoverty commitment. To disband it was to repudiate the national goal and to break faith with the past. Its existence, Shriver testified, recognized our moral and political responsibility to have an advocate for the poor at the national level, which made "a tremendous advance in the whole philosophy on which our Nation is based."[4] Shriver, Assistant Secretary Lisle C. Carter, Jr., of Health, Education, and Welfare, and Senator Joseph Clark of Pennsylvania all spoke of the agency's value in focusing national attention. Whitney Young put it succinctly: "The nation's promise to the poor as enunciated in 1964 is embodied in the OEO and to destroy the OEO is to destroy that promise."[5] Senator Robert Kennedy saw OEO as the primary instrument by which the poor could remain convinced of the legitimacy and good faith of the political process, and Roy Wilkins of the National Association for the Advancement of Colored People warned that, if OEO were disbanded or drastically cut, "I think we are in for upheaval and disturbance, because people will feel that the government is abandoning them."[6]

OEO opponents did not respond directly to this claim of symbolic value, but they proposed to "spin off" specific OEO programs—Head Start to the Office of Education, Job Corps to the Department of Labor, Neighborhood Youth Corps to Health, Education, and Welfare. Administration advocates responded to these specific proposals but tried to yoke together a defense of the individual programs and a reaffirmation of the OEO's symbolic value. Congressman William S. Moorhead of Pennsylvania, for example, noted, "Many of those who are quick to denounce the War on Poverty are equally quick to defend its specific component programs. . . . These people seem to feel that by removing the specific programs from the jurisdiction of OEO criticism of the antipoverty program will end."[7] The whole, Moorhead implied, was only the sum of its parts. Actually, *his* was the specious reasoning, since it was inconsistent with the administration's own premise. If OEO were important primarily for symbolic reasons, then there *was* something in the whole—namely, the symbolism—which was greater than the sum of the parts.

Some opponents of the program put forth a more direct contest. They accepted the fact that OEO was regarded as a symbol, but attempted to shift the symbol's referent. Whereas the Johnson administration might regard the Office of Economic Opportunity as symbolic of the nation's determination to fight poverty, opponents might regard it as symbolic of waste, maladministration, overextension of the federal government, and other such vices. Because OEO symbolized those evils, Congress could strike a blow against the evils by killing the symbol. Specific antipoverty programs, which would be transferred to other departments, would not be hurt. Several analysts of the 1967 congressional debates have offered just this explanation for many of the spinoff proposals. As the *New York Times,* for example, editorialized, "If the Administration loses the O.E.O., it loses political face. That would be construed as proof of failure in the war on poverty." Correspondent Joseph Loftus concluded that, for precisely that reason, opponents wanted to topple the agency "which, more than any other, has been a symbol of the Great Society."[8]

But now the administration supporters could play the other side of the fence, pointing to the merits of specific programs. As Shriver put it, "No responsible legislator has said: 'Stop Headstart,' 'Stop NYC,' 'Stop Foster Grandparents,' 'Stop legal services,' 'Close down your new health centers,' 'Close down the Job Corps,' 'Terminate VISTA.' "[9] If OEO were symbolic of great evils, how could it have spawned programs which were such a success? In this way the popular programs and the umbrella agency were tied together. But this was no declaration of unconditional war; it was a bureaucracy that stood as a symbol of an earlier national commitment. And therein lay the danger.

Aaron Wildavsky has described a concern with "purely symbolic" issues as the dilemma of the political liberal. If he loses a symbolic struggle, he is rendered impotent and therefore is in a worse position than before. But, if he wins, he *also* may be worse off, once it becomes apparent that the issue was *only* symbolic and that nothing has changed. There might follow a chain of recriminations in which the liberal's action would be decried as an empty gesture and his motives would be attacked as hypocritical.[10] Although referring specifically to race relations, Wildavsky's comments also are pertinent to the War on Poverty. Passage of the Economic Opportunity Amendments of 1967 evaded the first horn of the dilemma. Averting the second, however, depended on the future. If the nation's commitment to fight poverty became more a nostalgic reinvocation of the past than a permanent priority, representing OEO as the symbol of that commitment would invite frustration and disillusionment in 1968 and the years to come.

Selecting the Enemy. A second tactic of 1967 involved reformulation of the theory of poverty as a vicious circle, particularly as that theory found application in the Job Corps. The original idea had been for the Job Corps, by providing education and training for poor youths, to enable them to qualify for jobs paying wages above the poverty line, and thereby to exit from the vicious circle. Since the program emphasized, in Shriver's words, "altering society so poor people are able to raise *themselves* above the poverty level through their *own* efforts" (emphasis in original),[11] it was anticipated that it would be both popular and successful.

Events were to prove otherwise. Concurrent with the hearings on the 1965 Economic Opportunity Act amendments, the Job Corps was beset with outbreaks of "rowdyism, brawls, and violence." The dropout rate was alarmingly high, owing to delays in processing applications, inadequate preparation of the centers, mis-screening of enrollees, and mismatching of enrollees and centers. Congressmen complained that many Job Corps graduates were unable to find jobs upon completion of the program and that their fate prompted other enrollees to withdraw. The cost of training led many to believe that, even if the program were operating in optimal fashion, it would be impossible to train more than a fraction of the youths in poverty.[12]

Presidential Assistant Joseph Califano suggested that the Job Corps would pose "the major problem of the program."[13] To counter these prospects of trouble, the administration moved quickly in late 1966 and 1967 to alter the public conception of the Job Corps. The aim was to achieve what Kenneth Boulding has described as a change in symbolic systems through the accretion of new elements.[14] To the image of the Job Corps would be added new features, which effectively would alter the fundamental nature of the image. The changes made by the administration were summarized under the rubric "the new Job Corps."

The nature of the "new Job Corps" was painted in broad strokes in the 1967 annual report of OEO. It was "a Job Corps in which cost reduction and maximum efficiency go hand and [sic] hand; . . . in which lessons learned at one center provided more effective guidelines for all Job Corps centers; . . . in which only sound discipline and hard work are tolerated." In the administrative history of OEO, the components of the "new Job Corps" were identified as more stringent screening and selection procedures, barring persons with a history of antisocial behavior, maintaining curricular and disciplinary standards, creating advisory councils and a new placement system, providing better coordination and more systematic evaluation of effectiveness, and limiting the maximum size of the corps to 45,000 persons and the maximum cost per trainee to $7,500.[15]

The "new Job Corps" proved during 1967 to be both popular and successful. The withdrawal rate declined from 30 percent voluntary and 3 percent discharged to 19 percent voluntary and 2 percent discharged.[16] Discipline in the corps improved; Shriver wrote President Johnson in May, "Not one 'riot' has occurred in a Job Corps camp for 12 solid months, and not one draft card has been burned by a Job Corps enrollee or graduate." As if to underscore the magnitude of this accomplishment, Shriver invited the president to "compare this record with Harvard's treatment of McNamara, Dartmouth's treatment of George Wallace, and the riots at the University of Wisconsin at Madison."[17] The placement rate of graduates improved; a Louis Harris survey in January 1968 found that 76 percent of the male Job Corps graduates were working, in school, or in the military, at average postgraduate wages of $1.80 per hour, higher than the minimum wage at that time.[18] And support from the middle class and the business community was increasing, as Shriver would write the president in January 1968.[19]

The intent of the changes embodied in the phrase "the new Job Corps" was to change the image of the corps by anticipating congressional objections, removing the "sting" from the Job Corps and thereby making the program more palatable. That these changes would accomplish their end was uncertain even in the early fall. OEO's assistant director for congressional relations, George D. McCarthy, wrote to Barefoot Sanders, the White House aide in charge of congressional relations, on September 22 that little cooperation from Republicans could be expected, since Congressmen Quie and Goodell were determined to make the vote on the Job Corps a test of party loyalty.[20] In the end, however, the administration's tactic succeeded. When objections were raised to the Job Corps, many could be dismissed as anachronistic.

Republican proposals to repeal the Job Corps or to transfer it to other agencies of government were defeated, and
the corps survived intact.

A price was paid, however, for the success record of the
"new Job Corps." The administration had modified its
program to fit only those for whom the theory was easily
applicable. The tighter screening procedures amounted to
"creaming," accepting into the corps only those youths
who were likely to succeed. How much of the superior
record of the corps was attributable to administrative
improvement and how much to the artifact of selective
admission is impossible to determine. The administration's actions, however, did make it possible for critics to
argue that it was achieving the chimera of success only by
denying enrollment to those most in need of a program
such as the Job Corps. Either the theory of the poverty
cycle was not universally applicable or breaking the cycle
was far more difficult than had been supposed.

The Congress was presented with an alternative proposal which, although not incompatible with the trend of
the "new Job Corps," would have conveyed a different
impression. Senator Clark, like many others, was convinced that the problem of motivating corpsmen lay less in
faulty admission procedures than in the uncertainty that
jobs would be available after graduation. Rather than
restrict the corps to those most likely to qualify for
existing jobs, however, he proposed to expand the supply
of available jobs. To that end, he introduced the Emergency Employment Act of 1967, a $2.5 billion program
which he appended to the Economic Opportunity Act
amendments.

Major objections to Clark's proposal came from Senator Robert Byrd of West Virginia. He believed that there
was no shortage of jobs; he was concerned about philo-

sophical questions raised by the government's becoming
the employer of last resort; and he was convinced that the
employment program would be inflationary.[21] The Johnson administration shared this last concern and urged the
congressional leadership to strike this amendment.[22] Senator Byrd introduced a motion to strike which carried by a
vote of fifty-four to twenty-eight.

The administration had been confronted with the fact
that its solution to the poverty cycle did not seem to work.
Senator Clark's proposal would have modified the *solution* by adding emergency public employment to existing
training programs. His idea was politically palatable; a
Louis Harris poll revealed that 69 percent of the public
favored "setting up large-scale Federal work projects to
give jobs to the unemployed."[23] But the administration
chose instead to redefine the *problem,* making it more
applicable to the already-existing solution. The problem
of the poverty cycle was reinterpreted so that only some
of the poor—those with proper motivation and without
antisocial tendencies—could escape. But that view made
the exit from poverty seem to depend more on individual
personality traits than on cultural conditions, and it
strongly implied that those who remained behind were
poor because something was wrong with them. The "new
Job Corps," while popular and successful, was a return to
the dominant traditional view of the causes of poverty and
a retreat from the vision which had inspired consensus in
1964.

The War on Poverty also retreated from the view that
the problem was a matter of economics rather than race,
but here there may have been little choice. The riots of
1967 obliterated hopes of maintaining a distinction. Congressmen had even less sympathy for rioters than for
welfare recipients and more of a desire to exact retribu-

tion. Although it was sometimes charged that OEO had
instigated the riots, the data suggested that the primary
effect of the War on Poverty had been to prevent or to
cool riots. Some advocates, therefore, tried to link OEO
and the riots in a *favorable* way. Reiterating a recurrent
theme, they alleged that the antipoverty agency, in effect,
was also an antiriot office. Senator Jacob Javits of New
York announced, "In the antipoverty and emergency
employment legislation the Senate has before it the most
critically important bill of the year to avert a winter of
discontent and another summer of violence." And Congressman Carl Perkins of Kentucky lamented the fact that
"the many community action agencies which helped keep
the peace during the urban tensions of last summer are
now ending their program years without money to continue the important work they are doing."[24] If the disjunction between poverty and race were lost, OEO's partisans
strove to make the most of it. As previous experience had
demonstrated, though, these arguments could not quell
the continuing accusations that the poverty program had
offered direct or indirect incitement to violence. Accordingly, it seemed best that OEO's supporters not emphasize the program's impact on racial peace, choosing
instead to defend the 1967 legislation primarily on other
grounds.

Choosing the Weapons and Tactics. The primary weapon
in the public discourse of 1964 was a locally based, flexible
strategy rooted in community action. This element of the
War on Poverty proved to be the most controversial. In
1967, the Johnson administration made a rhetorical retreat by accepting an amendment introduced by Congresswoman Edith Green of Oregon. The "Green
amendment" would designate states, counties, or cities as

the community action agencies, unless those governments chose to select a public or private nonprofit agency in their stead. The amendment also required that one-third of the agency board members be public officials. It redefined in a fundamental way the nature of the local community as the antipoverty battleground.

The central objectives of the amendment were explained by President Johnson in his memoirs. The president, who labeled the amendment "the most important compromise" of the markup process, wrote, "we knew that with this amendment we could win the support of several Southern Democrats and solidify the support of Democrats from big cities who were under pressure for tighter local control."[25] Uniting northern and southern Democrats, of course, would reduce the likelihood that Republican spinoff proposals would be accepted. That likelihood was further diminished by the intemperate reaction of Congressman Goodell to the Green amendment. On the House floor, he denounced it, saying, "The amendment which was adopted in our committee might well be called the bosses and boll weevil amendment because it is an amendment for the big city hall bosses and for the southerners to completely denude community action of its potential."[26] Goodell's indiscreet manner angered many Democrats and may have encouraged them to support both the Green amendment and the overall administration position.

In defending her amendment, Mrs. Green maintained that it was restorative rather than radical. As she recalled 1964, "The Congress did not intend to create a new governmental substructure of powerful political bodies with the luxury of millions of Federal dollars to spend and none of the responsibilities of raising any of that money."[27] But OEO had perverted the intent of Congress, so new language was needed to clarify the legislative purpose. Denying that the Green amendment undermined broad-based local participation, supporters insisted on the contrary that it would *enhance* participation by preventing programs from being taken over by militant radicals. Senator Robert Byrd of West Virginia voiced his concern that community action programs had been "subverted by 'leadership' which seems to be ideologically opposed to what it openly refers to as 'the power structure,' or contemptuously calls 'the establishment.' "[28] The Green amendment would answer these concerns by reorienting the War on Poverty to the true enemy. As Mrs. Green expressed it, she sometimes wondered "whether it was city hall or poverty that was the enemy being attacked with Federal funds."[29]

The Green amendment provoked intense congressional debate. Its opponents argued that it was the failure of city government that had prompted the creation of independent community action agencies in the first place.[30] They argued that mayors did not *want* control, citing the defeat by the Conference of Mayors of a resolution requiring that projects be approved by a "responsible local agency of government."[31] Other arguments against the Green amendment were that it would reduce the involvement of the poor to tokenism, nullify the principle of "maximum feasible participation," subordinate the War on Poverty to the wishes of political hacks, and stifle flexibility and innovation in local programs. Accountability to the public, which the amendment's supporters praised, was thought to inhibit the chances of unpopular or experimental programs whose success might not be foretold in advance. The tendency might be for each community to adopt the most popular or well-established programs, rather than to continue to search for the best means to fight poverty.

In this argumentative encounter, the proponents of the Green amendment had the better of the exchange. Although the dispute over legislative history ultimately could not be resolved, in the riot-scarred year of 1967 it was not a persuasive position to argue to congressmen that they *ever* had intended to finance dissent and disruption or that control of federal funds should rest in organizations not accountable to the taxpayers.

Moreover, advocates for the Green amendment could argue that it refocused attention on the goal of fighting poverty, rather than on the controversial issue of participation, which after all was only a means to the end. Nothing was sacrosanct about participation in its own right, especially if it failed to achieve its goal. As Mrs. Green asked, "Is it the purpose of this legislation to foment discord in our cities and in rural communities? Or are we not trying to stamp out ignorance, disease, and poverty in America?" She added, "If it is the latter, it is the worth of the program that is important and not whether the poor are the architects."[32]

Despite the clamor of the Green amendment discussion, and although the amendment was seen as a major reorientation of community action, one might safely predict that it would produce little real change. For one thing, mayors *already* were heavily represented on governing boards. In June of 1967, answering the charge that the administration was contemplating a "sellout" to the local establishment, Shriver had told the Senate Labor and Public Welfare Committee's Subcommittee on Employment, Manpower, and Poverty, "The truth of the matter is that in nearly all cases locally elected officials already have representatives or themselves serve on local community action agencies."[33] Shriver also predicted, in his letter urging the president to sign the 1967 bill, that there would be little change in the number of community action agencies operated directly by public officials, and this prediction was accurate. At the time the amendment was passed, only 20 percent of existing community action agencies were administered by local governments. Within eight months of the passage of the 1967 act, 792 of the 1,018 governmental units affected took action to designate a local agency. Of these, 96.7 percent chose to continue existing agencies without change.[34]

A satisfactory modus vivendi had evolved at the local level. Community agencies proved to offer far less challenge to the power of the mayors than had been feared. Donald Haider has summarized the countervailing resources of local governments, writing that they proved "more resilient to challenges than expected, more accommodating, cooperative, and absorptive of O.E.O. activities than the mayors had figured."[35] Consequently, the Green amendment permitted Congress symbolically to ratify changes which *already* had occurred in the field.

Because the Green amendment produced little change in community action operations, Levitan judged it to have been a "tempest in a teapot."[36] But the tempest was rhetorically functional, in that it achieved a major change in the way in which community action was perceived. The difficulties of community action in 1967 resulted far more from its symbolic character—what it was thought to represent—than from the operational details of most projects. Hence the task of the administration was to alter the "social reality" of community action, to change what people perceived it to be. The Green amendment itself, and the fact that it stimulated such an intense congressional debate, brought about this result. Surely something important must have been at stake and therefore surely some major change had been achieved.

In the debates of 1964, much emphasis had been given to the choice of local communities as the battlefields of the War on Poverty, and this selection of battlefields was defended by reference to grass-roots direct democracy. Now the defense of local action retreated from a focus on *direct* to a focus on *representative* democracy. By this change in symbols, congressmen were convinced that they had repaired the damage to community action, while the local programs continued basically unchanged.

Community action, of course, had not been the only antipoverty weapon featured prominently in public discourse. Advocates of the war also stressed that it embodied manpower programs rather than welfare, and that it relied on sound and prudent management. On each of these themes, 1967 saw retreat as well. To be sure, it still was argued that OEO would save money for the nation by removing people from the welfare rolls.[37] But the increase in the rolls during the previous three years, in many cases the result of OEO's encouragement, did not make that claim persuasive. Moreover, it seemed that OEO itself now was viewed as a charity program, very similar to traditional welfare measures, rather than as an investment in human potential. In a lengthy and revealing analogy, Congresswoman Green compared OEO to a charity organization. The American people were the donors and OEO was only the disposal agency—neither donor nor recipient. Therefore, for OEO to object when questioned about whether its goals were being accomplished "makes just about as much sense as telling someone who makes a donation to charity that he has no right to know if his donation was spent for the stated purpose."[38]

The 1967 congressional session did not augur well for welfare programs. Restrictive amendments to the Social Security Act provided that employable adults must work in order to receive benefits and also placed a limit on the percentage of any state's population who could qualify for federal aid under the program of Aid to Families with Dependent Children. Congressional passage of these measures signaled an attitude toward the poor which could be characterized as parsimonious if not punitive. Given the existence of this attitude, and given the growing tendency for people to view the Economic Opportunity Act as being just like traditional welfare programs, it hardly would have been wise for the act's supporters to make more than perfunctory reference to the whole question of OEO's relationship to welfare.

At first glance, the administration's stance with respect to prudent management did not seem like a retreat at all. The theme had played well in earlier years and OEO now offered more of the same. But implicit in the 1967 stance was the recognition that earlier efforts had not been sufficient. The agency had not won the reputation it sought for careful and competent administration. Indeed, its credibility was suspect. Therefore OEO promised or accepted reforms which would produce even tighter administration. The discourse of 1967 reveals a pattern of acquiescence by the agency in moves which none too subtly suggested that its management had been inadequate.

For example, OEO yielded to demands that its operations be reviewed by outside auditors. Annual accountability to Congress meant little if credible information could not be obtained. And the administration's own data did not seem trustworthy. OEO stood accused of overselling its achievements and of conducting a more aggressive campaign of public relations than of antipoverty remedies. Congressman Robert Michel of Illinois, for instance, believed that "OEO has developed a paranoid survival instinct and is spending more time and money trying to convince the Congress of what a good job they are doing than they are in trying to do the job we have assigned them."[39] Few reliable sources of data existed outside the OEO, however. Congress therefore stipulated that the General Accounting Office (GAO) audit the effectiveness of antipoverty programs and the implementation of the 1967 amendments. The proposal for GAO audits was made by Senator Winston Prouty of Vermont. It was accepted by Senator Clark of Pennsylvania, chairman of the Committee on Labor and Public Welfare, although he believed it to be unnecessary, because "I would like to have the minority believe that we in the majority do pay careful heed to their recommendations and their suggestions in this whole field." In the House, the proposal for GAO audits was introduced by Congressman Dellenback of Oregon and was accepted without debate.[40]

Besides the need for outside review, Congress also had expressed concern that the administrative cost of the war was excessive and that money was wasted through maladministration. OEO and its supporters fought this concern more directly. First, they argued that the management of the programs was generally successful. Although there was administrative error in every program, the wisdom of the program ought not to be determined solely by judging its mistakes. Congressman Emanuel Celler of New York explained by analogy: "There is a fly in every ointment, but the fly and the ointment are not inseparable; the part does not vitiate the whole."[41]

A second response was to contend that OEO already had resolved many administrative problems internally. Personnel changes during 1966 had caused theorists and ideologues to be replaced by more pragmatic administrators. In its 1967 annual report, OEO claimed that its administrative costs were low—only 1.5 percent—and that its bureaucracy of 2,800 employees was small.[42] In an unsigned memorandum in the White House files, it was claimed that in 1967 the Johnson administration could offer a new, tighter bill, sounder administration after the program's early difficulties, and a program whose nature was conservative and which offered economic return.[43] The defensiveness in these claims is evident.

Third, Congress during 1967 made further amendments which were thought to limit administrative excess. For example, an amendment by Congressman Ashbrook of Ohio limited OEO "supergrades" (staff in government classifications GS-16, GS-17, and GS-18) to 1 percent of the total of the agency's employees. Another Ashbrook amendment eliminated the OEO director's authority to hire consultants. An amendment offered by Senator Monroney of Oklahoma limited the reimbursable administrative costs of any individual community action agency to 15 percent of the agency's total cost.[44]

Of these three responses to the charge of maladministration, the first enabled the agency to save face and may have limited the scope of possible attacks. The second anticipated congressional objections and precluded them by making concessions. The third response enabled congressmen who were so inclined to chastise OEO without having to defeat the antipoverty legislation.

Concerns about OEO's management also affected discussion about the appropriate level of funding for the agency. Initial hopes for a sharp increase in funds had been dashed, and the startup budget became the norm. The $1.773 billion authorized in 1967 permitted the refunding of ongoing programs but virtually no expansion. Against proposals to enlarge the scope of the war, it was argued that the *current* funds had not been spent wisely. As Congressman Brown of Ohio stated it, it would be a mistake to "throw money away on generally unproved or clearly unsuccessful programs and [to] continue to create a bad public reaction to the total OEO program."[45] The administration yielded with respect to the funding level. In a television interview on November 6, Shriver had threatened to resign if his agency were not given the funds "to do a substantial job." He refused, he said, to delude the poor into believing that action was taking place when insufficient funds were provided.[46] Evidently, he did not regard the congressional actions of 1967 as breaking faith with the poor, at least for the four months he was to remain at the helm of OEO.

A pattern can be detected in the specific issues related to the management of OEO. The claim to prudence, which the Johnson administration had made, still was of paramount importance to the Congress. No longer, however, was the Congress convinced that the administration in fact was being prudent. Although it defended its general record, the OEO, desiring to forestall congressional criticisms, made internal changes to tighten its administration. Even these changes, though, were not enough to satisfy the Congress. The penalty for the loss in credibility which the agency had suffered over the years was that it would have to endure congressionally imposed checks on discretion and administrative excess. Although unhappy with these moves, the OEO chose to yield to them, in order that it might survive.

II

If OEO's rhetorical stance in 1967 implied an internal retreat, the Johnson administration was determined to prevail in convincing Congress that it should extend the program's life. The basic strategy was to conciliate the Congress on as many specific points as possible while activating a slowly developing constituency in support of OEO.

There were, indeed, the beginnings of strong support at the local level. The Advisory Commission on Intergovernmental Relations concluded that, despite early problems, "much of the commotion" was subsiding. A similar study in 1967 by Daniel Yankelovich and his associates found community action projects generally to be "producing significant results and . . . acquiring a broad base of support among community leaders."[47] Mayors gave the antipoverty effort more support: only a year after denouncing community action, both the U.S. Conference of Mayors and the National League of Cities passed resolutions urging that the War on Poverty be funded at least to the full amount requested.[48] In late summer, twenty-two Republican mayors sent a telegram to their party's congressional leaders, urging OEO's continuation and expansion.[49]

Other voices were heard in support, too. OEO continued to stress the active involvement of business leaders as evidence of commitment from the business sector. OEO also received the support of the League of Women

Voters. By October and November, the agency could count over 450 newspapers, including many traditionally conservative organs, editorializing in its behalf. In his memoirs, President Johnson spoke of "wide-ranging support" marshaled for OEO from community groups across the nation.[50] For its part, the agency portrayed itself as the object of increasing support from a once-skeptical public. "The echo of the War on Poverty," declared the OEO's second annual report, "is no longer going against the wind—but is going with the wind." Another agency publication began, "Six months ago, gloom-mongers were beating the funereal drums for OEO. But look again."[51]

Still, these developments probably were not powerful enough to outweigh the difficulties affecting the poverty program. Simultaneously, therefore, the administration attempted directly to conciliate congressional opponents in order to reduce the number of points of dispute. The president's message of March 14 set the tone. It reasserted the importance of combating poverty, acknowledged and tried to answer many of the criticisms of OEO, discussed the difficulties of mounting a sustained effort, and requested larger budgets primarily for the national emphasis programs. Shriver, who now spent most of his time on congressional relations, focused on the national emphasis programs, stressed internal changes to "tighten up" management of OEO, and yielded to congressional amendments which either codified existing practice or made innocuous changes.

Not all members of the administration agreed with this approach. In a memorandum to White House aide Barefoot Sanders, who was in charge of congressional relations, Samuel V. Merrick, special assistant for congressional relations in the Labor Department, asserted that "the atmosphere has been to accommodate and this

seems to me to be the road to real disaster." Merrick
predicted that the administration's strategy would permit
the development of a bipartisan bill, "but it will be a bill
firmly on the road to emasculation."[52] The administration's approach did succeed, however, in reducing the
number of controversial issues. In the Senate, Joseph
Clark began debate on the 1967 extension of the Economic Opportunity Act by identifying only five key issues,
and in the House, Sam Gibbons of Florida was able to
distill the issues to two.

Since the Senate was thought to pose fewer obstacles to
the passage of the bill, consent by the upper chamber was
sought first. Senator Clark introduced debate by acknowledging that the burden of proof was on the proponents of
the Economic Opportunity Act. Although Clark did not
intend this statement as a major concession, it was an
explicit acknowledgment that the presumption—which
the administration had captured in 1964—now rested in
the hands of the program's adversaries. Clark then referred to an extensive study of OEO operations, which
had been made by his Committee on Labor and Public
Welfare in order to answer charges that OEO had not
been studied adequately. The results, he concluded, were
that poverty was still a major problem and that the basic
programs of the Office of Economic Opportunity were
sound and warranted continuation. A lengthy list of
OEO's accomplishments was offered for the record.[53]
Although much discussion ensued concerning the administrative details of the bill, there was little direct challenge
to the basic premises advanced by Senator Clark. In the
end, the Senate committee reported a bill authorizing a
half billion dollars more than the administration had
requested, and including a separate $2.5 billion program
of emergency employment and job creation, which the

administration opposed. The measure, without the employment provisions, passed the Senate on October 5, by a vote of sixty to twenty-one.

In the House, the outcome was far less certain. The objective of muting partisanship was aided by the election of Carl Perkins of Kentucky as chairman of the House Education and Labor Committee following the ouster of Adam Clayton Powell. Unlike his predecessor, Perkins consulted actively with the committee Republicans during deliberations. He then reportedly persuaded committee Democrats with the argument that he must not be made to appear less capable of providing for the poor than was Powell.[54] But any momentum which had developed in the House was arrested by the riots of 1967 and by the charge that OEO directly or indirectly was responsible for them. Despite evidence to the contrary, many members of Congress believed in late summer that to spend more money on social programs would be a waste of funds at best, and more likely a reward for riot. In September, Congressman Gibbons counted over 230 votes against any poverty bill, a dozen more than were needed for its defeat.[55]

Accordingly, Perkins delayed bringing the poverty bill to the floor until late fall, reportedly in the hope that post-riot tempers would cool.[56] This delay in reporting the bill also made action seem more urgent, lest admittedly desirable poverty projects be ended for want of funds. Perkins's belief that time was on his side was strengthened by the reaction to a series of seemingly vindictive actions taken by the House during the fall. Already, the House had refused to pass a special appropriation for rat control. In an amendment to the Juvenile Delinquency Prevention and Control Act of 1967, agencies funded by OEO were excluded from participation in projects supported by the new bill. On October 11 the House approved an amendment offered by Congressman Gurney of Florida, excluding OEO workers from a general pay raise granted to other federal employees. And on October 23 the House omitted OEO from the continuing resolution which provided operating funds at the previous year's level for agencies whose appropriations had not yet been passed.

In one sense, these moves were "cheap shots," undertaken precisely because they were cheap. They permitted congressmen from uncertain districts to oppose OEO, for purposes of home consumption, although on final passage many of these congressmen would vote for the administration's bill. Referring to the rider to the Juvenile Delinquency Act, for example, George D. McCarthy, OEO's assistant director for congressional relations, wrote to Barefoot Sanders, "We think that this endorsement presented an easy and virtually harmless way to cast a conservative vote on the war on poverty, and while we would not seek to minimize the difficulty we face in the House, that it would be erroneous to consider the vote as any legitimate test of our true strength."[57]

Meanwhile, the House amendments struck many people as both petulant and vindictive. Public sympathy for OEO as a victim of injustice helped to elicit last-minute support for the administration's bill, making Perkins's timing quite fortuitous. By November 3, twelve days before final passage and a week before the height of favorable public reaction, McCarthy could predict that the prospects for Democratic opposition to a Republican substitute bill were "fairly encouraging" and a White House head count predicted a 219-to-160 favorable vote on final passage.[58]

The final events came quickly. The authorization level, already reduced from the Senate's $2.496 billion figure to the administration's requested $2.06 billion, was cut further, to $1.6 billion, roughly the level of ongoing appropriations. Congressman Perkins then reintroduced the bill, which passed on November 15 by a vote of 283 to 129. The conference committee set the final level of authorizations at $1.773 billion, and the president signed the bill late in December. The bill was, as Shriver said in his letter recommending presidential approval, "a notable vindication of the War on Poverty."[59]

The Johnson administration's goal in 1967 was to save the poverty program, and its rhetorical stance helped it to succeed. This was a major accomplishment, since pursuit of the war had seemed uncertain earlier in the year. Sargent Shriver said that the action of the House in approving the 1967 amendments was "the greatest legislative victory he has ever been associated with."[60] The administration's triumph was the greater, since, by passing the 1967 amendments, Congress settled the question of whether antipoverty activities were regular and appropriate functions of government. On these grounds the basis for national consensus was laid.[61]

But passage of the 1967 bill meant assent to a far weaker proposition than the administration had sustained three years before. It is ironic that the 1967 act would be hailed as a legislative victory, since so much had been surrendered to secure its passage. OEO was forced to concede virtually every assumption which dominated its earlier discourse—the war metaphor, the view of poverty as a vicious circle, the community action motif, the disjunctions from welfare and race, and, perhaps most important, the refutation of the traditional ideology that people are poor because something is wrong with them. In short, OEO had lost control of the governing metaphors of public discussion. It was forced into a position in which it articulated no view of its overarching purpose but engaged in a series of ad hoc, tactical moves, hacking away with whatever resources were left, in a desperate quest for survival. Rather than the ends determining the means, precisely the reverse adaptation had occurred. The tactics which dominated the public discourse of 1967 themselves determined the ends which the War on Poverty could pursue. And since those tactics embodied retreat, it should not come as a surprise that the subsequent course of the war was a stalemate.

III

In a special report to the president, Shriver proclaimed 1967 to have been "the year in which the war against poverty achieved serious bipartisan support throughout the country and became a national commitment in the most meaningful sense." To support his judgment, Shriver cited the strong congressional support from members of both parties and the growing support for OEO among governors and mayors, business and labor groups, and religious, educational, service, and youth leaders.[62] Even the Green amendment was depicted as an improved means for accomplishing an already-accepted end, rather than as a mandate for OEO to direct its local efforts toward a different end. The independent study of the Green amendment, required by the 1967 law, concluded that its influence had been salutary, neither demoralizing the poor nor surrendering local boards to political patronage.[63] And what was true of the Green amendment proved true of most of the other changes made by Congress in 1967: the effective functioning of the poverty program was not impaired.

One of the changes, in fact, offered great promise to OEO. For the first time in the agency's history, the Congress granted it a two-year authorization. This authorization, not requested by the administration and proposed originally by Senator Clark, assured the continuation of OEO and its programs through the 1969 fiscal year.[64] The agency need not spend time and energies in 1968 on a fresh round of justifications. In short, 1968 could have been a year in which OEO consolidated its gains, established its programs on firm footing, refashioned its rhetoric, and built on its developing public support.

Instead, however, the agency spent the year in limbo. The president, preoccupied with Southeast Asia, appeared to have lost interest in the War on Poverty.[65] Even within OEO itself, there were signs of sagging energy. Although the debates of 1967 had preserved the office as a symbol of the nation's antipoverty commitment, the pressures of that year had sapped the morale and enthusiasm of the poverty warriors themselves. In some respects, they had become the creatures of their earlier symbolism; it was hard for them to be content with having only narrowly averted defeat. Shriver, having obtained his face-saving legislative victory, was ready to leave; in March, he was nominated to be ambassador to France. His deputy, Bertrand Harding, was named to succeed him, but the Senate, engaged in controversy over the nomination of Abe Fortas to be chief justice, never brought the Harding nomination to the floor. On March 31, the president announced his own intention not to seek reelection, making himself a "lame duck" and placing much of the government in the status of caretaker. The *only* sense in which OEO's position had been advanced beyond 1967 was that the agency stood as a symbol, communicating to the poor the government's concern for their needs.

Even the agency's future as a symbol, though, supposedly resolved the previous year, was not assured. The possibility of transferring OEO programs to other agencies was raised again, during consideration of the Higher and Vocational Education Amendments of 1968. Although the transfer proposal was defeated, the fact that it was even raised was a sign that the symbolic survival of 1967 had not completely settled all outstanding issues.

Nor was the administration willing in 1968 to commit increased resources to the poverty program. In order to win congressional approval of a proposed tax surcharge, President Johnson acceded to Congressman Wilbur Mills's demand for a reduction of $6 billion in federal spending. Still, the president reportedly asked Harding specifically to request for OEO an appropriation for the 1969 fiscal year equal to the full amount of the prior authorization. Even that amount, however, as Harding explained, "will fund no major substantive departure from what we have done in the past. In many cases it will simply permit us to continue programs at their current levels."[66] Those who had battled in the administration's behalf found that their battle had been of symbolic significance only. Paradoxically, in choosing to *defend* OEO as a symbol of commitment, they may have precluded its really *becoming* one. Congressmen who had been skeptical or dubious could salve their consciences with the knowledge that the continued existence of a federal agency would recapture the lost enthusiasm of 1964. The fact that the agency was there would be enough of a symbol of their concern for the poor. They need not remain committed enough to support the office's activities or to enlarge its budget.

Nevertheless, the president's valedictory messages could speak positively of accomplishment in reducing poverty in America. In his final Economic Report, Johnson listed "the advances in the war on poverty" as the achievement which gave him the greatest pride, and the elimination of poverty as the social challenge of the greatest concern. The accompanying annual report of the Council of Economic Advisers indicated that the poverty-income gap had dwindled to $9.7 billion and could be closed with but a modest redistribution of income. The council echoed its assertion of 1968, that eliminating poverty was "a concrete, realistic, and attainable goal in our generation."[67] In his budget message of January 15, 1969, Johnson pleaded especially for the continuation of OEO and for a 12 percent increase in its authorization. This message was a challenge to the incoming administration to build on what his own had begun. Johnson had made a similar challenge the previous October, asserting that the next president would have to continue the fight against poverty "to make sure those who have crossed the poverty line are not neglected and allowed to slip back."[68]

But no one could be certain what the next president would do. During the 1968 campaign, the Republicans fiercely had attacked OEO. A Republican campaign document linked summer riots to the Johnson administration's "reckless use of inflated promises and . . . resort to political sloganeering, which raised many expectations that were not realized."[69] Campaigning for the vice presidency, Governor Spiro T. Agnew of Maryland promised that a Republican administration would eliminate community action; in a speech to the American Political

Science Association, he dismissed the entire Johnson program as an "unsuccessful holding action."[70]

Early in 1968, one analyst had predicted that any Republican successor to Lyndon Johnson would want to scuttle OEO, if only for the partisan political reason of dismantling a visible symbol. By the following February, the same writer had concluded that politics would make the outright abolition of the agency impossible. Since its existence had been defended on symbolic grounds, its termination "would seem callous disregard for those deprived segments of American society, the Negro and other slum dwellers, [whom President Nixon] claims to care for."[71] Jonathan Spivak predicted, though, that the agency certainly would be renamed. The new president did not make even that much of a break from the past. Instead, Richard Nixon proclaimed, "From the experience of OEO, we have learned the value of having in the Federal Government an agency whose special concern is the poor."[72] Nixon named Congressman Donald Rumsfeld of Illinois to be director of OEO. At his confirmation hearings, Rumsfeld promised to preserve the agency's role as an innovative and experimental force, and spoke forcefully of the need for continued participation by the poor.[73]

There were signs, however, of uncertainty and drift. Rumsfeld toned down his agency's program and avoided all semblance of the military metaphor. Within a year, he had antagonized aggressive local antipoverty leaders, who thought he was de-emphasizing participation of the poor; militants within OEO, who objected to his calling the police to arrest black law students who held a demonstration at the agency's headquarters; local officials, who were angered by his threats to suspend funds to "ineffective" community action agencies; and Republicans in

Congress, who resented his lack of support for their 1969 plan to transfer control of antipoverty programs to the states.[74] He resigned the OEO directorship in 1970 and was brought inside the White House, eventually to become director of the Cost of Living Council and then ambassador to the North Atlantic Treaty Organization. Rumsfeld was succeeded by Frank Carlucci, who in turn was followed by Philip V. Sanchez. Finally, after his reelection, President Nixon in January 1973 named Howard Phillips to direct the OEO, reportedly with the instructions to terminate its activities and to dismantle its structure.[75] Ten years after it was created, it was gone.

7

The Impasse of the Liberal Argument

I

Although the War on Poverty ended in stalemate, it was not without enduring results. If it did not achieve all for which its proponents had hoped, it did legitimize a number of new ideas, influencing the thinking of social reformers and providing the institutional basis for a more complete attack in the future.

Citizen participation, for example, emerged as a key idea in the process of social change. To be sure, it had not always served the interests of the disadvantaged. But the principle of participation itself was important: the gap in status between rich and poor could be narrowed once the poor were regarded as active participants in a program rather than as social wards. Social welfare professionals during the late 1960s were rapidly shifting their perspective about the poor, their consciousness having been raised, in part, by the emphasis OEO gave to citizen participation.

Under Lyndon Johnson, OEO also legitimized the role of advocate for the poor, despite the fact that President

Nixon chose not to have the agency play this role. Just as farmers, laborers, businessmen, and other economic groups had their official spokesmen, the poor needed an advocate within the councils of government. Miller and Rein had predicted as early as 1965 that the major contribution of the War on Poverty might be to render legitimate the grievances of the poor.[1] If these grievances were recognized by the larger society as justified claims against the political system, then its members would need to consider the need for institutional change to redress them.

A third major idea nurtured by the War on Poverty was that government services should be decentralized. Community action programs embodied this idea; their descendants included neighborhood centers and revenue sharing. Neighborhood centers made programs more accessible to the poor, made the poor more aware of available services and programs, involved the poor in their planning, and reduced the institutional aura which had alienated the poor from traditional bureaucracies. Revenue sharing provided states and localities with funds to support such activities as the individual jurisdictions might find appropriate. In the absence of funds, participation in local decisionmaking was of little importance, for there was not much of consequence about which to decide.

A fourth positive contribution of the agency was the development of indigenous political leadership among the poor. One consequence of participation by the poor in community action, even if their inclusion had no immediate impact on policy, was to raise their own level of interest and political consciousness. As leaders of the poor gained in political sophistication and experience, they became more able to struggle for power within the confines of the established political system.[2] Political participation was conservative, in the sense that it strengthened the ties of the social fabric, while at the same time it allowed the poor to use the political system to press for attention to their needs. These were second-order effects of a rhetoric which defined community action as an instrument of democracy.

Although the Johnson administration espoused neither the proposal that the government become employer of last resort nor the proposal that the government become guarantor of an annual income, both ideas were stimulated and nourished by the experience of OEO—a fifth positive contribution. The emphasis on *opportunity* in the rhetoric surrounding the poverty program led to a concern for the availability of jobs. The president advocated a program called Job Opportunities in the Business Sector, under which private businesses would be encouraged by the prospect of federal subsidies to create jobs which could be filled by the hard-core unemployed. There were some optimistic forecasts for this program; in 1969, for instance, the OEO claimed that fifteen thousand companies already had hired and retrained more than 100,000 of the hard-core unemployed.[3] But since no statistics were kept on the number of successful placements, nor on the proportion of trainees who were poor, it was impossible to determine the employment program's effectiveness. A report of the General Accounting Office in 1968 also disclosed that most federal funds for private, on-the-job training were used to subsidize training that would have taken place in any case.[4]

From the experience of these job-creation efforts, however, it would not have required a great leap in inference to justify a government program of guaranteed public employment. The Johnson administration did not endorse such a program, and it discouraged Congress from establishing one, despite the fact that the president had been advised that there was strong public support for it.[5] The experience of OEO, however, laid the groundwork for discussion of a public employment program; the basic premises were all in place.

Similarly, OEO placed proposals for a guaranteed annual income on the agenda for public consideration. In the early 1960s, such proposals had been almost the exclusive property of academics who were concerned that automation was eliminating job opportunities, or of economic conservatives who saw a "negative income tax" as the means by which government could cease its involvement in social welfare programs.[6] But OEO officials saw the guaranteed income as a potential antipoverty weapon. Sargent Shriver reportedly included a negative income tax in his first five-year comprehensive plan to eliminate poverty,[7] and he continued to urge the idea upon the president. In his 1967 economic message, Johnson announced his intention to appoint a commission to study income maintenance proposals. Although proclaiming that a guaranteed income "may or may not prove to be practicable at any time" and that it was "almost surely beyond our means at this time," he counseled, "But we must examine any plan, however unconventional, which could promise a major advance."[8]

Finally, and perhaps of greatest significance among the ideas which OEO institutionalized, was the belief that national interest and concern properly ought to focus upon the poor. Breaking down complacency, stimulating national dialogue, and giving visibility to hidden issues all were means by which the agency promoted a will to act. That the government ought to combat poverty became an axiom of politics. Of course, the depth of national commitment at times was superficial, and its persistence was uncertain. But, at least for a time, President Johnson's War on Poverty expanded the nation's consciousness of fundamental social problems and inspired dedicated people to attack them.

Clearly, however, the choices reflected in the rhetoric of the War on Poverty could not be sustained. Even as the country institutionalized some of the Johnson administration's advances, it became profoundly disillusioned about its ability to conquer the foe and even about whether the victory was worth the cost.

Many Americans escaped from poverty between 1964 and 1969, but the Office of Economic Opportunity could claim little of the credit. Although OEO had established agencies and programs in most sections of the country, by 1968 it had reached directly no more than 6 percent of the poor.[9] In retrospect, the economic growth attributable to the war in Vietnam was the main causal force in reducing poverty. This news was discouraging to a nation wearying of war, hoping to achieve peace abroad and prosperity at home at the same time.

Other signs of disillusionment could be found, as well. Research studies questioned the long-run effectiveness of poverty programs. Perhaps the most discouraging research was the Westinghouse evaluation of Project Head Start, which concluded that its long-term effectiveness was minimal. Five years earlier, ambitious programs had been met with enthusiasm; in the climate of 1969, they were received with skepticism.

Pursuant to President Nixon's orders, OEO shifted from the direct operation of major programs to research and development of new antipoverty approaches, testing them on a limited basis for possible adoption by other agencies of government. Militancy was to be de-emphasized; community action agencies no longer were to serve as advocates for the poor against other groups of society. Many of the national emphasis programs finally were transferred to other government departments beginning in 1969, with manpower programs going to the Department of Labor and educational efforts going to Health, Education, and Welfare.

These shifts did not originate with the Republican president. Johnson aides had urged the outgoing president to recommend in his final State of the Union message that, once OEO programs were fully developed, they should be "delegated to established departments and agencies."[10]

It was the Johnson administration, too, which issued the retreat from militant community action efforts. At issue in 1968 was a controversial grant which OEO had made directly to The Woodlawn Organization in Chicago, over the objection of Mayor Daley, for the purpose of rehabilitating two Chicago gangs. Hearings on Bertrand Harding's nomination to be OEO director were delayed until he offered assurances that no more such projects would be funded by OEO. Although he defended the agency's decision in making the Chicago grant, Harding, in a letter to Senator Harry F. Byrd, made the desired promise.[11]

One of the clearest signs of disillusionment with the poverty program was the growing disenchantment with the concept of "maximum feasible participation." Participation came to be seen as a token gesture which gave the poor only the illusion of a voice in policymaking. When established political organizations believed that they might be threatened by the participation of the poor, they moved to reassert their interests. By carefully selecting their representatives, they might be able to achieve the power of veto over the community action agency, without being involved in its day-to-day decisionmaking. Representatives of the poor were included on local boards so that they might perceive that they had a stake in the existing system, not so that they might serve as catalysts for change. The goal of broadly representing all segments of the community, which had been used earlier to justify *increased* power for the poor, now could be used to *check* the power of the poor.

Even when meaningful participation was achieved, moreover, it did not necessarily lead to the desired ends. Dialogue among groups and interests offered no assurance of a solution which would be satisfactory to all concerned; it might instead, as former MFY executive Harold H. Weissman explained, "escalate conflicts to the point where democratic politics cannot resolve them." And Dale Rogers Marshall, summarizing research on community action, reported that, while some observers found participation to reduce hostility and alienation, others found that these qualities were increased, especially when participation of the poor in poverty programs failed to meet rising expectations.[12] It was, at best, an unclear verdict.

II

Since an overall assessment of President Johnson's War on Poverty must be mixed, a simple judgment of success or failure would fall wide of the mark. For whatever reasons, the incidence of poverty had dropped markedly by 1969. Still, the fact is that the War on Poverty was ended far short of the announced goal of total victory. Surveying the course of the war, sympathetic analysts have suggested that the administration should have altered specific tactics while pursuing the same basic course.

Perhaps, for example, legislation should have been drafted with less haste; perhaps Congress should have been given more time for intelligent debate. Perhaps Johnson set his budgetary sights too low and should have sought a higher initial appropriation. Maybe it was a mistake to give so much emphasis to community action programs and the principle of "maximum feasible participation." Maybe Johnson should have been as concerned with the details of administration as he was with the legislative process. And it often has been suggested that Johnson could have accomplished more, had he claimed less. These alternatives, however, would have made little real difference to the rhetorical history of the antipoverty program, or else they were not known to be available in 1964. There were pressures for participation spawned by the mid-1960s that were independent of the poverty program; the same could be said for efforts to cut domestic federal spending. And the president could not know in 1964 that a future Congress would be in a receptive mood. Delay could prove fatal, and it certainly would not respond to the immediate need. Inspiration was what the country needed then, and Lyndon Johnson met that need through exhortation and challenge.

Other critics have suggested that the problem lay more with strategy than tactics. Poverty should have been linked to a symbol which would appeal to the self-interest of all. The Social Security program is the nation's outstanding example of such a symbolic link. Although not all benefit *equally* from the program, all stand to gain. Conceived in controversy, the Social Security program quickly acquired broad national support. Despite changes in the concept of individual equity which were begun as early as 1939, Social Security profits from the myth that it is a form of insurance.[13]

In contrast to a unitary system, the War on Poverty was divisive in its orientation. By asking the nonpoor to sacrifice on behalf of the poor, it depended ultimately upon a moral appeal, stated most succinctly by Sargent Shriver when he testified that the War on Poverty was an act of expiation, "of humbling and prostrating ourselves before the Creator."[14] But continued public support for a divisively oriented program resting on a moral appeal could not be assumed. The middle class could not be expected permanently to support a program from which its members not only did not stand to benefit but eventually lost relative status or advantage. A unitary orientation to the antipoverty program would require that benefits be included for the nonpoor. The political scientist James Q. Wilson described these benefits as "side payments," writing that to implement social change often required "giving other people as a condition of acquiescence something that they want. The total package becomes much bigger, and a single change tends to be imbedded in a cluster of simultaneous changes."[15] Wilson added that such an approach, while economically "inefficient" and costly, might be politically of great value. It could cement the support of the affluent, who would have no incentive to diminish the program and every incentive to enlarge and enhance it.

Economic security might have been the unifying symbol—the analogy to Social Security is obvious. Several sources of economic insecurity could have been identified and redressed through transfer payments: dislocation resulting from economic bottlenecks and sectoral labor shortages, catastrophic illness and disability which would exhaust the savings of even the well-to-do, technological unemployment caused by planned cuts in defense spending, poverty which prevented minimal conditions of subsistence, and training required for the new jobs created through automation. In sum, then, the administration might have proposed an income strategy without defining it as a strategy *against poverty*.

This idea was in the wind in 1964. In the same week that the Economic Opportunity Act was proposed to Congress, the outline for a unitary system to combat poverty was published in a report by a small group called the Ad Hoc Committee on the Triple Revolution. Describing vast changes wrought in society by cybernetics, military technology, and advances in civil rights, the report recommended basic changes in government policy, such as the adoption of a guaranteed income to provide economic security in a world in which the number of productive jobs was expected to decline sharply because of automation.[16] This report was quickly brought to Shriver's attention.[17] The president might have taken a leaf from the Triple Revolutionists. Although it is uncertain, of course, he might have been able to steer such a program through Congress in 1964, and it might have avoided some of the dangerous ambiguities of the War on Poverty.

From the perspective of hindsight, however, one can see in the fate of Social Security the likely results of such a venture. The political gain from expanding the benefits would have proved irresistible; the gap between receipts and expenditures would have widened. To avert economic chaos, it would have been necessary somehow to reduce benefits. In a world of shrinking resources, one could easily imagine the divisive competition between groups and classes which it was the very purpose of the unifying symbol to avoid.

III

Explaining the stalemate of the War on Poverty takes one beyond the level of tactics and strategy, to ideology. The course of the war sharply illustrates the impasse of the liberal argument in contemporary American politics. The liberal occupies the middle ground between the conservative and the radical. He or she believes the existing order to be fundamentally good yet very much in need of reform. Change must occur within the system, however, and through orderly processes rather than confrontation or revolution. The means are as important as the ends. Indeed, the liberal sees government itself as a benign force for change and envisions its role as a counterweight to organized special interests and a guarantor of individual rights.

Moreover, modern liberalism assumes the importance of economic growth.[18] If growth were to cease, what would follow would be a war between groups and sections for distribution of a pie of fixed size. In contrast, growth allows the pie to be enlarged. Then the incremental economic resources can be allocated in favor of the disadvantaged, gradually improving their station without worsening the conditions of those relatively well off. The limited welfare state means that the poor can gain without strain to the rich. Reform can be achieved without the specter of redistribution.[19]

These premises are clearly incrementalist and relatively noncontroversial. But in the 1960s the public was not calling for the liberal agenda. Throughout the twentieth century the liberal has not merely responded to public opinion but has sought to evoke it. Liberals, in effect, made themselves advocates for a *latent* public opinion which would assert itself if properly stimulated. They presumed, in other words, to "stand in" for the public. Their duty was to define the agenda of national concerns by raising public consciousness of problems and posing solutions to them.

But why was the public only latent? Because, liberals believed, American society was in a kind of stalemate. Resources were there to solve problems but the will was lacking. Special interests organized themselves effectively to block reform, meanwhile narcotizing the public into a kind of false consciousness. Therefore, effective action would require somehow bypassing this clash of interests. Liberals sought to do so by rendering the conflict moot. They redefined issues, appealing not to interests but to more abstract, transcendent symbols which would subsume the bickering. Issues were defined in terms of principles which would command wide support.[20] For Johnson, the abolition of poverty and injustice served as such principles. As was true of other liberals, it seemed that, by evading difficult choices between competing interests, he had cut through them. The ambiguous symbol not only facilitated consensus but also was lofty and noble enough to justify the pains and costs required to achieve the goal.

Hence the liberal's situation made it necessary to clothe incrementalist programs in an absolutist rhetoric. To create optimism about the feasibility and value of social change, strategic selection of condensation symbols is crucial. One writer expressed this idea in the aphorism, "Great societies are first believed in, then made."[21] But the appeal of the visionary, absolutist condensation symbol contained its own dilemmas. It encouraged the evaluation of a liberal president largely by what he accomplished in the symbolic world, exaggerating the influence of the symbolic over the tangible. His programs were measured not against what the conditions had been before he began but against the vision which his own rhetoric had proclaimed. Inevitably, incrementalist measures would fall short. So here was the dilemma: Excessively forceful symbolic choices could not be sustained in incrementalist action, but less forceful symbolic choices might well have been ineffective in arousing a latent public in the first place.

There were other dilemmas as well. The liberal was an advocate of change, but once he was in power and his programs were in place, he was defending a new status quo. And once the liberal programs were institutionalized in the middle ground, they were open to attack from both extremes. As the historian Allen Matusow succinctly summarizes, conservatives charged that they had inherent flaws—"violation of market logic, covert service to special interests, and perversion by bureaucrats." Meanwhile, as he points out, "No less vindicated were those leftist critics who dismissed liberals as pseudo-reformers unwilling to address the only real issue—the maldistribution of wealth and power in America."[22] And the dilemma of the middle ground is that one cannot abandon it for either extreme without doing violence to one's own assumptions of a benign order which nevertheless is in need of reform. Those assumptions, too, contained their dilemmas. How, after all, can one attack and defend the existing system at the same time? The liberal assumed that the society was not fundamentally flawed but misdirected; the combination of an aroused public opinion, active participation in decisionmaking, and the incentives of federal funds would arrest its attention and prove sufficient inducements to change. This line of thought, now so seemingly naive, made faulty assumptions about the motives of political actors. It greatly overestimated the possibility of institutional change and severely minimized the ability of established interests to co-opt the reform impulse and redirect it to serve their own agenda. The basic dilemma is still there.

To define one's goals in the loftiest terms is to arouse expectations and to court disappointment when the tangible benefits of legislation fall short of its avowed goals, as inevitably they will. On the defensive, unused to supporting the status quo and yet unable to abandon his or her premises, the liberal is vulnerable. The War on Poverty illustrates how the liberal's middle ground was eroded from both poles. Many sympathizers of the *objective* moved leftward, concluding that poverty was but a symptom of a more fundamental illness requiring redistribution of wealth and power. Because the War on Poverty could not countenance this admission that society was flawed, Matusow proclaims for it the epitaph, "Declared but Never Fought."[23]

But the radical critique could not hold a candle to the conservative reaction against the War on Poverty. In an oft-quoted passage, Moynihan has noted that the American public, though liberal in practice, is ideologically conservative.[24] The gap between absolutist rhetoric and incrementalist policy nurtured a conservative ideology, which was further stimulated by the public misperception that legislative programs are really of the same magnitude as their symbolic dimension would suggest. From the persistence of poverty and inequality into the 1970s, it became fashionable to conclude that the War on Poverty had failed and that its failure was proof of the futility of liberal reform. In reaction to the Johnson administration, conservatives concluded that the liberals' record showed the dangers of government regulation of private enterprise, denied that a strong president was an appropriate instrument for social reform, and established that government was the enemy rather than the friend of the people.

The conservative reaction was particularly potent in the case of the War on Poverty, because the traditional poverty ideology had been only compromised and not abandoned. Gradually, over six centuries, government had assumed responsibility for the poor, but in limited ways and without directly contesting the widespread belief that poverty was primarily a personal problem and, in some sense, evidence of individual failure. As a consequence of the conservative reaction, the War on Poverty took on a different cast and tone; antipoverty programs came to be valued *primarily* for their stabilizing effect. Peter Schrag could describe as the irony of the Great Society the fact that the survival of its programs might depend less upon their effectiveness in raising the educational and social attainment of the poor (their original objective) than upon their ability not to disturb the status quo as perceived by the majority.[25]

Nor was this trend a unique response to civil disorders. Social programs need the support of protective constituencies if they are to survive. Since the poor lack the political power to comprise a sufficient base of support for social programs, support from the middle class also must be obtained. The middle class, however, will not be likely to support programs for social reconstruction which challenge its economic self-interest or its social status, but will, as Jones wrote, "support a change in the personalities of lower-class individuals." The latter change, of course, not only does not threaten the interests of the middle class but in fact provides reassurance. "Accordingly," Jones concludes, "government programs, no matter how innovative, must eventually become rehabilitative."[26]

The War on Poverty had been launched on the strength of its ability to appeal to both the liberal and the conservative presumption. But its failure to perform at the level promised by its rhetoric undercut its balanced appeal. If liberals stayed in the middle ground, they had nothing to defend. If they drew the more radical conclusion that major changes in society and culture were needed, they came to lack confidence "that the problems plaguing the nation were within the competence of any single party or individual."[27] Having said that, however, what further response was available to the liberal except numbness? The liberal argument had reached an impasse. It was during the administration of Lyndon Johnson that the old New Deal coalition came apart and, as Theodore H. White described it, "folk-wisdom not only ran out of solutions, it ran out of common standards of judgment."[28]

Reflecting on their demise at the end of the 1960s, some liberals began to wonder why, in effect, they had to promise the moon in order to achieve the smallest bits of reform. Perhaps the way out of the liberals' dilemma was to lower the level of expectations by espousing a less lofty vision in the first place. This hypothesis received a test during the presidency of Jimmy Carter, who came into office pledged to end the "imperial presidency" which had led to Watergate. Although he once referred to a national energy policy as the "moral equivalent of war," he tended to discuss issues without offering an overarching broad vision. Such an attempt to technologize the public sphere rests on the assumption that issues and problems are self-evident; people will see the facts and act upon them; there is no role for rhetoric to play. The results were

President Carter's self-inflicted sense of blandness and malaise. Carter, as the historian William E. Leuchtenburg notes, "could not offer a standard around which his partisans could rally"; his failure was less in policy than in the lack of an overall vision.[29]

It is more complicated than that. A vision of what might be is part of the glue of society. The need is not to eschew symbolism, even were that possible, but to select symbols which indeed do transcend, rather than temporarily subsume, conflicts of interest. In the early 1980s, liberals made what may be the first attempts to surmount their impasse, by defining new positions on such issues as a nuclear freeze and aid to education. It is far too soon to know whether these or other issues will reinvigorate the liberal argument. At this writing, liberals remain, in Matusow's phrase, "defensive and circumspect"[30] under the shadow of Ronald Reagan. But there are cycles in the strength of political appeals, and the time will come when summoning the people with a vision of vast possibilities will again be a persuasive appeal. What remains to be seen is whether the rhetorical dilemmas of the War on Poverty will recur or whether liberal advocates will be able to shift the argument to a new level, selecting symbols which control the subsequent discussion while avoiding the impasse.

Notes

Chapter 1

1. Richard Neustadt, *Presidential Power: The Politics of Leadership* (New York: Wiley, 1960), esp. chaps. 2 and 3.

2. The distinction between truth and reality is explored in Celeste Condit Railsback, "Beyond Rhetorical Relativism: A Structural-Material Model of Truth and Objective Reality," *Quarterly Journal of Speech* 69 (Nov. 1983):351–63. For a discussion of how reality is socially constructed, see especially Peter Berger and Thomas Luckmann, *The Social Construction of Reality: A Treatise in the Sociology of Knowledge* (Garden City, N.Y.: Doubleday, 1966).

3. Joel Charon, *Symbolic Interactionism: An Introduction, an Interpretation, an Integration* (Englewood Cliffs, N.J.: Prentice-Hall, 1979), p. 40.

4. The concept of definition of the situation draws from the work of Mead, Dewey, and Schutz, especially George Herbert Mead, *Mind, Self, and Society* (Chicago: University of Chicago Press, 1934); John Dewey, *Human Nature and Conduct* (New York: Holt, 1922); and Alfred Schutz, "On Multiple Realities," in *Collected Papers I: The Problem of Social Reality* (The Hague: Martinus Nijhoff, 1962), pp. 207–59.

5. J. Robert Cox, "Argument and the 'Definition of the Situation,' " *Central States Speech Journal* 32 (Fall 1981):200.

6. On unconditional surrender, see James W. Hikins, "The Rhetoric of 'Unconditional Surrender' and the Decision to Drop the Atomic Bomb," *Quarterly Journal of Speech* 69 (Nov. 1983):379–400. For a symbolic interactionist view of the presidency, see Robert E. Denton, Jr., *The Symbolic Dimensions of the American Presidency: Description and Analysis* (Prospect Heights, Ill.: Waveland Press, 1982).

7. See especially Murray Edelman, *The Symbolic Uses of Politics* (Urbana: University of Illinois Press, 1964); *Politics as Symbolic Action: Mass Arousal and Quiescence* (Chicago: Markham, 1971).

8. This view of the field is embodied in the report of the 1970 National Developmental Conference on Rhetoric. See Lloyd F. Bitzer and Edwin Black, eds., *The Prospect of Rhetoric* (Englewood Cliffs, N.J.: Prentice-Hall, 1971).

9. For a view that the study of public address captures the changes in ideas in the process of transmission, see Ernest J. Wrage, "Public Address: A Study in Social and Intellectual History," *Quarterly Journal of Speech* 33 (Dec. 1947):451–57.

10. Richard Weaver has suggested that a person's mode of argument provides a more reliable index to true beliefs than does an explicit statement of principles, and he offers assessments of Edmund Burke and Abraham Lincoln to bear out his contention (see Richard Weaver, *The Ethics of Rhetoric* [Chicago: Regnery, 1953], esp. pp. 57–114). For a similar view, see Bernard L. Brock, "A Definition of Four Political Positions and Their Rhetorical Characteristics" (Ph.D. diss., Northwestern University, 1965).

11. James W. Ceaser, Glen E. Thurow, Jeffrey Tulis, and Joseph M. Bessette, "The Rise of the Rhetorical Presidency," in *Essays in Presidential Rhetoric,* ed. Theodore Windt and Beth Ingold (Dubuque: Kendall/Hunt, 1983), pp. 3–22 (originally published in *Presidential Studies Quarterly* 11 [Spring 1981]:158–71).

12. Woodrow Wilson, *Papers,* ed. Arthur S. Link (Princeton: Princeton University Press, 1975), vol. 19, p. 42.

13. Wilson, *Papers,* vol. 19, p. 42.

14. Ceaser, Thurow, Tulis, and Bessette, "The Rise of the Rhetorical Presidency," p. 10.

15. Chaim Perelman and L. Olbrechts-Tyteca, *The New Rhetoric,* trans. John Wilkinson and Purcell Weaver (Notre Dame, Ind.: University of Notre Dame Press, 1969), pp. 415–26. See also Chaim Perelman, *The Realm of Rhetoric,* trans. William Kluback (Notre Dame, Ind.: University of Notre Dame Press, 1982), pp. 126–37.

16. For a detailed examination of Johnson's redefinition through dissociation, see David Zarefsky, "Lyndon Johnson Redefines 'Equal Opportunity': The Beginnings of Affirmative Action," *Central States Speech Journal* 31 (Summer 1980):85–94.

17. Charles L. Stevenson, *Ethics and Language* (New Haven: Yale University Press, 1944), pp. 206–26.

18. Edward Sapir, "Symbolism," *Encyclopaedia of the Social Sciences,* ed. Edwin R. A. Seligman (New York: Macmillan, 1934), p. 492.

19. G. Thomas Goodnight, "The Liberal and the Conservative Presumption: On Political Philosophy and the Foundations of Public Argument," *Proceedings of the [First] Summer Conference on Argumentation,* ed. Jack Rhodes and Sara Newell (Falls Church, Va.: Speech Communication Association, 1980), pp. 304–37.

20. John Morton Blum, *The Progressive Presidents: Theodore Roosevelt, Woodrow Wilson, Franklin D. Roosevelt, Lyndon B. Johnson* (New York: Norton, 1980).

21. Ernest G. Bormann, "Fantasy and Rhetorical Vision: The Rhetorical Criticism of Social Reality," *Quarterly Journal of Speech* 58 (Dec. 1972):398. This essay elaborates the approach of fantasy theme analysis as a means of understanding public discourse. But see G. P. Mohrmann, "An Essay on Fantasy Theme Criticism," *Quarterly Journal of Speech* 68 (May 1982):109–32, for a critical view of the assumptions and procedures underlying this approach.

22. The derivation and meaning of the "Great Society" phrase are reviewed in David Zarefsky, "The Great Society as a

Rhetorical Proposition," *Quarterly Journal of Speech* 65 (Nov. 1979):364–78.

23. The creation of expectations through the use of symbols illustrates Kenneth Burke's concept of form as "an arousing and fulfillment of desires." He writes that a literary work "has form in so far as one part of it leads a reader to anticipate another part, to be gratified by the sequence" (Kenneth Burke, *Counter-Statement* [1931; reprint ed., Berkeley and Los Angeles: University of California Press, 1968], p. 124). Of course, one would be gratified only if one's expectations were met—a potential difficulty when symbols lead people to vast expectations.

24. Kenneth Burke, *Attitudes toward History* (1937; reprint ed., Boston: Beacon Press, 1959), pp. 225–29.

25. See David Zarefsky, Carol Miller-Tutzauer, and Frank E. Tutzauer, "Reagan's Safety Net for the Truly Needy: The Rhetorical Uses of Definition," *Central States Speech Journal* 35 (Summer 1984):113–19.

26. Leland M. Griffin, "The Rhetoric of Historical Movements," *Quarterly Journal of Speech* 38 (Apr. 1952):184–88; "A Dramatistic Theory of the Rhetoric of Movements," *Critical Responses to Kenneth Burke,* ed. William H. Rueckert (Minneapolis: University of Minnesota Press, 1969), pp. 456–79.

27. See E. E. Schattschneider, *The Semisovereign People* (New York: Holt, Rinehart, and Winston, 1960), pp. 16–18, in which the author discusses the scope of conflict as a strategic question.

28. Paul Wilkinson, *Social Movement* (New York: Praeger, 1971), p. 14.

Chapter 2

1. Lyndon Baines Johnson, *The Vantage Point: Perspectives of the Presidency, 1963–1969* (New York: Holt, Rinehart, and Winston, 1971), p. 74.

2. Cited in Philip W. Borst, "President Johnson and the 89th Congress: A Functional Analysis of a System under Stress" (Ph.D. diss., Claremont Graduate School, 1968), p. 24.

3. Doris Kearns, *Lyndon Johnson and the American Dream* (New York: Harper and Row, 1976), p. 412. Kearns quotes these figures from a memorandum from Horace Busby to the president dated January 14, 1964.

4. See especially William E. Leuchtenburg, *In the Shadow of FDR: From Harry Truman to Ronald Reagan* (Ithaca: Cornell University Press, 1983), pp. 121–60.

5. Harry McPherson, *A Political Education* (Boston: Atlantic, Little, Brown, 1972), p. 196.

6. The figure is cited by Arthur M. Schlesinger, Jr., *A Thousand Days: John F. Kennedy in the White House* (Boston: Houghton Mifflin, 1965), p. 978.

7. Douglass Cater, "The Politics of Poverty," *Reporter* 30 (Feb. 13, 1964):17; Terry Sanford, in House Committee on Education and Labor, *Economic Opportunity Act of 1964,* hearings, 88th Cong., 2d sess., 1964, vol. 2, p. 924 (hereafter *1964 House Committee Hearings*).

8. Elinor Graham, "The Politics of Poverty," in *Poverty as a Public Issue,* ed. Ben B. Seligman (New York: Free Press, 1965), p. 243.

9. Cited in Sargent Shriver, *Point of the Lance* (New York: Harper and Row, 1964), p. 107. Shriver attempted to rebut this poll in a speech to the American Society of Newspaper Editors on April 18, 1964, in which he claimed that success could be achieved because the antipoverty effort had the support "of those American people who actually know what the battle is all about."

10. Byron G. Lander, "The Emergence of Poverty as a Political Issue in 1964" (Ph.D. diss., University of Missouri, 1967), pp. 2, 176.

11. Michael Harrington, *The Other America* (New York: Macmillan, 1962).

12. Harrington, *The Other America,* pp. 155, 168.

13. Sar A. Levitan, *The Great Society's Poor Law: A New*

Approach to Poverty (Baltimore: Johns Hopkins University Press, 1969), p. 13.

14. Bayard Rustin, "From Protest to Politics: The Future of the Civil Rights Movement," in *Poverty in America: A Book of Readings,* ed. Louis A. Ferman, Joyce L. Kornbluh, and Alan Haber (Ann Arbor: University of Michigan Press, 1965), p. 464.

15. Kearns, *Lyndon Johnson and the American Dream,* p. 188.

16. Johnson, *The Vantage Point,* p. 79.

17. Murray Edelman has described how ambiguity can reinforce political mythology. Listeners are encouraged "to realize [their] sometimes desperate wish to entrust responsibility to someone who can cope by finding in the striking rhetoric an assurance of clear-sightedness and determination" (Edelman, *Politics as Symbolic Action,* p. 80).

18. Among these books are Ben H. Bagdikian, *In the Midst of Plenty* (Boston: Beacon Press, 1964), and Hubert H. Humphrey, *War on Poverty* (New York: McGraw-Hill, 1964).

19. Murray Kempton, "The Essential Sargent Shriver," *New Republic* 150 (Mar. 28, 1964):12.

20. Daniel P. Moynihan, "What Is Community Action?" *Public Interest* 5 (Fall 1966):7; Frances Fox Piven, "The Great Society as Political Strategy," *Columbia Forum* 13 (Summer 1970):18.

21. Kearns, *Lyndon Johnson and the American Dream,* p. 188.

22. Phil Landrum, quoted in *Congressional Record* 110 (Aug. 5, 1964):18206.

23. Walter Reuther, quoted in *1964 House Committee Hearings,* vol. 1, p. 422; Raymond R. Tucker, quoted in *1964 House Committee Hearings,* vol. 2, pp. 786–87; *Poverty,* H. Doc. 88-243, 88th Cong., 2d. sess., 1964, p. 3; Lyndon B. Johnson, *Economic Report of the President, Together with the Annual Report of the Council of Economic Advisers* (Washington: U.S. Government Printing Office, 1964), p. 55; W. Willard Wirtz,

quoted in *1964 House Committee Hearings,* vol. 1, p. 184; John G. Tower, quoted in *Congressional Record* 110 (July 22, 1964):16616.

24. Orville Freeman, quoted in *1964 House Committee Hearings,* vol. 1, p. 246, and in Senate Committee on Labor and Public Welfare, *Economic Opportunity Act of 1964,* hearings, 88th Cong., 2d sess., 1964, p. 49 (hereafter *1964 Senate Committee Hearings*).

25. These programs rested heavily on a theory of delinquency advanced in Richard Cloward and Lloyd Ohlin, *Delinquency and Opportunity* (London: Routledge and Kegan Paul, 1961). For accounts of the delinquency projects, see Peter Marris and Martin Rein, *Dilemmas of Social Reform: Poverty and Community Action in the United States* (New York: Atherton, 1969); Daniel L. Knapp, "Scouting the War on Poverty: Social Reform Politics in the Kennedy Administration" (Ph.D. diss., University of Oregon, 1970).

26. See, for example, "Government's Drive on Poverty Will Emphasize Local Initiative," *New York Times,* Jan. 15, 1964, p. 21.

27. Concerning these events, see John F. Bibby and Roger H. Davidson, *On Capitol Hill: Studies in the Legislative Process* (New York: Holt, Rinehart, and Winston, 1967), p. 231; James L. Sundquist, "The End of the Experiment?" in *On Fighting Poverty: Perspectives from Experience* (New York: Basic Books, 1969), p. 238. President Johnson's account of the events is slightly different. According to him, it was he who encouraged Kermit Gordon and Walter Heller to broaden the program's scope beyond a limited number of demonstration areas. In his memoirs, Johnson wrote, "I was certain that we could not start small and hope to propel a program through Congress. It had to be big and bold and hit the whole nation with real impact" (Johnson, *The Vantage Point,* p. 73).

28. Levitan, *The Great Society's Poor Law,* p. 121.

29. Anthony J. Celebrezze, quoted in *1964 House Committee Hearings,* vol. 1, p. 139; Phil Landrum, quoted in *1964 House Committee Hearings,* vol. 1, p. 190.

30. Richard Whately, *Elements of Rhetoric* (1828; reprint ed., Boston: James Munroe, 1852), pt. 1, chap. 3, sec. 2.

31. An excellent discussion of the strategic value of labeling situations as crises may be found in Murray Edelman, *Political Language: Words That Succeed and Policies That Fail* (New York: Academic Press, 1977), pp. 43–49.

32. Lyndon B. Johnson, *Public Papers of the Presidents: Lyndon B. Johnson, 1963–64* (Washington: U.S. Government Printing Office, 1965), vol. 1, p. 779.

33. Millard Simpson, in *Congressional Record* 110 (July 23, 1964):16777; A. Willis Robertson, quoted in *Congressional Record* 110 (July 22, 1964):16616.

34. House Committee on Education and Labor, *Economic Opportunity Act of 1964*, H. Rept. 88-1458, 88th Cong., 2d sess., 1964, p. 68 (hereafter *1964 House Committee Report*).

35. Senate Committee on Labor and Public Welfare, *Economic Opportunity Act of 1964*, S. Rept. 88–1218, 88th Cong., 2d sess., 1964, p. 69 (hereafter *1964 Senate Committee Report*).

36. Cited in Louise Lander, ed., *War on Poverty* (New York: Facts on File, 1967), pp. 11–12. Nixon made this statement at a press conference in Dayton, Ohio, on April 30, 1964.

37. Peter H. B. Frelinghuysen, in *1964 Senate Committee Hearings,* p. 184.

38. Frelinghuysen's committee statement may be found in *1964 House Committee Hearings,* vol. 1, p. 140; his floor statement, in *Congressional Record* 110 (Aug. 5, 1964):18211.

39. Johnson, *Public Papers, 1963–64,* vol. 1, p. 597.

40. Richard J. Daley, quoted in *1964 House Committee Hearings,* vol. 2, p. 763.

41. Stewart L. Udall, quoted in *1964 House Committee Hearings,* vol. 1, p. 346; Johnson, *Public Papers, 1963–64,* vol. 1, p. 611.

42. Johnson, *Economic Report of the President* (1964), p. 15; Johnson, *Public Papers, 1963–64,* vol. 1, p. 780. A slight variation on this theme was Shriver's argument that, while all the pertinent knowledge did not yet exist, it soon would be discovered. In his convocation address at Texas Tech College,

he made a comparison to the space program, saying, "We do not know how to go to the moon yet either, but we are going to get there" (Shriver, *Point of the Lance,* p. 61).

43. Robert F. Kennedy, in *1964 House Committee Hearings,* vol. 1, p. 306; Hubert H. Humphrey, *War on Poverty,* p. 14.

44. Johnson, *The Vantage Point,* p. 285.

45. *1964 Senate Committee Report,* p. 6. The phrase, "the other America," is an apparent reference to Michael Harrington's work of that title.

46. Johnson, *Public Papers, 1963–64,* vol. 1, p. 183.

47. Quoted in *1964 House Committee Hearings,* vol. 2, p. 1128.

48. Graham, "The Politics of Poverty," pp. 244–46.

49. Charles Mohr, "Shriver Confers on Poverty Here," *New York Times,* Apr. 1, 1964, p. 17.

50. Whitney Young, Jr., quoted in *1964 House Committee Hearings,* vol. 1, p. 632.

51. For example, Congressman Dominick V. Daniels of New Jersey commented, "There is a grim irony in extending, through a public accommodations section, the right to a man to use a restaurant, but deny [*sic*] him the training necessary for him to make enough money to feed his family adequately" (*Congressional Record* 110 [Aug. 6, 1964]:18276).

52. *1964 Senate Committee Report,* p. 7.

53. Jack Conway, in *1964 Senate Committee Hearings,* vol. 3, p. 1542, Robert F. Kennedy, in *1964 Senate Committee Hearings,* pp. 208–209; Pat McNamara, in *Congressional Record* 110 (July 22, 1964):16613; Warren Magnuson, in *Congressional Record* 110 (July 23, 1964):16743.

54. Shriver, *Point of the Lance,* p. 100.

55. "The Office of Economic Opportunity during the Administration of President Lyndon B. Johnson," Lyndon Baines Johnson Library, pp. 183, 185 (hereafter "OEO Administrative History"). In general, see Sar A. Levitan, "Planning the Anti-Poverty Strategy," *Poverty and Human Resources Abstracts* 2 (Mar.–Apr. 1967):8. Levitan maintains that the phrase was introduced following a suggestion of Richard W. Boone on

February 4. Moynihan sets the date as February 23. For his view, see Moynihan, "What Is Community Action?" p. 6.

56. Adam Yarmolinsky attributed authorship to Boone, who claimed it (see "A Planner Talks on Role of Poor," *New York Times,* Oct. 29, 1967, p. 41). In his dissertation, Lombard refers to a claim by Boone that the original phrase was "maximum participation" and that "feasible" was inserted during the House committee deliberations (Rudolph Joseph Lombard, "Achieving 'Maximum Feasible Participation' of the Poor in Anti-Poverty Elections" [Ph.D. diss., Syracuse University, 1970], p. 23). If correct, this claim would explain Powell's alleged role. The reported attribution of authorship to Powell is cited in Barbara Carter, "Sargent Shriver and the Role of the Poor," *Poverty: Power and Politics,* ed. Chaim I. Waxman (New York: Grosset and Dunlap, 1968), p. 208.

57. [Kenneth B. Clark and Jeannette Hopkins], *A Relevant War against Poverty: A Study of Community Action Programs and Observable Social Change* (New York: Metropolitan Applied Research Center, 1968), p. 22.

58. Gordon W. Allport, "The Psychology of Participation," *Psychological Review* 52 (May 1945):119; Charles I. Schottland, quoted in *1964 House Committee Hearings,* vol. 2, p. 1086.

59. Illustrative of the witnesses who justified participation in this fashion was Walter Reuther (see *1964 House Committee Hearings,* vol. 1, p. 462).

60. Robert F. Kennedy, in *1964 House Committee Hearings,* vol. 1, p. 308; Sargent Shriver, in *1964 Senate Committee Hearings,* pp. 169–71.

61. Anne Austin Murphy, "Involving the Poor in the War against Poverty" (Ph.D. diss., University of North Carolina, 1970), p. 27.

62. Johnson, *The Vantage Point,* p. 75.

63. S. M. Miller and Pamela Roby, "Poverty: Changing Social Stratification," in *On Understanding Poverty: Perspectives from the Social Sciences,* ed. Daniel P. Moynihan (New York: Basic Books, 1968), p. 71; Eric F. Goldman, *The Tragedy of Lyndon Johnson* (New York: Knopf, 1969), p. 41.

64. Gilbert Steiner, *Social Insecurity: The Politics of Welfare* (Chicago: Rand McNally, 1966), p. 3.

65. Walter Heller, in *1964 House Committee Hearings,* vol. 1, p. 29; Roman Pucinski, in *Congressional Record* 110 (June 3, 1964):12518, and (Aug. 6, 1964):18298; Pat McNamara, in *Congressional Record* 110 (July 22, 1964):16661; Ralph Yarborough, in *Congressional Record* 110 (July 22, 1964):16630.

66. Johnson, *Public Papers, 1963–64,* vol. 1, pp. 411, 480, 483; vol. 2, pp. 989, 1360.

67. Phil Landrum, quoted in *Congressional Record* 110 (Aug. 5, 1964):18208.

68. John C. Donovan, *The Politics of Poverty* (New York: Pegasus, 1967), p. 118; Murphy, "Involving the Poor," p. 26; "OEO Administrative History," p. 21; "Why Should Conservatives Support the War on Poverty?" unsigned memorandum, May 26, 1964, Executive File WE 9, Box 25, Lyndon Baines Johnson Library. Levitan argues, furthermore, that the expectation of cuts in the defense budget was a major factor in the support of the poverty program by businesses seeking a new opportunity for government contracts. See Levitan, *The Great Society's Poor Law,* p. 83.

69. Humphrey, *War on Poverty,* p. 25.

70. Lyndon B. Johnson, "Statement on 'The Great Society,' " cabinet meeting, Nov. 19, 1964, Executive File WE 9, Box 25, Lyndon Baines Johnson Library.

71. Sargent Shriver, quoted in *1964 Senate Committee Hearings,* p. 55.

72. Sargent Shriver, quoted in *1964 House Committee Hearings,* vol. 3, p. 1535.

73. Johnson, *The Vantage Point,* p. 76.

74. Bibby and Davidson, *On Capitol Hill,* p. 232n.

75. Harry M. Scoble, "The Political Scientist's Perspective on Poverty," in *Poverty: New Interdisciplinary Perspectives,* ed. Thomas Weaver and Alan Magid (San Francisco: Chandler, 1969), p. 137.

76. Donovan, *The Politics of Poverty,* p. 34.

77. Graham, "Poverty and the Legislative Process," p. 257.

78. Roman Pucinski, quoted in *1964 House Committee Hearings,* vol. 2, p. 773.

79. Murphy, "Involving the Poor," p. 28.

80. Adam Clayton Powell, in *1964 House Committee Hearings,* vol. 1, p. 64; vol. 3, p. 1150.

81. *1964 Senate Committee Report,* p. 71.

82. Warren G. Magnuson, quoted in *Congressional Record* 110 (July 23, 1964):16743.

83. Cited in Alfred Steinberg, *Sam Johnson's Boy: A Close-Up of the President from Texas* (New York: Macmillan, 1968), p. 660.

84. Johnson, *The Vantage Point,* p. 80.

85. Rowland Evans and Robert Novak, "The Yarmolinsky Affair," *Esquire* 63 (Feb. 1965):80–81.

Chapter 3

1. Kenneth Burke, *Attitudes toward History* (1937; reprint ed., Boston: Beacon Press, 1959), p. 139.

2. Thomas Payne, quoted in Senate Committee on Labor and Public Welfare, *Examination of the War on Poverty,* hearings, 90th Cong., 1st sess., 1967, vol. 4, p. 1294 (hereafter *1967 Senate Committee Hearings*).

3. Senate Committee on Labor and Public Welfare, *Economic Opportunity Amendments of 1966,* S. Rept. 89-1666, 89th Cong., 2d sess., 1966, p. 3 (hereafter *1966 Senate Committee Report*). Specifically, according to the figures fewer than 30 percent of poor children had been affected by Head Start; only 10 percent of the elderly poor and 15 percent of the rural poor had been affected by any OEO program; and only 25 percent of school dropouts between the ages of sixteen and twenty-one had been affected by the Job Corps or the Neighborhood Youth Corps.

4. Gregory Farrell, "The View from the City: Community Action in Trenton," *On Fighting Poverty: Perspectives from Experience,* ed. James L. Sundquist (New York: Basic Books,

1969), p. 151; Paul Jacobs, *Prelude to Riot: A View of Urban America from the Bottom* (New York: Random House, 1966), p. 286.

5. McPherson, *A Political Education,* p. 298; John Kenneth Galbraith, *Who Needs the Democrats?* (New York: Signet Books, 1970), pp. 60–62.

6. See, for instance, Erwin Knoll and Jules Witcover, "Maximum Feasible Publicity: The War on Poverty's Campaign to Capture the Press," *Columbia Journalism Review* 5 (Fall 1966):34–35; Richard W. Boone, in *1967 Senate Committee Hearings,* vol. 1, p. 230; and House Committee on Education and Labor, *Economic Opportunity Act Amendments of 1967,* hearings, 90th Cong., 1st sess., 1967, vol. 4, p. 3018 (hereafter *1967 House Committee Hearings*).

7. Nan Robertson, "A New Era in Naming Projects," *New York Times,* Feb. 13, 1966, p. 55. Robertson reports, for instance, that Shriver insisted upon approving all titles. Among the proposed names for the agency were "War on Poverty" and "War against Poverty." The former was rejected because its initials would offend Italians; the latter, because its initials sounded "like a pop art word." Nor did Shriver wish to imitate the "alphabet agencies" of the New Deal.

8. U.S. Office of Economic Opportunity, *Public Affairs Handbook* (Washington: U.S. Government Printing Office, 1967), pp. 2, 6, 12; Herbert Kramer, "Communicating," *Communities in Action* 1 (1966):3.

9. Knoll and Witcover, "Maximum Feasible Publicity," p. 33.

10. House Committee on Education and Labor, "Minority Views," *Economic Opportunity Act Amendments of 1967,* H. Rept. 90-866, 90th Cong., 1st sess., 1967, p. 193 (hereafter *1967 House Committee Report*).

11. Knoll and Witcover, "Maximum Feasible Publicity," p. 40.

12. See Levitan, *The Great Society's Poor Law,* pp. 98–99.

13. Johnson, *Public Papers, 1965* (Washington: U.S. Government Printing Office, 1966), vol. 1, p. 200.

14. Sargent Shriver, quoted in House Committee on Education and Labor, *Examination of War on Poverty Program,* hearings, 89th Cong., 1st sess., 1965, p. 27 (hereafter *1965 House Committee Hearings*).

15. Sargent Shriver, "Poverty in the United States—What Next?" in *The Social Welfare Forum, 1965* (New York: Columbia University Press, 1965), pp. 62–64.

16. U.S. Office of Economic Opportunity, *The Quiet Revolution: Second Annual Report, Fiscal Year 1966* (Washington: U.S. Government Printing Office, 1967), p. 4.

17. U.S. Office of Economic Opportunity, *A Nation Aroused: First Annual Report* (Washington: U.S. Government Printing Office, 1966), p. 7.

18. Sargent Shriver, quoted in House Committee on Education and Labor, *1966 Amendments to the Economic Opportunity Act of 1964,* hearings, 89th Cong., 2d sess., vol. 1, p. 146 (hereafter *1966 House Committee Hearings*).

19. U.S. Office of Economic Opportunity, *Public Affairs Handbook,* p. 30.

20. Roman Pucinski, quoted in *Congressional Record* 112 (Sept. 27, 1966):24002; Robert F. Kennedy, quoted in *Congressional Record* 112 (Oct. 3, 1966):24794.

21. Johnson, *Public Papers, 1965,* vol. 1, p. 199; *Public Papers, 1967* (Washington: U.S. Government Printing Office, 1968), vol. 1, p. 641.

22. Sargent Shriver, quoted in Senate Committee on Labor and Public Welfare, *Amendments to the Economic Opportunity Act of 1964,* hearings, 89th Cong., 2d sess., 1966, p. 47 (hereafter *1966 Senate Committee Hearings*).

23. Joseph A. Kershaw, *Government against Poverty* (Washington: Brookings Institution, 1970), p. 147. Kershaw had been director of the Office of Research, Plans, Programs, and Evaluation during much of the time that this five-year plan was prepared. See also "OEO Administrative History."

24. Levitan, *The Great Society's Poor Law,* p. 97.

25. Sargent Shriver, in Senate Committee on Government

Operations, *Federal Role in Urban Affairs,* 90th Cong., 1st sess., vol. 2, p. 448 (hereafter cited only as *Federal Role in Urban Affairs*). Shriver maintained that the 1976 target date would require a commitment to the War on Poverty equal to half the fiscal dividend (the increase in governmental revenues predicted to result from the rising gross national product), and insisted that he had said as much to the original committee.

26. Robert A. Levine, in *1967 Senate Committee Hearings,* vol. 9, p. 2754.

27. "More Nonsense on Poverty," *New York Times,* June 28, 1966, p. 44.

28. George Murphy, quoted in *1967 Senate Committee Hearings,* vol. 1, p. 10.

29. Roman Pucinski, in House Committee on Education and Labor, *Antipoverty in the District of Columbia,* hearings before the Task Force on Antipoverty in the District of Columbia, 89th Cong., 2d sess., 1966, p. 57 (hereafter *Antipoverty in D.C.*).

30. Edith Green, quoted in *1967 House Committee Hearings,* vol. 1, pp. 813–14.

31. Blue Carstenson, *1967 Senate Committee Hearings,* vol. 1, p. 251. Carstenson was assistant legislative director of the National Farmers Union.

32. Ben B. Seligman, *Permanent Poverty: An American Syndrome* (Chicago: Quadrangle, 1968), p. 178.

33. Charles Goodell, in *1967 House Committee Hearings,* vol. 1, p. 84.

34. Roman Pucinski, in *Antipoverty in D.C.,* pp. 57, 59.

35. William H. Ayres, *Congressional Record* 111 (July 20, 1965):17488; House Committee on Education and Labor, *Economic Opportunity Act Amendments of 1966,* H. Rept. 89-1568, 89th Cong., 2d sess., 1966, p. 91 (hereafter *1966 House Committee Report*); Charles Goodell, in House Committee on Rules, *Economic Opportunity Act Amendments of 1966,* hearings, 89th Cong., 2d sess., 1966, vol. 3, p. 124 (hereafter *1966 Rules Committee Hearings*).

36. George Murphy, in *1967 Senate Committee Hearings,*

vol. 1, pp. 11, 19; Winston L. Prouty, in *1967 Senate Committee Hearings,* vol. 4, p. 1341; Dave Martin, in *Congressional Record* 112 (Sept. 26, 1966):23773.

37. A. V. Sorensen, in *Federal Role in Urban Affairs,* vol. 4, p. 1049; Charles Goodell, in *1966 Rules Committee Hearings,* vol. 4, p. 136; Paul Fino, "Controversy over the Federal Job Corps," *Congressional Digest* 47 (Jan. 1968):23; A. Philip Randolph, in *Federal Role in Urban Affairs,* vol. 9, p. 1892; John Lindsay, in *1967 Senate Committee Hearings,* vol. 6, p. 1833; Augustus F. Hawkins, in *Congressional Record* 113 (Nov. 15, 1967):32637; Hugh Scott, in *Congressional Record* 113 (Sept. 26, 1967):26806; George Murphy, in *1967 Senate Committee Hearings,* vol. 10, p. 3302; Winston L. Prouty, in *1967 Senate Committee Hearings,* vol. 9, p. 2723.

38. This episode is described in Levitan, *The Great Society's Poor Law,* p. 289; and in *1967 House Committee Hearings,* vol. 3, p. 1667.

39. Kenneth B. Clark, in *1967 Senate Committee Hearings,* vol. 1, p. 307; Robert A. Levine, *The Poor Ye Need Not Have with You: Lessons from the War on Poverty* (Cambridge, Mass.: MIT Press, 1970), p. 92; S. M. Miller and Pamela Roby, "The War on Poverty Reconsidered," in *Poverty: Views from the Left,* ed. Jeremy Larner and Irving Howe (New York: Morrow, 1968), p. 69.

40. Cited in *Federal Role in Urban Affairs,* vol. 18, p. 3894.

41. Robert C. Weaver, in *Federal Role in Urban Affairs,* vol. 18, p. 3699; Herbert J. Gans, in *Federal Role in Urban Affairs,* vol. 11, p. 2410; William F. Haddad, "Mr. Shriver and the Savage Politics of Poverty," *Harper's* 231 (Dec. 1965):50.

42. "Humphrey's Stand Criticized by Ford," *New York Times,* July 23, 1966, p. 9; Albert H. Quie, in *Congressional Record* 112 (Sept. 26, 1966):23767; A. V. Sorensen, in *Federal Role in Urban Affairs,* vol. 4, p. 1050; David R. Jones, "G.O.P. Links Riots to Johnson Policy," *New York Times,* June 3, 1968, pp. 1, 38.

43. The Lemberg data are cited in Walter Lorenzo Walker, "The War on Poverty and the Poor: A Study of Race, Poverty,

and a Program" (Ph.D. diss., Brandeis University, 1969), p. 47. For comparison, see Angus Campbell and Howard Schuman, "Racial Attitudes in Fifteen American Cities," and Peter H. Rossi, Richard A. Berk, David P. Boesel, Bettye K. Eidson, and W. Eugene Groves, "Between White and Black: The Faces of American Institutions in the Ghetto," in *Supplemental Studies for the National Advisory Commission on Civil Disorders* (New York: Praeger, 1968), pp. 1–67, 69–215.

44. Nan Robertson, "Reuther Asks for More Poverty Funds," *New York Times*, Apr. 14, 1966, p. 25.

45. Andrew Kopkind, "By or For the Poor?" in *Poverty: Power and Politics*, ed. Chaim I. Waxman (New York: Grosset and Dunlap, 1968), p. 227.

46. The quotations from Shriver's remarks are based on Louise Lander, ed., *War on Poverty* (New York: Facts on File, 1967), p. 140.

47. Nan Robertson, "Shriver Explains Convention Boos," *New York Times*, Apr. 19, 1966, p. 44.

48. Kopkind, "By or For the Poor?" p. 226.

49. James S. Coleman, *Community Conflict* (Glencoe: Free Press, 1957).

50. Charles Goodell, in *1967 House Committee Hearings*, vol. 1, p. 813.

51. Sargent Shriver, in *1967 House Committee Hearings*, vol. 4, pp. 3468–3469.

52. Knoll and Witcover, "Maximum Feasible Publicity," p. 34; Office of Economic Opportunity, *A News Summary of the War on Poverty* 2 (Aug. 28, 1967):2.

53. Knoll and Witcover, "Maximum Feasible Publicity," p. 34; Arthur B. Shostak, "Old Problems and New Agencies: How Much Change?" *Power, Poverty, and Urban Policy*, ed. Warner Bloomberg, Jr., and Henry J. Schmandt (Beverly Hills, Calif.: Sage Publications, 1968), p. 78.

54. Johnson, *Public Papers, 1967*, vol. 1, p. 333; *Public Papers, 1968–69* (Washington: U.S. Government Printing Office, 1970), vol. 2, p. 1062. Similar explanations were offered in "OEO Administrative History," p. 661.

55. Charles Goodell, in *Congressional Record* 112 (Sept. 27, 1966):23987.

56. Stephan Thernstrom, *Poverty, Planning, and Politics in the New Boston: The Origins of ABCD* (New York: Basic Books, 1969), p. 47.

57. Frances Fox Piven, "Federal Intervention in the Cities: The New Urban Programs as a Political Strategy," *Handbook on the Study of Social Problems,* ed. Erwin O. Smigel (Chicago: Rand McNally, 1971), p. 604.

58. Richard F. Fenno, Jr., *The Power of the Purse: Appropriations Politics in Congress* (Boston: Little, Brown, 1966), pp. 280, 286, 337, 338.

59. David Braybrooke and Charles E. Lindblom, *A Strategy of Decision* (New York: Free Press, 1963), p. 31.

60. Fenno, *The Power of the Purse,* pp. 17, 99–100, 316.

61. Fenno, *The Power of the Purse,* p. 370. Examples include the Federal Bureau of Investigation, the Food and Drug Administration, the Bureau of Narcotics, the Customs Bureau, and the Immigration and Naturalization Service.

62. Albert H. Quie, in *1966 Rules Committee Hearings,* vol. 3, p. 111.

63. See, for example, "Minority Views," *1966 House Committee Report,* p. 92; *Congressional Record* 112 (Sept. 26, 1966):23761.

64. See, for example, Goldman, *The Tragedy of Lyndon Johnson,* p. 242; Rowland Evans and Robert Novak, *Lyndon B. Johnson: The Exercise of Power* (New York: New American Library, 1966), pp. 107, 109. See also Kearns, *Lyndon Johnson and the American Dream,* p. 204, on Johnson's tendency to withdraw from possible conflict.

65. Sam Gibbons, quoted in *Congressional Record* 112 (Sept. 26, 1966):23763.

66. Levine, *The Poor Ye Need Not Have with You,* p. 62.

67. Letter from Elmer B. Staats to Sargent Shriver, Aug. 27, 1965, in "OEO Administrative History," documentary supplement; memorandum from Sargent Shriver to Charles L.

Schultze, Dec. 17, 1965, in "OEO Administrative History," documentary supplement. See also "OEO Administrative History," pp. 608, 622.

68. Sargent Shriver, Senate Committee on Labor and Public Welfare, *Expand the War on Poverty,* hearings, 89th Cong., 1st sess., 1965, p. 75 (hereafter *1965 Senate Committee Hearings*); "Shriver Discounts Politics on Poverty," *New York Times,* Apr. 19, 1965, p. 59.

69. Memorandum from Charles L. Schultze to the President, Dec. 28, 1966, Executive File WE 9, Box 28, Lyndon Baines Johnson Library.

70. Winston Prouty, in *Congressional Record* 112 (Oct. 3, 1966):24793.

71. *Congressional Record* 112 (Oct. 4, 1966):25138. In describing his amendment, Dirksen said that President Johnson "fulminated like Hurricane Inez" about congressional authorizations which exceeded the administration's budget. See L. Lander, *War on Poverty,* p. 40.

72. On the alleged reduction in the OEO budget request, see the colloquy between Sargent Shriver and Joseph S. Clark, in *1967 Senate Committee Hearings,* vol. 9, p. 2712; Joseph S. Clark, in *Congressional Record* 112 (Sept. 30, 1966):24735; Winston Prouty, in *Congressional Record* 112 (Oct. 3, 1966):24793; "OEO Administrative History," pp. 559, 610.

73. Sargent Shriver, quoted in Donovan, *The Politics of Poverty,* p. 91. Kearns argues that this judgment of priorities was made because President Johnson had not sought to generate a wartime mood of sacrifice (Kearns, *Lyndon Johnson and the American Dream,* p. 298).

74. Wayne Morse, quoted in *Congressional Record* 112 (Oct. 4, 1966):25121.

75. John V. Lindsay, in *1966 Senate Committee Hearings,* pp. 237–38.

76. Memorandum from Charles L. Schultze to the President, Nov. 7, 1966, Executive File WE 9, Box 28, Lyndon Baines Johnson Library.

77. Letter from Sargent Shriver to Charles L. Schultze, Oct. 1, 1965, Reports on Enrolled Legislation, P.L. 89-253, Lyndon Baines Johnson Library.

78. Johnson, *Economic Report of the President* (1967), p. 16; Johnson, *Public Papers, 1968–69,* vol. 1, p. 720.

79. Johnson, *Public Papers, 1967,* vol. 1, pp. 657, 54.

80. These causes are suggested by Donald H. Haider, "Governors and Mayors View the Poverty Program," *Current History* 61 (Nov. 1971):274; Samuel E. Deets, "The Anti-Poverty Program: A Study in Professionalized Reform" (Ph.D. diss., University of Cincinnati, 1970), p. 177. An inspection of government documents will suggest that the administration did not want to make this equation. In the 1967 annual report of the Council of Economic Advisers, community action was discussed under the heading "Urban Problems"; Head Start and related programs were discussed under "Education." The section headed "Poverty" was concerned mainly with income maintenance (Johnson, *Economic Report of the President* [1967], pp. 20, 159).

Chapter 4

1. B. F. Sisk, quoted in *Congressional Record* 112 (Sept. 26, 1966):23755. Sisk was quoting from the 1966 report of the House Committee on Education and Labor. See *1966 House Committee Report.*

2. For example, Willard Wirtz, in *1966 Senate Committee Hearings,* p. 128; Johnson, *Public Papers, 1965,* vol. 1, p. 482.

3. U.S. Office of Economic Opportunity, *A Nation Aroused: First Annual Report, Fiscal Year 1965* (Washington: U.S. Government Printing Office, 1966), p. 33; *1966 House Committee Hearings,* vol. 2, p. 780; Robert F. Kennedy, in *Federal Role in Urban Affairs,* vol. 10, p. 2176.

4. Levine, *The Poor Ye Need Not Have with You,* pp. 132, 142.

5. Senate Committee on Labor and Public Welfare, *Review*

of Economic Opportunity Programs by the Comptroller General of the United States Made Pursuant to Title II of the 1967 Amendments to the Economic Opportunity Act of 1964, Joint Committee Print, 91st Cong., 1st sess., p. 67 (hereafter *Review by the Comptroller General*).

6. Levine, *The Poor Ye Need Not Have with You,* p. 129; Kershaw, *Government against Poverty,* p. 30; Johnson, *Public Papers, 1967,* vol. 1, p. 494.

7. John N. Erlenborn, in *Congressional Record* 112 (Sept. 29, 1966):24416.

8. Kenneth B. Clark, in *1967 Senate Committee Hearings,* vol. 1, p. 300; Stokely Carmichael and Charles V. Hamilton, *Black Power: The Politics of Liberation in America* (New York: Vintage Books, 1967), p. 161.

9. Kershaw, *Government against Poverty,* p. 30; Richard A. Cloward and Robert Ontell, "Our Illusions about Training," *American Child* 47 (1965):10.

10. Sargent Shriver, in *1966 House Committee Hearings,* vol. 1, p. 151.

11. Willard Wirtz, in *1966 House Committee Hearings,* vol. 1, p. 348; William H. Ayres, in *Congressional Record* 112 (Sept. 26, 1966):23769; A. Philip Randolph, in *Federal Role in Urban Affairs,* vol. 9, p. 1993.

12. *1967 House Committee Report,* p. 14; U.S. Office of Economic Opportunity, *As the Seed Is Sown: Fourth Annual Report, 1968* (Washington: U.S. Government Printing Office, 1969), p. 69.

13. Willard Wirtz, cited in *1967 House Committee Hearings,* vol. 2, p. 1262; John W. Gardner, in *1966 Senate Committee Hearings,* p. 209.

14. James Ridgeway, "The More Glorious War," *New Republic* 154 (Mar. 26, 1966):7.

15. "Individual Views of Senator Murphy," *1966 Senate Committee Report,* p. 91. The same theme is noted in "OEO Administrative History," pp. 93, 94, 496.

16. Paul Fino, in *Congressional Record* 112 (Sept. 27, 1966):23976.

17. See Levitan, *The Great Society's Poor Law,* p. 285; "OEO Administrative History," p. 482n.

18. Sargent Shriver, in *1966 Senate Committee Hearings,* p. 60.

19. Sargent Shriver, in *1966 Senate Committee Hearings,* p. 59; Shriver, in House Committee on Appropriations, *Supplemental Appropriation Bill, 1967,* hearings, 89th Cong., 2d sess. (1966), vol. 1, p. 10.

20. U.S. Office of Economic Opportunity, *The Quiet Revolution,* p. 18.

21. Letter from Sargent Shriver to the Editor, *Washington Post,* Mar. 15, 1965, Executive File WE 9, Box 26, Lyndon Baines Johnson Library.

22. Sargent Shriver, in House, *Supplemental Appropriation Bill, 1967,* vol. 1, p. 9.

23. Adam Clayton Powell, in *1966 House Committee Hearings,* vol. 1, p. 288; memorandum from Sargent Shriver to the President, Oct. 20, 1965, Executive File WE 9, Box 26, Lyndon Baines Johnson Library.

24. Robert F. Kennedy, *Congressional Record* 112 (Oct. 3, 1966):24795. The administration had rejected an employment program when it decided not to include in the original Economic Opportunity Act Senator Gaylord Nelson's proposal that a job-creation program be financed by a special five-cent tax on cigarettes (see Daniel P. Moynihan, "The Professors and the Poor," *Commentary* 46 [Aug. 1968]:22; "5-Cent Rise Asked in Cigarette Tax," *New York Times,* Jan. 28, 1964, p. 14).

25. *Review by the Comptroller General,* p. 8.

26. Sargent Shriver, in *1967 Senate Committee Hearings,* vol. 9, p. 2950.

27. Johnson, *Economic Report of the President* (1968), p. 142; *Economic Report of the President* (1969), p. 159; memorandum from Sargent Shriver to the President, Jan. 4, 1968, Executive File WE 9, Box 31, Lyndon Baines Johnson Library.

28. President's Commission on Income Maintenance Programs, *Poverty amid Plenty: The American Paradox* (Washington: U.S. Government Printing Office, 1969), p. 37.

29. U.S. Office of Economic Opportunity, *The Watershed, A New Look at the War on Poverty* (Washington: U.S. Government Printing Office, 1967), p. 3.

30. See Cater, "The Politics of Poverty," pp. 16–20.

31. Walker, "The War on Poverty and the Poor," p. 20. The riot study is quoted in *Federal Role in Urban Affairs,* vol. 18, p. 3894.

32. Cited in Walker, "The War on Poverty and the Poor," p. 40. Similar findings were obtained in a supplemental study for the National Advisory Commission, popularly known as the Kerner Commission (see Angus Campbell and Howard Schuman, "Racial Attitudes in Fifteen American Cities," in *Supplemental Studies for the National Advisory Commission on Civil Disorders* [New York: Praeger, 1968], p. 41).

33. Walker, "The War on Poverty and the Poor," p. 55.

34. Walker, "The War on Poverty and the Poor," pp. 33, 41, 124.

35. Kenneth B. Clark, "The Negro and the Urban Crisis," in *Agenda for the Nation,* ed. Kermit Gordon (Washington: Brookings Institution, 1968), pp. 129–30; [Clark and Hopkins], *A Relevant War against Poverty,* p. 185.

36. Walker, "The War on Poverty and the Poor," p. 1.

37. Cited in William F. Soskin, "Riots, Ghettos, and the 'Negro Revolt,' " *Unemployment, Race, and Poverty,* ed. Arthur M. Ross and Herbert Hill (New York: Harcourt, Brace, and World, 1967), p. 225.

38. Quoted in Homer Bigart, " 'System' Blamed for Negro Riots," *New York Times,* Aug. 2, 1967, p. 17.

39. Sterling Tucker, *Beyond the Burning: Life and Death of the Ghetto* (New York: Association Press, 1968), p. 10.

40. On inability to delay gratification, see Warren C. Haggstrom, "The Power of the Poor," in *Poverty: Power and Politics,* ed. Chaim I. Waxman (New York: Grosset and Dunlap, 1968), pp. 114–15; S. M. Miller, Frank Riessman, and Arthur A. Seagull, "Poverty and Self-Indulgence: A Critique of the Non-Deferred Gratification Pattern," in *Poverty in America,* ed. Louis A. Ferman, Joyce L. Kornbluh, and Alan Haber

(Ann Arbor: University of Michigan Press, 1965), p. 286. On fatalism, see, for example, E. S. Battle and J. B. Rotter, "Children's Feeling of Personal Control as Related to Social Class and Ethnic Group," *Journal of Personality* 31 (1963):489. The classic study on social-class differences in linguistic habits is Basil Bernstein, "Some Sociological Determinants of Perception," *British Journal of Sociology* 9 (1958):159–74; for an adaptation of this theme to the United States, see Catherine S. Chilman, "Child-Rearing and Family Life Patterns of the Very Poor: Implications for Home Economists," *Working with Low-Income Families* (Washington: American Home Economics Association, 1965), p. 51. On low levels of aspiration, see Herbert H. Hyman, "The Value Systems of Different Classes," *Class, Status, and Power,* ed. Reinhard Bendix and Seymour Martin Lipset, 2d ed. (New York: Free Press, 1966), p. 490.

41. A. R. Mahrer, "The Role of Expectancy in Delayed Reinforcement," *Journal of Experimental Psychology* 42 (1956):101–106, cited in Miller, Riessman, and Seagull, "Poverty and Self-Indulgence," p. 299.

42. Haggstrom, "The Power of the Poor," p. 117; Vernon L. Allen, ed., *Psychological Factors in Poverty* (Chicago: Markham, 1970), p. 251; Helene Levens, "Organizational Affiliation and Powerlessness: A Case Study of the Welfare Poor," *Social Problems* 16 (Summer 1968):26.

43. See, generally, Frederick Williams, ed., *Language and Poverty* (Chicago: Markham, 1971).

44. David C. McClelland, "Toward a Theory of Motive Acquisition," *American Psychologist* 20 (1965):321–33.

45. The President's Commission on Income Maintenance found in 1966 that 70 percent of the nonaged heads of poor families worked for some part of the year and that most of the remainder were ill, disabled, or women with young children and absent husbands (President's Commission on Income Maintenance Programs, *Poverty amid Plenty,* p. 3).

46. See especially, Charles A. Valentine, *Culture and Poverty: Critique and Counter-Proposals* (Chicago: University of Chicago Press, 1968); Allen, *Psychological Factors,* p. 372;

Louis Kriesberg, *Mothers in Poverty* (Chicago: Aldine, 1970), p. 290.

47. Kenneth B. Clark, in *Federal Role in Urban Affairs*, vol. 13, p. 2758.

48. On the social function of victimage, see especially Kenneth Burke, *Permanence and Change* (1935; reprint ed., Indianapolis: Bobbs-Merrill, 1965), pp. 283–94. Ryan has provided an operational definition of victimage in regard to social problems, consisting of four steps: (1) identify a social problem; (2) study those who are affected by it, and determine in what ways they are different from others; (3) identify the differences to be the cause of the problem; (4) devise governmental intervention addressed to the differences, rather than to the true underlying causes. Ryan applies this process to a range of contemporary social problems (see William Ryan, *Blaming the Victim* [New York: Random House, 1971], esp. pp. 5, 8).

49. William L. O'Neill, *Coming Apart: An Informal History of America in the 1960's* (Chicago: Quadrangle, 1971), p. 128.

50. George Gallup, "Two Basically Different Views Held on Causes of Poverty," *Poverty and Affluence,* ed. Robert E. Will and Harold G. Vatter, 2d ed. (New York: Harcourt, Brace, and World, 1970), p. 45; Robert H. Lauer, "The Middle Class Looks at Poverty," *Urban and Social Change Review* 5 (Fall 1971):8.

51. Scott Briar, "Welfare from Below: Recipients' Views of the Public Welfare System," *California Law Review* 54 (1966):380, 382; Neil Gilbert and Joseph W. Eaton, "Who Speaks for the Poor?" *Journal of the American Institute of Planners* 36 (Nov. 1971):415; Joel F. Handler and Ellen Jane Hollingsworth, *The "Deserving Poor": A Study of Welfare Administration* (Chicago: Markham, 1971), p. 146.

52. Richard A. Cloward and Richard M. Elman, "The First Congress of the Poor," *Nation* 202 (Feb. 7, 1966):148.

53. T. M. Tomlinson, "The Development of a Riot Ideology among American Negroes," *Racial Violence in the United States,* ed. Allen D. Grimshaw (Chicago: Aldine, 1969), p. 232.

54. "Los Angeles Riot Study—Negro Attitudes toward the Riot," quoted in *Federal Role in Urban Affairs,* vol. 18, p. 3874.

55. The Lemberg study is quoted in *Federal Role in Urban Affairs,* vol. 20, p. 4314; the Rossi study, in Rossi, Berk, Boesel, Eidson, and Groves, "Between White and Black," pp. 88–89, 129.

56. Ralph S. Locher, in *Federal Role in Urban Affairs,* vol. 4, p. 1035.

57. Robert M. Fogelson, *Violence as Protest* (Garden City, N.Y.: Doubleday, 1971), pp. 12–13. See also Lewis A. Coser, *Continuities in the Study of Social Conflict* (New York: Free Press, 1967), p. 97; Paul Jacobs, *Prelude to Riot: A View of Urban America from the Bottom* (New York: Random House, 1966), p. 9; Edelman, *Politics as Symbolic Action,* p. 124.

58. Fogelson, *Violence as Protest,* pp. 179–80. The poll was reported originally in the Sept. 8, 1967, issue of *Congressional Quarterly.*

59. Winston L. Prouty, in *1967 Senate Committee Hearings,* vol. 10, p. 3272.

60. Leo Bernstein, in *1967 House Committee Hearings,* vol. 4, pp. 3537, 3557; Frank Addonizio, in *1967 House Committee Hearings,* vol. 4, pp. 3540, 3557.

61. Sargent Shriver, in *1967 House Committee Hearings,* vol. 4, pp. 3419–3421; Shriver, in *Federal Role in Urban Affairs,* vol. 20, p. 4320; memorandum from Sargent Shriver to the President, Sept. 12, 1967, Executive File WE 9, Box 30, Lyndon Baines Johnson Library.

62. Senate Committee on Labor and Public Welfare, *Economic Opportunity Amendments of 1967,* S. Rept. 90-563, 90th Cong., 1st sess., 1967, p. 38 (hereafter *1967 Senate Committee Report*).

63. Sargent Shriver, in *1967 House Committee Hearings,* vol. 4, p. 3418.

64. Paul Fino, quoted in *Congressional Record* 112 (Sept. 27, 1966):23975; James C. Gardner, quoted in *1967 House Committee Hearings,* vol. 4, p. 3478.

65. Details of the approval, and subsequent cancellation, of

the Black Arts Theatre grant may be found in "OEO Administrative History," pp. 118–22.

66. J. David Greenstone and Paul E. Peterson, "Reformers, Machines, and the War on Poverty," in *City Politics and Public Policy*, ed. James Q. Wilson (New York: Wiley, 1968), p. 288.

67. Whitney Young, in *1967 Senate Committee Hearings*, vol. 7, p. 2202. See also Whitney Young, in *Federal Role in Urban Affairs*, vol. 14, p. 2923.

68. National Advisory Commission on Civil Disorders, *Report* (New York: Bantam Books, 1968), p. 140.

69. Robert A. Levine, quoted in *1967 House Committee Hearings*, vol. 2, p. 1050.

70. Jake Pickle, quoted in *Congressional Record* 112 (Sept. 27, 1966):23979.

71. Quoted in U.S. Office of Economic Opportunity, *A News Summary of the War on Poverty* 2 (July 31, 1967):2.

72. Cited in Joseph A. Loftus, "Role of Poverty Funds as Riot Deterrent Assayed," *New York Times*, July 26, 1967, p. 18.

73. For example, see Tomlinson, "The Development of a Riot Ideology," p. 230; Rossi, Berk, Boesel, Eidson, and Groves, "Between White and Black," p. 74; *Federal Role in Urban Affairs*, vol. 20, p. 4311. The last citation is to a reprint of the text of the riot study done at the Lemberg Center of Brandeis University.

74. Quoted in "Riots Held Peril to Poverty Drive," *New York Times*, Aug. 1, 1967, p. 17.

75. Sargent Shriver, "New Weapons in Fighting Poverty," *Public Welfare* 24 (Jan. 1966):10.

Chapter 5

1. Sargent Shriver, in *Federal Role in Urban Affairs*, vol. 2, pp. 393, 397; Shriver, "Draft Message on the Disadvantaged," Executive File SP 2-3/1967/WE 9, Box 8, Lyndon Baines Johnson Library. The president did not use this language in his address to Congress.

2. Theodore M. Berry, in *1966 Senate Committee Hearings,* p. 49.

3. U.S. Office of Economic Opportunity, *The Quiet Revolution,* p. 11.

4. Theodore C. Sorensen, *The Kennedy Legacy* (New York: Macmillan, 1969), p. 334.

5. Sargent Shriver, "The Controversy over the Federal Antipoverty Program: Pro and Con," *Congressional Digest* 45 (Mar. 1966):82.

6. Robert F. Wagner, quoted in *1964 House Committee Hearings,* vol. 2, p. 728; Richard J. Daley, quoted in *1964 House Committee Hearings,* vol. 2, p. 768; Raymond R. Tucker, in *1964 House Committee Hearings,* vol. 2, p. 790; C. Beverly Briley, in *1964 House Committee Hearings,* vol. 3, p. 1467; William F. Walsh, quoted in *1964 House Committee Hearings,* vol. 2, p. 822.

7. John F. Shelley, quoted in Donovan, *The Politics of Poverty,* p. 55; Robert F. Wagner, in *1965 House Committee Hearings,* p. 483; Sam Yorty, quoted by George Murphy, in *1965 Senate Committee Hearings,* p. 40.

8. The details of the Shelley-Yorty resolution are drawn largely from Ben A. Franklin, "Mayors Challenge Antipoverty Plan," *New York Times,* June 1, 1965, p. 30; Franklin, "Mayors Shelve Dispute," p. 20; Joseph A. Loftus, "Mayors Assured of Poverty Role," *New York Times,* June 8, 1965, p. 49. Humphrey's sentiments are described in Loftus, p. 49.

9. See, generally, Lester W. Milbrath, *Political Participation* (Chicago: Rand McNally, 1965), esp. pp. 70, 78. See also Zahava D. Blum and Peter H. Rossi, "Social Class Research and Images of the Poor: A Bibliographic Review," in *On Understanding Poverty: Perspectives from the Social Sciences,* ed. Daniel P. Moynihan (New York: Basic Books, 1968), pp. 358–59; Tomlinson, "The Development of a Riot Ideology," p. 229; National Advisory Commission on Civil Disorders, *Report,* p. 286.

10. Michael Lipsky and Margaret Levi, "Community Organization as a Political Resource," in *People and Politics in*

Urban Society, ed. Harlan Hahn (Beverly Hills, Calif.: Sage Publications, 1972), p. 175. See also Schattschneider, *The Semisovereign People,* p. 105.

11. Sargent Shriver, in *Federal Role in Urban Affairs,* vol. 2, p. 397.

12. Sargent Shriver, in *1965 House Committee Hearings,* p. 20.

13. Sargent Shriver, "Poverty in the United States—What Next?" in *The Social Welfare Forum, 1965* (New York: Columbia University Press, 1965), pp. 60–61.

14. Shriver, "The Controversy," p. 82.

15. James H. Scheuer, in *1966 House Committee Hearings,* vol. 1, pp. 139–40.

16. Elmer J. Holland, in *1967 House Committee Hearings,* vol. 4, p. 3581.

17. U.S. Office of Economic Opportunity, *Community Action Program Guide, Volume I: Instructions for Applicants* (Washington: U.S. Government Printing Office, 1965), pp. 16, 21.

18. Sargent Shriver, in *Federal Role in Urban Affairs,* vol. 6, p. 1277. For a similar expression of Shriver's view, see letter from Sargent Shriver to Adam Clayton Powell, Aug. 26, 1966, "OEO Administrative History."

19. Albert H. Quie, in *1966 House Committee Hearings,* vol. 1, p. 498. See also Adam Clayton Powell, in *Federal Role in Urban Affairs,* vol. 6, p. 1277.

20. Bernard Boutin, in *1966 House Committee Hearings,* vol. 2, p. 825.

21. Seligman, *Permanent Poverty,* p. 211.

22. Adam Clayton Powell, in *1965 House Committee Hearings,* p. 2. In retrospect, the major effect of the Shriver-Powell feud may have been to forestall criticism from other Democrats who were dissatisfied with the poverty program but who were forced to rally to its defense as an antidote to Powell's attack. This argument is made, for example, in "Powell Backs Poverty-Program Extension Following Soothing Letter from Shriver," *Wall Street Journal* 165 (May 13, 1965):4.

23. For example, see Albert H. Ouie, in *Congressional Record* 112 (Sept. 29, 1966):24423; Peter H. B. Frelinghuysen, in *Congressional Record* 112 (Sept. 29, 1966):24424; Augustus F. Hawkins, in *1966 House Committee Hearings,* vol. 1, p. 492; Haynes Johnson, "The Other War: A Frontline Report," *Progressive* 30 (June 1966):14; Senate Committee on Labor and Public Welfare, "Minority Views," *Economic Opportunity Act Amendments of 1965,* S. Rept. 89-599, 89th Cong., 1st sess., 1965, p. 60 (hereafter *1965 Senate Committee Report*); Kenneth B. Clark, in *Federal Role in Urban Affairs,* vol. 13, p. 2759; Saul Alinsky with Marion K. Sanders, "A Professional Radical Moves in on Rochester," *Harper's* 231 (July 1965):54.

24. Johnson, *Public Papers, 1965* (Washington: U.S. Government Printing Office, 1966), vol. 1, p. 453.

25. "Shriver Discounts Politics on Poverty," *New York Times,* Apr. 19, 1965, p. 59.

26. Charles E. Silberman, "The Mixed-Up War on Poverty," *Fortune* 72 (Aug. 1965):160.

27. Kenneth Hahn, quoted in House Committee on Education and Labor, *Antipoverty Programs in New York City and Los Angeles,* hearings before the Subcommittee on the War on Poverty Program, 89th Cong., 1st sess., 1965, p. 104; Roman Pucinski, quoted in *1965 House Committee Hearings,* p. 386.

28. A. V. Sorensen, in *Federal Role in Urban Affairs,* vol. 4, p. 1053; Hugh Addonizio, quoted in John Herbers, "M'Cone Says U.S. Could Be Ruined by Racial Strife," *New York Times,* Aug. 23, 1967, p. 33; Sam Yorty, in *Federal Role in Urban Affairs,* vol. 3, p. 692; John F. Shelley, in *1967 Senate Committee Hearings,* vol. 9, p. 3497.

29. Joseph A. Loftus, "Wide Policy Role for the Poor Opposed by Budget Bureau," *New York Times,* Nov. 5, 1965, p. 1; "U.S. Aide Denies a Poverty Shift," *New York Times,* Nov. 7, 1965, p. 70.

30. Memorandum from Charles L. Schultze to the President, Sept. 18, 1965, "Office of Economic Opportunity" Folder, Bill Moyers Files, Box 56, Lyndon Baines Johnson Library. Another sign of the president's attitude is his reaction to a letter he

received from James Rowe. Rowe described protests financed by the poverty program in Syracuse and claimed that something similar was occurring in Washington "to organize sit-in groups, protest marches, housing strikes, etc." Johnson had penciled in the margin: "Bill [Moyers]—For God's sake get on top of this and put a stop to it at once. L." (letter from James Rowe to the President, June 29, 1965, "Office of Economic Opportunity" Folder, Bill Moyers Files, Box 56, Lyndon Baines Johnson Library).

31. Joseph W. Sullivan, "Some Lawmakers Seek to Curb Local Control of Antipoverty Projects," *Wall Street Journal* 167 (Feb. 16, 1966):14.

32. Jonathan Spivak, "Spotlight on Shriver: Bold Methods Get War against Poverty Moving But Lead to Confusion," *Wall Street Journal* 165 (June 4, 1965):14.

33. Albert H. Quie, in *1965 House Committee Hearings,* p. 28.

34. "52 Poverty Units Warned Funds Will Stop Unless Poor Get Posts," *New York Times,* Mar. 10, 1967, p. 24; Sargent Shriver, in *1967 House Committee Hearings,* vol. 1, p. 80. Shriver's assertion provoked a rebuttal from Congressman Charles Goodell of New York. "Frankly, I think this is absurd," Goodell said. "It is just so far from being the truth and it does not do us any good to have it covered up" (Charles Goodell, in *1967 House Committee Hearings,* vol. 3, p. 1634).

35. Greenstone and Peterson, "Reformers, Machines, and the War on Poverty," p. 281.

36. Richard J. Daley, in *1967 Senate Committee Hearings,* vol. 13, p. 4131.

37. Dale Rogers Marshall, "Public Participation and the Politics of Poverty," *Race, Change, and Urban Society,* ed. Peter Orleans and William Russell Ellis, Jr. (Beverly Hills, Calif.: Sage Publications, 1971), p. 460; Ralph Kramer, *Participation of the Poor: Comparative Community Case Studies in the War on Poverty* (Englewood Cliffs, N.J.: Prentice-Hall, 1969), p. 191; *1967 House Committee Hearings,* vol. 5, p. 4035.

38. Kenneth B. Clark, quoted in *1967 Senate Committee*

Hearings, vol. 1, p. 299; [Clark and Hopkins], *A Relevant War against Poverty,* p. 225.

39. On the use of politics to provide reassurance to the mass public while distributing tangible benefits to the elites, see Murray Edelman, *The Symbolic Uses of Politics,* esp. chap. 1; Edelman, *Politics as Symbolic Action.*

40. *1966 House Committee Hearings,* vol. 2, p. 910.

41. Johnson, *Economic Report of the President* (1968), p. 140.

42. Senate Committee on Labor and Public Welfare, *Examination of the War on Poverty: Staff and Consultants' Reports,* 90th Cong., 1st sess., 1967, vol. 4, p. 930; Jerome P. Cavanagh, in *1967 Senate Committee Hearings,* vol. 1, p. 86; Sam Yorty, in *1967 Senate Committee Hearings,* vol. 12, p. 3773; John Lindsay, in *1967 Senate Committee Hearings,* vol. 6, p. 1834; Deton J. Brooks, in *1967 Senate Committee Hearings,* vol. 13, p. 4144.

43. Walter Williams and John W. Evans, "The Politics of Evaluation: The Case of Head Start," *Annals of the American Academy of Political and Social Science* 385 (Sept. 1969):122.

44. Johnson, *Public Papers, 1965,* vol. 2, p. 954; *Public Papers, 1967,* vol. 1, p. 152.

45. The most significant study in this regard is that prepared by the Westinghouse Corporation, as described in Williams and Evans, "The Politics of Evaluation," pp. 118–32.

46. See Jules Witcover and Erwin Knoll, "Politics and the Poor: Shriver's Second Thoughts," *Reporter* 33 (Dec. 30, 1965):23.

47. Austin C. Wehrwein, "Shriver Defends Poverty Program," *New York Times,* Dec. 7, 1965, p. 27.

48. Adam Clayton Powell, quoted in *1965 House Committee Hearings,* p. 488.

49. Joseph A. Loftus, "Shriver, Refusing to Shift, Backs Policy Role of the Poor," *New York Times,* Nov. 6, 1965, p. 1.

50. Sargent Shriver, in *1966 House Committee Hearings,* vol. 1, p. 176.

51. William C. Selover, "U.S. Poor Gain Foothold in Local Programs," *Christian Science Monitor,* Aug. 2, 1966, p. 10.

52. *1967 Senate Committee Report,* p. 37; Howard W. Hallman, in *Examination of the War on Poverty: Staff and Consultants' Reports,* vol. 4, p. 899.

53. Levitan, *The Great Society's Poor Law,* p. 64.

54. R. Kramer, *Participation of the Poor,* p. 266.

55. *1967 House Committee Report,* p. 21.

56. Memorandum from William H. Crook to Bill Moyers, May 3, 1966, Executive File WE 9, Box 27, Lyndon Baines Johnson Library; letter from Sargent Shriver to the President, n.d. (stamped "Rec'd 8-30-66"), Executive File WE 9, Box 27, Lyndon Baines Johnson Library. The Crook memorandum also was forwarded by Moyers to the president.

57. Sargent Shriver, in House, *Supplemental Appropriation Bill, 1967,* vol. 1, pp. 11, 14.

58. On these points, see Whitney Young, in *1967 House Committee Hearings,* vol. 3, p. 2283; Levitan, *The Great Society's Poor Law,* p. 315; James L. Sundquist, in collaboration with David W. Davis, *Making Federalism Work* (Washington: Brookings Institution, 1969), p. 48.

59. On this point, see Howard W. Hallman, "The Community Action Program: An Interpretative Analysis," in *Power, Poverty, and Urban Policy,* ed. Warner Bloomberg, Jr., and Henry J. Schmandt (Beverly Hills, Calif.: Sage Publications, 1968), p. 289.

60. Sundquist, *Making Federalism Work,* p. 62.

61. Richard A. Cloward, in *1965 Senate Committee Hearings,* p. 275.

62. Saul D. Alinsky, *Reveille for Radicals* (Chicago: University of Chicago Press, 1946), pp. 29, 88; Saul Alinsky with Marion K. Sanders, "The Professional Radical: Conversations with Saul Alinsky," *Harper's* 230 (June 1965):45; Sanford D. Horwitt, "Saul D. Alinsky and a Rhetoric of the Power Strategy as a Means of Social Change" (Ph.D. diss., Northwestern University, 1970), p. 171.

63. Horwitt, "Saul D. Alinsky," p. 179.

64. Homer Bigart, "9 in Youth Project Linked to Leftists," *New York Times,* Aug. 18, 1964, p. 1; Clayton Knowles,

"Screvane Report Scores Practices of Youth Agency," *New York Times*, Nov. 10, 1964, p. 1.

65. On the MFY experience, see Herbert Krosney, *Beyond Welfare: Poverty in the Supercity* (New York: Holt, Rinehart, and Winston, 1966). MFY was not the only early program which experienced these dilemmas of social change. In Boston, Mayor Collins complained vehemently when an employee of Action for Boston Community Development was encouraging residents to protest against the lack of street lamps and other physical facilities. Collins apparently did not believe that fomenting dissatisfaction was part of ABCD's role (see Thernstrom, *Poverty, Planning, and Politics*, p. 112).

66. Edith Green, quoted in *1967 House Committee Hearings*, vol. 4, pp. 3577–78.

67. Mitchell Sviridoff, quoted in *1966 Senate Committee Hearings*, p. 203.

68. John H. Buchanan, Jr., quoted in *Congressional Record* 112 (Sept. 26, 1966):24463; Joel T. Broyhill, quoted in *Congressional Record* 113 (Nov. 15, 1967):32703; Paul Fino, "Controversy Over the Federal Job Corps," *Congressional Digest* 47 (Jan. 1968):27.

69. For example, Frank Riessman, *Strategies against Poverty* (New York: Random House, 1969), pp. 4–9; Riessman, "The Myth of Saul Alinsky," *Dissent* 14 (July–Aug. 1967):471–74; James J. Vanecko, "Community Mobilization and Institutional Change: The Influence of the Community Action Program in Large Cities," *Social Science Quarterly* 50 (Dec. 1969):629.

70. Joseph S. Clark, quoted in *1966 Senate Committee Hearings*, pp. 158–59. Clark expressed a similar view the next year. See *1967 Senate Committee Hearings*, vol. 4, p. 1504.

71. Sargent Shriver, in *1967 Senate Committee Hearings*, vol. 9, p. 2823.

72. Senate, *Examination of the War on Poverty: Staff and Consultants' Reports*, vol. 5, p. 1242.

73. Roman Pucinski, in *1965 House Committee Hearings*, p. 588; Johnson, *Public Papers, 1967*, vol. 1, p. 628.

74. Shriver, "Poverty in the United States—What Next?" p. 58.

75. Wilbur J. Cohen, in Senate Committee on Appropriations, *Departments of Labor and Health, Education and Welfare Appropriations, Fiscal Year 1969,* hearings, 90th Cong., 2d sess. (Washington: U.S. Government Printing Office, 1968), vol. 1, p. 583.

76. Frances Fox Piven and Richard A. Cloward, *Regulating the Poor: The Functions of Public Welfare* (New York: Random House, 1971), p. 198.

77. Abraham Ribicoff, in *Federal Role in Urban Affairs,* vol. 1, p. 94.

78. Shriver, "New Weapons in Fighting Poverty," pp. 9–14.

79. Lombard, "Achieving 'Maximum Feasible Participation' of the Poor," p. 153.

80. For example, see Graham, "The Politics of Poverty," p. 235; Saul D. Alinsky, "The War on Poverty—Political Pornography," *Journal of Social Issues* 21 (1965):45.

81. Martin Luther King, Jr., in *Federal Role in Urban Affairs,* vol. 14, p. 2973.

82. Fenno, *The Power of the Purse,* pp. 332, 336; Aaron Wildavsky, *The Politics of the Budgetary Process* (Boston: Little, Brown, 1964), p. 12.

83. Each of these instances was widely discussed. All but the last four are listed in "Minority Views," *1966 House Committee Report,* pp. 95ff. On James Farmer's proposed literacy project, see M. S. Handler, "Farmer Dropping Literacy Project," *New York Times,* July 4, 1966, p. 16. The concern for the Washington, D.C., attendance records is discussed in *Antipoverty in D.C.,* passim. Levine, *The Poor Ye Need Not Have with You,* p. 70, refers to the leaks of internal disagreements to newspaper reporters. The difficulties of obtaining an OEO telephone directory are considered in *Congressional Record* 111 (July 20, 1965):17498ff.

84. Sargent Shriver, quoted in *1966 House Committee Hearings,* vol. 1, p. 490.

85. House Committee on Education and Labor, "Minority Views," *Economic Opportunity Amendments of 1965,* H. Rept. 89-428, 89th Cong., 1st sess., 1965, p. 56 (hereafter *1965 House Committee Report*).

86. "Individual Views of Senator Murphy," *1966 Senate Committee Report,* p. 89; "Drive on Poverty is Scored by G.O.P.," *New York Times,* Jan. 15, 1966, p. 17.

87. William H. Ayres, quoted in *1966 Rules Committee Hearings,* vol. 3, p. 100.

88. James J. Delaney, quoted in *1966 Rules Committee Hearings,* vol. 4, p. 156.

89. Charles Goodell, quoted in *1967 House Committee Hearings,* vol. 4, p. 3318.

90. William H. Ayres, quoted in *Congressional Record* 112 (Sept. 26, 1966):23765; Glenn Andrews, quoted in *Congressional Record* 112 (Sept. 28, 1966):24132.

91. Kenneth Burke, *Attitudes toward History* (1937; reprint ed., Boston: Beacon Press, 1959), p. 78.

92. Adam Clayton Powell, cited in U.S. Office of Economic Opportunity, *A News Summary of the War on Poverty* 1 (Sept. 6, 1966):1; "Hays Says Powell Should Quit Post," *New York Times,* Aug. 31, 1966, p. 31. Shriver's caustic reply, reported in the Aug. 31 story in the *Times,* was, "I have never known that Congressman Powell considered himself an expert on administration—either public or private."

93. Albert H. Quie, *Congressional Record* 112 (Sept. 27, 1966):23954; Joseph A. Loftus, "House Republicans Call for Shriver's Resignation," *New York Times,* Sept. 28, 1966, p. 36; "Shriver Ouster Is Urged," *New York Times,* Aug. 20, 1967, p. 52; "Prohibitionists Scorn Shriver," *New York Times,* Sept. 3, 1966, p. 5.

94. U.S. Office of Economic Opportunity, *The Watershed,* pp. 8, 10, 11.

95. For example, William C. Selover, "$2.5 billion effort drags," *Christian Science Monitor,* Aug. 1, 1966, p. 7; Roscoe Drummond, quoted by John Brademas, in *Congressional Record* 112 (Sept. 27, 1966):23977.

Chapter 6

1. Joseph A. Loftus, "Antipoverty Drive Is Facing Cutbacks in Realigned House," *New York Times,* Nov. 13, 1966, p. 50; Marjorie Hunter, "Revisions in Poverty Law Sought to Abate Criticism," *New York Times,* Apr. 10, 1967, p. 12.

2. "Poll of Congress Opposes Tax Rise," *New York Times,* Dec. 23, 1966, p. 13.

3. Lee Rainwater and W. L. Yancey, *The Moynihan Report and the Politics of Controversy* (Cambridge, Mass.: MIT Press, 1967), p. 481.

4. Sargent Shriver, in *1967 Senate Committee Hearings,* vol. 10, p. 3148.

5. Sargent Shriver, in *1967 House Committee Hearings,* vol. 1, p. 77; Lisle C. Carter, Jr., in *1967 House Committee Hearings,* vol. 2, p. 1287; Joseph S. Clark, in *Congressional Record* 113 (Sept. 22, 1967):26542; Whitney Young, quoted in *1967 Senate Committee Hearings,* vol. 7, p. 2203.

6. Robert F. Kennedy, in *Congressional Record* 113 (Sept. 27, 1967):27084; Roy Wilkins, quoted in *Federal Role in Urban Affairs,* vol. 7, p. 1521.

7. William S. Moorhead, *1967 House Committee Hearings,* vol. 2, p. 1456.

8. "Poverty: More and More a Party Issue," *New York Times,* Oct. 1, 1967, sec. 4, p. 2; Joseph A. Loftus, "Poverty and the G.O.P.," *New York Times,* Nov. 11, 1967, p. 17.

9. Sargent Shriver, in *Supplemental Appropriation Bill, 1967,* vol. 1, p. 13.

10. Aaron Wildavsky, "The Empty-head Blues: Black Rebellion and White Reaction," *Public Interest* 11 (Spring 1968):4.

11. Memorandum from Sargent Shriver to the President, Oct. 20, 1965, Executive File WE 9, Box 26, Lyndon Baines Johnson Library.

12. Problems of discipline are described in "OEO Administrative History," p. 496. For the factors alleged to contribute to the dropout rate, see "OEO Administrative History," p. 498.

Among the members of Congress who complained of the graduates' inability to find jobs were Winston Prouty, in *Congressional Record* 113 (Oct. 3, 1967):27614; and Charles Percy, in *Congressional Record* 113 (Oct. 3, 1967):27568.

13. Memorandum from Joseph Califano to the President, Feb. 23, 1967, Executive File FG 11-15-1, Box 1, Lyndon Baines Johnson Library. Califano attributed this judgment to Sam Gibbons.

14. Kenneth Boulding, *Conflict and Defense* (New York: Harper, 1962), p. 103.

15. U.S. Office of Economic Opportunity, *The Tide of Progress: Third Annual Report, Fiscal Year 1967* (Washington: U.S. Government Printing Office, 1968), p. 57; "OEO Administrative History," p. 526.

16. Cited in L. Lander, *War on Poverty*, p. 111.

17. Memorandum from Sargent Shriver to the President, May 20, 1967, Executive File WE 9-1, Box 45, Lyndon Baines Johnson Library.

18. Cited in "OEO Administrative History," p. 539.

19. Memorandum from Sargent Shriver to the President, Jan. 19, 1968, Executive File FG 11-15-1, Box 1, Lyndon Baines Johnson Library.

20. Memoranda from George D. McCarthy to Barefoot Sanders, Sept. 22 and 29, 1967, Reports on Legislation, Box 38, Lyndon Baines Johnson Library.

21. For a listing of his objections, see Robert C. Byrd, in *Congressional Record* 113 (Oct. 3, 1967):27623.

22. Memorandum from Barefoot Sanders to the President, Sept. 18, 1967, Reports on Legislation, Box 38, Lyndon Baines Johnson Library; memorandum from George D. McCarthy to Barefoot Sanders, Sept. 22, 1967, Reports on Legislation, Box 38, Lyndon Baines Johnson Library.

23. Cited by Joseph S. Clark, in *Congressional Record* 113 (Oct. 3, 1967):27634.

24. Jacob Javits, quoted in *Congressional Record* 113 (Sept. 27, 1967):27061; Carl D. Perkins, quoted in *Congressional Record* 113 (Nov. 7, 1967):31408.

25. Johnson, *The Vantage Point,* p. 83.

26. Charles Goodell, quoted in *Congressional Record* 113 (Nov. 7, 1967):31414.

27. Edith Green, quoted in *Congressional Record* 113 (Nov. 7, 1967):31416.

28. Robert C. Byrd, quoted in *Congressional Record* 113 (Oct. 3, 1967):27619.

29. Edith Green, quoted in *Congressional Record* 113 (Nov. 14, 1967):32364.

30. For example, see Leonard Farbstein, in *Congressional Record* 113 (Nov. 9, 1967):31886. The OEO itself had stated that the amendment "would result in a drastic revision of the present concept of Community Action." See U.S. Office of Economic Opportunity, *A News Summary of the War on Poverty* 2 (Oct. 23, 1967):1.

31. Lawrence E. Davies, "Mayors Reject Shift on Poverty Role," *New York Times,* June 22, 1967, p. 44. The National League of Cities and National League of Counties, however, both supported the Green amendment. Cited by Edith Green, in *Congressional Record* 113 (Nov. 15, 1967):32648. The mayors' lack of interest in control did not necessarily reflect their intense commitment to neighborhood-level power. In many cases, it may have been politically expedient for community action projects to exist autonomously. Then those projects, rather than the mayor's office, could bear the onus for social turmoil.

32. Edith Green, quoted in *Congressional Record* 113 (Nov. 7, 1967):31417.

33. Sargent Shriver, quoted in *1967 Senate Committee Hearings,* vol. 9, p. 2697.

34. Letter from Sargent Shriver to Charles L. Schultze, n.d. (stamped "Rec'd Dec 15 1967"), Reports on Enrolled Legislation, P.L. 90-222, Lyndon Baines Johnson Library; William C. Selover, "The View from Capitol Hill: Harassment and Survival," in *On Fighting Poverty: Perspectives from Experience,* ed. James L. Sundquist (New York: Basic Books, 1969), p. 177; Levitan, *The Great Society's Poor Law,* p. 67. Shriver did hedge

his prediction by saying, in the same letter, "However, this will not be the situation in all instances, and the jurisdictional and procedural problems created in the transition will be both varied and great." The trend identified by Levitan continued as the remaining governmental units made similar decisions.

35. Donald H. Haider, "Governors and Mayors View the Poverty Program," *Current History* 61 (Nov. 1971):277. Similar retrospective judgments were made by Ralph Kramer, *Participation of the Poor,* p. 263; Dale Rogers Marshall, *The Politics of Participation in Poverty* (Berkeley and Los Angeles: University of California Press, 1971), pp. 72–75.

36. Levitan, *The Great Society's Poor Law,* p. 67.

37. See, for example, U.S. Office of Economic Opportunity, *The Watershed,* passim; memorandum, "OEO—Our Cause in Capsule," unsigned and undated, OEO Folder, Irvine Sprague Files, Box 2, Lyndon Baines Johnson Library.

38. Edith Green, in *Congressional Record* 113 (Nov. 14, 1967):32364.

39. Robert H. Michel, quoted in *Congressional Record* 113 (Nov. 14, 1967):32351. For a similar judgment by a Democrat, see Edith Green, in *Congressional Record* 113 (Nov. 14, 1967):32364.

40. Winston Prouty, in *Congressional Record* 113 (Sept. 29, 1967):27378; Joseph S. Clark, quoted in *Congressional Record* 113 (Sept. 29, 1967):27379; John R. Dellenback, in *Congressional Record* 113 (Nov. 15, 1967):32691. The comptroller general's report, released in 1969, gave OEO generally a favorable evaluation. See Senate Committee on Labor and Welfare, *Review by the Comptroller General.*

41. Emanuel Celler, quoted in *Congressional Record* 113 (Nov. 9, 1967):31891.

42. U.S. Office of Economic Opportunity, *The Tide of Progress,* p. 5. On internal changes of personnel, see Levine, *The Poor Ye Need Not Have with You,* p. 64.

43. Memorandum, "OEO—Our Cause in Capsule," unsigned and undated, OEO Folder, Irvine Sprague Files, Box 2, Lyndon Baines Johnson Library.

44. John Ashbrook, in *Congressional Record* 113 (Nov. 15, 1967):32688; Ashbrook, in *Congressional Record* 113 (Nov. 15, 1967):32694; A. S. Mike Monroney, in *Congressional Record* 113 (Oct. 4, 1967):27865. The Ashbrook amendment on supergrades originally failed on a 74–74 tie vote, but passed, 118–110, when tellers were demanded.

45. Clarence J. Brown, Jr., quoted in *Congressional Record* 113 (Nov. 8, 1967):31761.

46. Cited in Joseph A. Loftus, "Shriver to Quit Poverty Agency Unless He Gets Funds to Do Job," *New York Times,* Nov. 7, 1967, p. 1.

47. U.S. Advisory Commission on Intergovernmental Relations, *Intergovernmental Relations in the Poverty Program,* Report A-29 (Washington: U.S. Government Printing Office, 1966), p. 161; "Poverty Projects Gaining Favor among Leaders in Communities," *New York Times,* Apr. 16, 1967, p. 46.

48. Cited in testimony of John V. Lindsay, in *1966 Senate Committee Hearings,* p. 232; Jerome P. Cavanagh, in *1967 Senate Committee Hearings,* vol. 1, p. 87.

49. U.S. Office of Economic Opportunity, *A News Summary of the War on Poverty* 2 (Oct. 16, 1967):3.

50. Selover, "The View from Capitol Hill," p. 175; Johnson, *The Vantage Point,* p. 82; Levitan, *The Great Society's Poor Law,* p. 102; Levine, *The Poor Ye Need Not Have with You,* p. 75; memorandum from Sargent Shriver to the President, Nov. 9, 1967, Executive File WE 9, Box 30, Lyndon Baines Johnson Library.

51. U.S. Office of Economic Opportunity, *The Quiet Revolution,* pp. 4–5; U.S. Office of Economic Opportunity, *The Watershed,* pp. 1–3.

52. Memorandum from Samuel V. Merrick to Barefoot Sanders, Sept. 29, 1967, Reports on Legislation, Box 38, Lyndon Baines Johnson Library.

53. Joseph S. Clark, in *Congressional Record* 113 (Sept. 22, 1967):26540–26541, 26548; Clark, in *Congressional Record* 113 (Sept. 25, 1967):26658–26659.

54. See Sar A. Levitan, "Is OEO Here to Stay?" *Poverty and Human Resources Abstracts* 3 (Mar.–Apr. 1968):3.

55. Levitan, *The Great Society's Poor Law*, p. 102.

56. Joseph A. Loftus, "Poverty and the G.O.P.," *New York Times*, Nov. 11, 1967, p. 17; Loftus, "How Poverty Bill Was Saved in House," *New York Times*, Dec. 25, 1967, p. 26. Perkins claimed that the delay in bringing the bill to the floor was attributable to the committee's lengthy hearings and the markup sessions on the bill (Carl D. Perkins, in *Congressional Record* 113 [Nov. 7, 1967]:31406).

57. Memorandum from George D. McCarthy to Barefoot Sanders, Sept. 29, 1967, Reports on Legislation, Box 38, Lyndon Baines Johnson Library.

58. Memorandum from George D. McCarthy to Barefoot Sanders, Nov. 3, 1967, Reports on Legislation, Box 40, Lyndon Baines Johnson Library; "House Worksheet, OEO Bill (S. 2388), Final Head Count, 11/4/67," OEO Folder, Irvine Sprague Files, Box 2, Lyndon Baines Johnson Library.

59. Letter from Sargent Shriver to Charles L. Schultze, n.d. (stamped "Rec'd Dec 15 1967"), Reports on Enrolled Legislation, P.L. 90-222, Lyndon Baines Johnson Library.

60. U.S. Office of Economic Opportunity, *A News Summary of the War on Poverty* 2 (Nov. 20, 1967):1.

61. Alfred J. Kahn, *Studies in Social Policy and Planning* (New York: Russell Sage Foundation, 1969), p. 61, characterized the 1967 act as "routinization of charisma."

62. Sargent Shriver, "War on Poverty, Report to the President," *Weekly Compilation of Presidential Documents* 4 (1968):50.

63. The details of the Yankelovich study are from U.S. Office of Economic Opportunity, *A News Summary of the War on Poverty* 4 (Mar. 31, 1969):1–2; U.S. National Advisory Council on Economic Opportunity, *Continuity and Change in Antipoverty Programs: Second Annual Report*, 1969, pp. 27–28.

64. The administration approved Senator Clark's plan for a

two-year authorization, provided that the figure for the second year remain open. Otherwise, the Budget Bureau feared that the total cost of the bill would seem so high that final passage would be jeopardized (memorandum from Charles L. Schultze to the President, June 28, 1967, Executive File LE/WE 9, Box 10, Lyndon Baines Johnson Library).

65. For example, only bare mention was made of the War on Poverty in the 1968 State of the Union address (Johnson, *Public Papers, 1968–69,* vol. 1, p. 31). See also the views of Selover, "The View from Capitol Hill," pp. 179, 185.

66. The president's concession to Congressman Mills limited his flexibility with respect to antipoverty spending. Acting Secretary of the Treasury Joseph W. Barr had advised Johnson that the best way to avert congressional onslaughts on antipoverty programs was to gain passage of the tax bill, so that it would not be *necessary* to cut domestic spending (memorandum from Joseph W. Barr to the President, Apr. 5, 1968, Executive File WE 9, Box 31, Lyndon Baines Johnson Library). But the concession to Mills *required* that domestic spending be limited and made the prospects for any substantial increase in OEO's budget virtually nil. Bertrand M. Harding's testimony in *Departments of Labor and Health, Education, and Welfare Appropriations, Fiscal Year 1969,* Hearings, U.S. Senate Committee on Appropriations, 90th Cong., 2d sess., 1968, vol. 2, p. 2560, contains the request for a full appropriation. Harding's statement that no major new programs would be funded is from House Committee on Appropriations, *Departments of Labor and Health, Education, and Welfare Appropriations for 1969,* hearings, 90th Cong., 2d sess., 1968, vol. 6, p. 7.

67. Johnson, *Economic Report of the President* (1969), p. 21; John Herbers, "U.S. Could End Poverty in 8 Years, Report Says," *New York Times,* Jan. 17, 1969, p. 15. The council's 1968 statement may be found in Johnson, *Economic Report of the President* (1968), p. 129.

68. John Herbers, "Poverty: New Emphasis Placed on Aid to the Poor," *New York Times,* Jan. 16, 1969, p. 23; "Johnson

Stresses Antipoverty Drive," *New York Times,* Oct. 24, 1968, p. 29.

69. David R. Jones, "G.O.P. Links Riots to Johnson Policy," *New York Times,* June 3, 1968, p. 1.

70. Ben A. Franklin, "Agnew Makes Bid for 'Protest' Vote," *New York Times,* Oct. 8, 1968, p. 33; Homer Bigart, "Agnew Calls for 'Thinning Out' of the Slums," *New York Times,* Sept. 6, 1968, p. 32.

71. Jonathan Spivak, "Poverty Agency Periled by Bureaucratic Rivals, Budget, Political Woes," *Wall Street Journal* 171 (Apr. 3, 1968):1; Spivak, "OEO under Fire: A Study in Durability," *Wall Street Journal* 173 (Feb. 4, 1969):18.

72. *Antipoverty Programs, Message from the President of the United States Transmitting Information Regarding Proposed Action Relative to the Administration of Head Start and Job Corps Programs,* H. Doc. 91-74, 91st Cong., 1st sess., 1969, p. 2.

73. Senate Committee on Labor and Public Welfare, *Nomination, Hearing, May 13, 1969, on Donald Rumsfeld of Illinois to be Director, Office of Economic Opportunity,* hearings, 91st Cong., 1st sess., 1969, pp. 7–8.

74. These antagonisms are described in Jonathan Spivak, "New Antipoverty Chief Plays Down Militancy and Stresses Research," *Wall Street Journal* 175 (Jan. 7, 1970):1.

75. In June 1973 a federal district court held that Phillips was occupying the directorship illegally, since his name had not been submitted for Senate confirmation. Judge William B. Jones also ruled that the president could not terminate OEO without congressional approval. Subsequently, President Nixon named Alvin Arnett to be director of OEO, but Nixon vowed to continue his efforts to phase out OEO's operations. In July he transferred many of the office's programs to other agencies, leaving only community action, legal services, and economic development, administered by a staff of 350 employees with a token budget (see Marjorie Hunter, "House and Nixon Act to Aid O.E.O.," *New York Times,* June 27, 1973; "Poverty Programs are Transferred," *New York Times,* July 13, 1973, p. 22).

Chapter 7

1. S. M. Miller and Martin Rein, "The War on Poverty: Perspectives and Prospects," in *Poverty as a Public Issue,* ed. Ben B. Seligman (New York: Free Press, 1965), p. 315.

2. Piven and Cloward, *Regulating the Poor,* pp. 274, 276. Piven and Cloward pronounce the War on Poverty a success in incorporating blacks into the political system. See also Daniel P. Moynihan, *Maximum Feasible Misunderstanding: Community Action in the War on Poverty* (New York: Free Press, 1969), p. 129.

3. U.S. Office of Economic Opportunity, *Business and OEO: Partnership against Poverty* (Washington: U.S. Government Printing Office, 1969), inside front cover.

4. Cited in Howard M. Wachtel, "Looking at Poverty from a Radical Perspective," *Review of Radical Political Economy* 3 (Summer 1971):13.

5. The president was so advised in a memorandum from Fred Panzer, June 14, 1968, Executive File WE 9, Box 32, Lyndon Baines Johnson Library.

6. See, for example, Robert Theobald, *Free Men and Free Markets* (New York: Potter, 1963); Milton Friedman, *Capitalism and Freedom* (Chicago: University of Chicago Press, 1962).

7. Joseph A. Loftus, "Tax Aid to Poor Urged by Shriver," *New York Times,* Dec. 15, 1965, p. 1.

8. Johnson, *Economic Report of the President* (1967), p. 17.

9. Seligman, *Permanent Poverty,* p. xi.

10. Memorandum from Jim Gaither to Harry McPherson, Dec. 31, 1968, Executive File SP-4/1969, Box 34, Lyndon Baines Johnson Library.

11. Joseph A. Loftus, "Poverty Agency Rules Out Financing for Gangs," *New York Times,* Sept. 4, 1968, p. 26. The friction surrounding the Chicago grant was caused in part by OEO's decision to fund The Woodlawn Organization directly, bypassing the citywide community action agency which allegedly was controlled by Mayor Daley.

12. Harold H. Weissman, "A Conservative Strategy for Social Planning in the Seventies," in *Social Work Practice, 1970* (New York: Columbia University Press, 1970), p. 9; Marshall, "Public Participation and the Politics of Poverty," p. 474.

13. Gilbert Steiner, "Policy Options for Welfare Reform," *Monthly Labor Review* 94 (March 1971):24. The analogy to insurance is palpably false; individual contributions do not build up reserves but are used to finance current payments. The program probably is as much a welfare program as is public assistance. Yet the convenient fiction of "insurance" is the glue that holds together social support for the program. See Robinson Hollister, "Social Mythology and Reform: Income Maintenance for the Aged," *Annals of the American Academy of Political and Social Science* 415 (Sept. 1974):19–40.

14. Sargent Shriver, quoted in *1965 House Committee Hearings,* p. 22.

15. James Q. Wilson, "An Overview of Theories of Planned Change," *Centrally Planned Change,* ed. Robert Morris (New York: National Association of Social Workers, 1964), p. 22.

16. John D. Pomfret, "Guaranteed Income Asked for All, Employed or Not," *New York Times,* Mar. 23, 1964, pp. 1, 20. It frequently is forgotten, because of the subsequent advocacy of the guaranteed annual income as an *antipoverty* mechanism, that many of its early proponents urged it as a response to *automation.*

17. Leonard J. Duhl, chief of the planning staff of the National Institute of Mental Health, wrote Shriver on March 25, calling his attention to the report in the March 23 *New York Times* and suggesting that the federal government take the lead by announcing that the issues involved in the report had been studied for more than a year (letter from Leonard J. Duhl to Sargent Shriver, "Poverty" Folder, Bill Moyers Files, Box 39, Lyndon Baines Johnson Library).

18. See, for example, Harry K. Girvetz, *The Evolution of Liberalism* (New York: Collier Books, 1963), p. 353.

19. In 1963, Robert Lampman of the Council of Economic Advisers wrote to Walter Heller, "Probably a politically accept-

able program must avoid completely the use of the term 'inequality' or of the term *'redistribution'* of income or wealth" (quoted in Allen J. Matusow, *The Unraveling of America: A History of Liberalism in the 1960s* [New York: Harper and Row, 1984], p. 220). Matusow adds, "It was not only the terms that were spurned, but the policies they implied."

20. For an elaboration of these ideas, see Blum, *The Progressive Presidents.*

21. Weissman, "A Conservative Strategy," p. 20.

22. Matusow, *The Unraveling of America,* p. 107.

23. Matusow, *The Unraveling of America,* p. 270.

24. Daniel P. Moynihan, *The Politics of a Guaranteed Income* (New York: Random House, 1973), pp. 316–17.

25. Peter Schrag, "Autopsy for a Great Society," *Saturday Review* 50 (June 17, 1967):63.

26. James A. Jones, "Federal Efforts to Solve Contemporary Social Problems," in *Handbook on the Study of Social Problems,* ed. Erwin O. Smigel (Chicago: Rand McNally, 1971), p. 586.

27. Herbert S. Parmet, *The Democrats: The Years after FDR* (New York: Oxford University Press, 1976), p. 310.

28. Theodore H. White, *The Making of the President 1968* (New York: Pocket Books, 1970), p. 518.

29. William E. Leuchtenburg, *In the Shadow of FDR: From Harry Truman to Ronald Reagan* (Ithaca: Cornell University Press, 1983), p. 208.

30. Matusow, *The Unraveling of America,* p. 439.

Selected Bibliography

Extensive use was made of materials in the Lyndon Baines Johnson Library in Austin, Texas. The unpublished administrative history of the Office of Economic Opportunity, the White House Central Files, and files of several of the president's aides are located there. Newspapers also were consulted frequently; especially helpful were articles by Homer Bigart, Ben A. Franklin, John Herbers, Marjorie Hunter, and Joseph A. Loftus in the *New York Times,* by William C. Selover in the *Christian Science Monitor,* and by Jonathan Spivak in the *Wall Street Journal.* The following books, periodical articles, public documents, and unpublished material also proved to be particularly useful.

Books

Alinsky, Saul D. *Reveille for Radicals.* Chicago: University of Chicago Press, 1946.
Allen, Vernon L., ed. *Psychological Factors in Poverty.* Chicago: Markham, 1970.
Bachrach, Peter, and Morton Baratz. *Power and Poverty.* New York: Oxford University Press, 1970.
Bagdikian, Ben H. *In the Midst of Plenty.* Boston: Beacon Press, 1964.

Bell, Jack. *The Johnson Treatment: How Lyndon B. Johnson Took over the Presidency and Made It His Own.* New York: Harper and Row, 1965.

Bibby, John F., and Roger H. Davidson. *On Capitol Hill: Studies in the Legislative Process.* New York: Holt, Rinehart, and Winston, 1967.

Bloomberg, Warner, Jr., and Henry J. Schmandt, eds. *Power, Poverty, and Urban Policy.* Beverly Hills, Calif.: Sage Publications, 1968.

Brager, George A., and Francis P. Purcell, eds. *Community Action against Poverty.* New Haven: College and University Press, 1967.

Bremner, Robert H. *From the Depths: The Discovery of Poverty in the United States.* New York: New York University Press, 1956.

Burke, Kenneth. *Attitudes toward History.* 1937. Reprint. Boston: Beacon Press, 1959.

Clark, Kenneth B. *Dark Ghetto: Dilemmas of Social Power.* New York: Harper and Row, 1965.

[Clark, Kenneth B., and Jeannette Hopkins]. *A Relevant War against Poverty: A Study of Community Action Programs and Observable Social Change.* New York: Metropolitan Applied Research Center, 1968.

Cloward, Richard A., and Lloyd Ohlin. *Delinquency and Opportunity.* New York: Free Press, 1960; London: Routledge and Kegan Paul, 1961.

Crook, William H., and Ross Thomas. *Warriors for the Poor.* New York: Morrow, 1969.

Donovan, John C. *The Politics of Poverty.* New York: Pegasus, 1967.

Downs, Anthony. *Inside Bureaucracy.* Boston: Little, Brown, 1967.

Edelman, Murray. *Politics as Symbolic Action: Mass Arousal and Quiescence.* Chicago: Markham, 1971.

Evans, Rowland, and Robert Novak. *Lyndon B. Johnson: The Exercise of Power.* New York: New American Library, 1966.

Fenno, Richard F., Jr. *The Power of the Purse: Appropriations Politics in Congress.* Boston: Little, Brown, 1966.

Ferman, Louis A., Joyce L. Kornbluh, and Alan Haber, eds. *Poverty in America: A Book of Readings.* Ann Arbor: University of Michigan Press, 1965.

Fogelson, Robert M. *Violence as Protest.* Garden City, N.Y.: Doubleday, 1971.

Goldman, Eric F. *The Tragedy of Lyndon Johnson.* New York: Knopf, 1969.

Gordon, Kermit, ed. *Agenda for the Nation.* Washington: Brookings Institution, 1968.

Greenstone, J. David, and Paul E. Peterson. "Reformers, Machines, and the War on Poverty." In *City Politics and Public Policy,* ed. James Q. Wilson. New York: Wiley, 1968.

Hahn, Harlan, ed. *People and Politics in Urban Society.* Beverly Hills, Calif.: Sage Publications, 1972.

Handler, Joel F. *Reforming the Poor: Welfare Policy, Federalism, and Morality.* New York: Basic Books, 1972.

Harrington, Michael. *The Other America.* Baltimore: Penguin Books, 1963.

Johnson, Lyndon Baines. *The Vantage Point: Perspectives of the Presidency, 1963–1969.* New York: Holt, Rinehart, and Winston, 1971.

Kahn, Alfred J. *Studies in Social Policy and Planning.* New York: Russell Sage Foundation, 1969.

Kearns, Doris. *Lyndon Johnson and the American Dream.* New York: Harper and Row, 1976.

Kershaw, Joseph A., with the assistance of Paul N. Courant. *Government against Poverty.* Washington: Brookings Institution, 1970.

Kramer, Ralph. *Participation of the Poor: Comparative Community Case Studies in the War on Poverty.* Englewood Cliffs, N.J.: Prentice-Hall, 1969.

Krosney, Herbert. *Beyond Welfare: Poverty in the Supercity.* New York: Holt, Rinehart, and Winston, 1966.

Lander, Louise, ed. *War on Poverty.* New York: Facts on File, 1967.

Levine, Robert A. *The Poor Ye Need Not Have with You: Lessons from the War on Poverty.* Cambridge, Mass.: MIT Press, 1970.

Levitan, Sar A. *The Great Society's Poor Law: A New Approach to Poverty.* Baltimore: Johns Hopkins University Press, 1969.

Lipsky, Michael. *Protest in City Politics.* Chicago: Rand McNally, 1970.

McPherson, Harry. *A Political Education.* Boston: Atlantic, Little, Brown, 1972.

Marris, Peter, and Martin Rein. *Dilemmas of Social Reform: Poverty and Community Action in the United States.* New York: Atherton, 1969.

Marshall, Dale Rogers. *The Politics of Participation in Poverty.* Berkeley and Los Angeles: University of California Press, 1971.

Matusow, Allen J. *The Unraveling of America: A History of Liberalism in the 1960s.* New York: Harper and Row, 1984.

Moynihan, Daniel P. *Maximum Feasible Misunderstanding: Community Action in the War on Poverty.* New York: Free Press, 1969.

————, ed. *On Understanding Poverty: Perspectives from the Social Sciences.* New York: Basic Books, 1968.

National Advisory Commission on Civil Disorders. *Report.* New York: Bantam Books, 1968.

————. *Supplemental Studies.* New York: Praeger, 1968.

Orleans, Peter, and William Russell Ellis, Jr., eds. *Race, Change, and Urban Society.* Beverly Hills, Calif.: Sage Publications, 1971.

Piven, Frances Fox, and Richard A. Cloward. *Regulating the Poor: The Functions of Public Welfare.* New York: Random House, 1971.

Rein, Martin. *Social Policy: Issues of Choice and Change.* New York: Random House, 1970.

Riessman, Frank. *Strategies against Poverty.* New York: Random House, 1969.

Ryan, William. *Blaming the Victim*. New York: Random House, 1971.

Seligman, Ben B. *Permanent Poverty: An American Syndrome*. Chicago: Quadrangle, 1968.

———, ed. *Poverty as a Public Issue*. New York: Free Press, 1965.

Shriver, Sargent. *Point of the Lance*. New York: Harper and Row, 1964.

Smigel, Erwin O., ed. *Handbook on the Study of Social Problems*. Chicago: Rand McNally, 1971.

Steinberg, Alfred. *Sam Johnson's Boy: A Close-Up of the President from Texas*. New York: Macmillan, 1968.

Sundquist, James L., in collaboration with David W. Davis. *Making Federalism Work*. Washington: Brookings Institution, 1969.

———, ed. *On Fighting Poverty: Perspectives from Experience*. New York: Basic Books, 1969.

Thernstrom, Stephan. *Poverty, Planning, and Politics in the New Boston: The Origins of ABCD*. New York: Basic Books, 1969.

Tomlinson, T. M. "The Development of a Riot Ideology among American Negroes." In *Racial Violence in the United States*, ed. Allen D. Grimshaw. Chicago: Aldine, 1969.

Valentine, Charles A. *Culture and Poverty: Critique and Counter-Proposals*. Chicago: University of Chicago Press, 1968.

Waxman, Chaim I., ed. *Poverty: Power and Politics*. New York: Grosset and Dunlap, 1968.

Wildavsky, Aaron. *The Politics of the Budgetary Process*. Boston: Little, Brown, 1964.

Articles

Alinsky, Saul D. "The War on Poverty—Political Pornography." *Journal of Social Issues* 21 (1965):41–47.

Alinsky, Saul D., with Marion K. Sanders. "The Professional

Radical: Conversations with Saul Alinsky." *Harper's* 230 (June 1965):37–47.

Bachrach, Peter. "A Power Analysis: The Shaping of Antipoverty Policy in Baltimore." *Public Policy* 18 (Winter 1970):155–86.

Briar, Scott. "Welfare from Below: Recipients' Views of the Public Welfare System." *California Law Review* 54 (1966):370–85.

Burke, Edmund M. "Citizen Participation Strategies." *Journal of the American Institute of Planners* 34 (Sept. 1968):287–94.

Cater, Douglass. "The Politics of Poverty." *Reporter* 30 (Feb. 13, 1964):16–20.

Cavala, Bill, and Aaron Wildavsky. "The Political Feasibility of Income by Right." *Public Policy* 18 (Spring 1970):321–54.

Cloward, Richard A., and Richard M. Elman. "The First Congress of the Poor." *Nation* 202 (Feb. 7, 1966):148–51.

Cloward, Richard A., and Frances Fox Piven. "The Weight of the Poor: A Strategy to End Poverty." *Nation* 202 (May 2, 1966):510–17.

Davidson, Roger H. "The Politics of Anti-Poverty." *Nation* 208 (Feb. 24, 1969):233–37.

———. "The War on Poverty: Experiment in Federalism." *Annals of the American Academy of Political and Social Science* 385 (Sept. 1969):1–13.

Evans, Rowland, and Robert Novak. "The Yarmolinsky Affair." *Esquire* 63 (Feb. 1965):80–82, 122–23.

Glazer, Nathan. " 'To Produce a Creative Disorder': The Grand Design of the Poverty Program." *New York Times Magazine,* Feb. 27, 1966, pp. 21, 64, 69–73.

Haider, Donald H. "Governors and Mayors View the Poverty Program." *Current History* 61 (Nov. 1971):273–78, 302–303.

Knoll, Erwin, and Jules Witcover. "Maximum Feasible Publicity: The War on Poverty's Campaign to Capture the Press." *Columbia Journalism Review* 5 (Fall 1966):33–40.

Krause, Elliott A. "Functions of a Bureaucratic Ideology: 'Citizen Participation.' " *Social Problems* 16 (Fall 1968):129–43.

Kravitz, Sanford, and Ferne K. Kolodner. "Community Action: Where Has It Been? Where Will It Go?" *Poverty and Human Resources Abstracts* 4 (July–Aug. 1969):9–17.

Lander, Byron G. "Group Theory and Individuals: The Origin of Poverty as a Political Issue in 1964." *Western Political Quarterly* 24 (1971):514–26.

Lauer, Robert H. "The Middle Class Looks at Poverty." *Urban and Social Change Review* 5 (Fall 1971):8–10.

Levitan, Sar A. "Can the War on Poverty Rise above Partisan Politics?" *Poverty and Human Resources Abstracts* 2 (Sept.–Oct. 1967):19–22.

_____. "The Community Action Program: A Strategy to Fight Poverty." *Annals of the American Academy of Political and Social Science* 385 (Sept. 1969):63–75.

Moynihan, Daniel P. "The Professors and the Poor." *Commentary* 46 (Aug. 1968):19–28.

_____. "What Is Community Action?" *Public Interest* 5 (Fall 1966):3–8.

Piven, Frances Fox. "The Great Society as Political Strategy." *Columbia Forum* 13 (Summer 1970):17–22.

Raab, Earl. "A Tale of Three Wars: Which War and Which Poverty?" *Public Interest* 3 (Spring 1966):45–56.

Rein, Martin, and S. M. Miller. "Citizen Participation and Poverty." *Connecticut Law Review* 1 (1968):221–43.

Riessman, Frank. "Mobilizing the Poor." *Commonweal* 82 (May 21, 1965):285–89.

_____. "The Myth of Saul Alinsky." *Dissent* 14 (July–Aug. 1967):469–78.

Shriver, Sargent. "New Weapons in Fighting Poverty." *Public Welfare* 24 (Jan. 1966):9–14.

Silberman, Charles E. "The Mixed-Up War on Poverty." *Fortune* 72 (Aug. 1965):156–61, 218, 223–24, 226.

Wildavsky, Aaron. "The Empty-head Blues: Black Rebellion and White Reaction." *Public Interest* 11 (Spring 1968):3–16.

Williams, Walter, and John W. Evans. "The Politics of Evaluation: The Case of Head Start." *Annals of the American Academy of Political and Social Science* 385 (Sept. 1969):118–32.

Public Documents

Johnson, Lyndon B. *Economic Report of the President, Together with the Annual Report of the Council of Economic Advisers.* Washington: U.S. Government Printing Office, 1964, 1967, 1968, 1969.

——. *Public Papers of the Presidents, Lyndon B. Johnson, 1963–64* (2 vols.), *1965* (2 vols.), *1966* (2 vols.), *1967* (2 vols.), *1968–69* (2 vols.). Washington: U.S. Government Printing Office, 1965–70.

President's Commission on Income Maintenance Programs. *Poverty amid Plenty: The American Paradox.* Washington: U.S. Government Printing Office, 1969.

U.S. Advisory Commission on Intergovernmental Relations. *Intergovernmental Relations in the Poverty Program.* Report A-29. Washington: U.S. Government Printing Office, 1966.

U.S. Congress. *Congressional Record.* Vols. 110 (1964), 111 (1965), 112 (1966), 113 (1967), 114 (1968).

——. House. Committee on Appropriations. *Departments of Labor and Health, Education, and Welfare Appropriations for 1969.* Hearings. 90th Cong., 2d sess., 1968. Vol. 6.

——. Committee on Education and Labor. *Economic Opportunity Act Amendments of 1966.* Report to Accompany H.R. 15111. H. Rept. 89-1568. 89th Cong., 2d sess., 1966. (Cited in notes as *1966 House Committee Report.*)

——. *Economic Opportunity Act Amendments of 1967.* Hearings. 90th Cong., 1st sess., 1967. 5 vols. (Cited in notes as *1967 House Committee Hearings.*)

——. *Economic Opportunity Act Amendments of 1967.* H. Rept. 90-866. 90th Cong., 1st sess., 1967. (Cited in notes as *1967 House Committee Report.*)

——. *Economic Opportunity Act of 1964.* Hearings before the Subcommittee on the War on Poverty Program. 88th Cong., 2d sess., 1964. 3 vols. (Cited in notes as *1964 House Committee Hearings.*)

——. *Economic Opportunity Act of 1964.* Report to Accompany H.R. 11377. H. Rept. 88-1458. 88th Cong., 2d sess., 1964. (Cited in notes as *1964 House Committee Report.*)

———. *Economic Opportunity Amendments of 1965.* Report to Accompany H.R. 8283. H. Rept. 89-428. 89th Cong., 1st sess., 1965. (Cited in notes as *1965 House Committee Report.*)

———. *Examination of War on Poverty Program.* Hearings before the Subcommittee on the War on Poverty Program. 89th Cong., 1st sess., 1965. (Cited in notes as *1965 House Committee Hearings.*)

———. *1966 Amendments to the Economic Opportunity Act of 1964.* Hearings before the Subcommittee on the War on Poverty Program. 89th Cong., 2d sess., 1966. 2 vols. (Cited in notes as *1966 House Committee Hearings.*)

———. Committee on Rules. *Economic Opportunity Act Amendments of 1966.* Hearings. 89th Cong., 2d sess., 1966. 5 vols. (Cited in notes as *1966 Rules Committee Hearings.*)

———. Senate. Committee on Finance. *Social Security Amendments of 1967.* Hearings. 90th Cong., 1st sess., 1967. 3 vols. (Cited in notes as *Senate Social Security Hearings.*)

———. Committee on Government Operations. *Federal Role in Urban Affairs.* Hearings before the Subcommittee on Executive Reorganization. 90th Cong., 1st sess., 1967. 21 vols.

———. Committee on Labor and Public Welfare. *Amendments to the Economic Opportunity Act of 1964.* Hearings before the Subcommittee on Employment, Manpower, and Poverty. 89th Cong., 2d sess., 1966. (Cited in notes as *1966 Senate Committee Hearings.*)

———. *Economic Opportunity Act Amendments of 1965.* Report to Accompany H.R. 8283. S. Rept. 89-599. 89th Cong., 1st sess., 1965. (Cited in notes as *1965 Senate Committee Report.*)

———. *Economic Opportunity Act of 1964.* Hearings before the Select Subcommittee on Poverty. 88th Cong., 2d sess., 1964. (Cited in notes as *1964 Senate Committee Hearings.*)

———. *Economic Opportunity Act of 1964.* Report to Accompany S. 2642. S. Rept. 88-1218. 88th Cong., 2d sess., 1964. (Cited in notes as *1964 Senate Committee Report.*)

————. *Economic Opportunity Amendments of 1966.* Report to Accompany S. 3164. S. Rept. 89-1666. 89th Cong., 2d sess., 1966. (Cited in notes as *1966 Senate Committee Report.*)

————. *Economic Opportunity Amendments of 1967.* S. Rept. 90-563. 90th Cong., 1st sess., 1967. (Cited in notes as *1967 Senate Committee Report.*)

————. *Examination of the War on Poverty.* Hearings before the Subcommittee on Employment, Manpower, and Poverty. 90th Cong., 1st sess., 1967. 15 vols. (Cited in notes as *1967 Senate Committee Hearings.*)

————. *Examination of the War on Poverty: Staff and Consultants' Reports.* Prepared by the Community Action Association of Pittsburgh for the Subcommittee on Employment, Manpower, and Poverty. 90th Cong., 1st sess., 1967. 8 vols.

————. *Expand the War on Poverty.* Hearings before the Select Subcommittee on Poverty. 89th Cong., 1st sess., 1965. (Cited in notes as *1965 Senate Committee Hearings.*)

————. *Review of Economic Opportunity Programs by the Comptroller General of the United States Made Pursuant to Title II of the 1967 Amendments to the Economic Opportunity Act of 1964.* 91st Cong., 1st sess., 1969. Joint Committee Print.

U.S. Department of Health, Education, and Welfare. *Having the Power, We Have the Duty.* Report of the Advisory Council on Public Welfare. Washington: U.S. Government Printing Office, 1966.

U.S. Office of Economic Opportunity. *As the Seed Is Sown: Fourth Annual Report, 1968.* Washington: U.S. Government Printing Office, 1969.

————. *Community Action Program Guide, Volume I: Instructions for Applicants.* Washington: U.S. Government Printing Office, 1965.

————. *A Nation Aroused: First Annual Report, Fiscal Year 1965.* Washington: U.S. Government Printing Office, 1966.

————. *A News Summary of the War on Poverty.* Washington: U.S. Government Printing Office. Vols. 1 (1966–67), 2 (1967–68), 4 (1969–70).

_____. *The Quiet Revolution: Second Annual Report, Fiscal Year 1966.* Washington: U.S. Government Printing Office, 1967.

_____. *The Tide of Progress: Third Annual Report, Fiscal Year 1967.* Washington: U.S. Government Printing Office, 1968.

_____. *The Watershed, A New Look at the War on Poverty.* Washington: U.S. Government Printing Office, 1967.

Unpublished Works

Deets, Samuel E. "The Anti-Poverty Program: A Study in Professionalized Reform." Ph.D. diss., University of Cincinnati, 1970.

Horwitt, Sanford D. "Saul D. Alinsky and a Rhetoric of the Power Strategy as a Means of Social Change." Ph.D. diss., Northwestern University, 1970.

Knapp, Daniel L. "Scouting the War on Poverty: Social Reform Politics in the Kennedy Administration." Ph.D. diss., University of Oregon, 1970.

Lander, Byron G. "The Emergence of Poverty as a Political Issue in 1964." Ph.D. diss., University of Missouri, 1967.

Lombard, Rudolph Joseph. "Achieving 'Maximum Feasible Participation' of the Poor in Anti-Poverty Elections." Ph.D. diss., Syracuse University, 1970.

Murphy, Anne Austin. "Involving the Poor in the War against Poverty." Ph.D. diss., University of North Carolina, 1970.

Walker, Walter Lorenzo. "The War on Poverty and the Poor: A Study of Race, Poverty, and a Program." Ph.D. diss., Brandeis University, 1969.

Index

267

ABOUT THE AUTHOR

David Zarefsky teaches communication studies and is associate dean of the School of Speech, Northwestern University. He received his B.S., M.A., and Ph.D. degrees from Northwestern University. His publications include several essays on the rhetoric of the Johnson presidency and two textbooks: *Contemporary Debate* and *Forensic Tournaments: Planning and Administration.*